The Divine Nature of Power

Chinese Ritual Architecture at the Sacred Site of Jinci

Harvard-Yenching Institute
Monograph Series 62

Published by the Harvard University Asia Center
for the Harvard-Yenching Institute and
distributed by Harvard University Press
Cambridge (Massachusetts) and London 2007

The Divine Nature of Power

Chinese Ritual Architecture at the Sacred Site of Jinci

Tracy Miller

Printed in the United States of America

The Harvard-Yenching Institute, founded in 1928 and headquartered at Harvard University, is a foundation dedicated to the advancement of higher education in the humanities and social sciences in East and Southeast Asia. The Institute supports advanced research at Harvard by faculty members of certain Asian universities and doctoral studies at Harvard and other universities by junior faculty at the same universities. It also supports East Asian studies at Harvard through contributions to the Harvard-Yenching Library and publication of the *Harvard Journal of Asiatic Studies* and books on premodern East Asian history and literature.

Cataloging-in-Publication Data

Miller, Tracy, 1966–

The divine nature of power : Chinese ritual architecture at the sacred site of Jinci / Tracy Miller.

p. cm. -- (Harvard-Yenching Institute monograph series ; 62)

Includes bibliographical references and index.

ISBN-13: 978-0-674-02513-4 (cl : alk. paper)

ISBN-10: 0-674-02513-X (cl : alk. paper)

1. Jin ci (Taiyuan, Shanxi Sheng, China) 2. Architecture and religion. 3. Architecture and state--China--Taiyuan (Shanxi Sheng) I. Harvard University. Asia Center. II. Harvard-Yenching Institute. III. Title.

NA6047.T357M55 2007

726'.1951095117--dc22

2006100699

Index by the author

♾ Printed on acid-free paper

Frontispiece: Ms. Liu as Village Girl, Bronze with Gilding, Dressing Tower first floor, 1563 (Ding et al., *Jinci*, pl. 74; courtesy Wenwu chubanshe; for more details, see Fig. 7.2, p. 160)

Last number below indicates year of this printing

16 15 14 13 12 11 10 09 08 07

The color reproduction of images in this book was generously supported by the College of Arts and Science, Vanderbilt University.

For
Peter, Aileen, and Lindsay

Acknowledgments

The core of this project began with a dissertation written under the guidance of Professors Nancy Steinhardt, Terry Kleeman, and Victor Mair within the Department of Asian and Middle Eastern Studies at the University of Pennsylvania. I thank Professors Kleeman and Mair for reading the text and my translations with critical eyes, and for answering questions and giving advice as the project increasingly wandered into the realm of local religion. Professor Steinhardt deserves special thanks for her unwavering support of my research, for encouraging me to explore the remote locations of China for buildings with which to compare the Sage Mother Hall, and for her careful reading of both the dissertation and a draft version of the manuscript. She is the model of responsibility as an advisor, and my appreciation of her only increases with time.

I have received financial and institutional support at various stages during my research and writing. My initial fieldwork in Mainland China was supported by a grant from the Committee on Scholarly Communication with China, and I was hosted at that time by Qinghua University in Beijing. My writing was funded by a dissertation-writing grant from the University of Pennsylvania, during which time the Institute of History and Philology at Academia Sinica generously provided office space and access to the Fu Ssu-nien Library, as well as to the "human resources" that make the Institute truly a Sinologists' paradise. The conversion of the dissertation into a manuscript took place during a sabbatical supported by the Chiang Ching-kuo Foundation. The College of Arts and Science at Vanderbilt also supported the sabbatical, in addition to providing funding for the color production of images in this book. Vanderbilt University's Research Scholars' Grant Fund allowed me another trip to Jinci for additional photographs. I am grateful for the support that has made this project possible.

I depended on the help of numerous friends and colleagues who offered their thoughts and suggestions as this book has developed. In Beijing, I am indebted to Lou Qingxi, Guo Daiheng, Lü Zhou, and the late Xu Bo'an at Qinghua University; Yang Hongxun for providing me with numerous opportunities to present my work in China; and Fu Xinian and Zhang Yuhuan for taking the time to meet with me in Beijing. Han Dongzhu freely offered advice and helped make introductions. I was fortunate to be at Qinghua at the same time as James Robson, who has continued to share his thoughts with me on Chinese religion. Lauren Nemroff, and her well-connected sister Courtney, made my stay in Beijing much more interesting. My sincere thanks to all of them.

In Shanxi Chai Zejun took the time to talk with me extensively about the architecture of that province. Peng Hai was kind enough to help me gain access to images of Jinci held at the Jinci Museum. The staff of the Jinci Museum graciously allowed me to reproduce these images. Song Naizhong spent hours with me at Jinci, sharing his experiences and discussing the architecture and development of the site. Li Baogen and Niu Yongming made trips to Gaoping like going home. I thank them all for their time and their help. Many of the historic buildings I studied for comparison with the Sage Mother hall are not open for public viewing. I would also like to thank the people in the towns and villages of Southern Shanxi who took time out of their schedules to open the doors of temples so that I could examine them more carefully.

At Academia Sinica I benefited from discussions about my work with Chen Wen-yi, Fan I-chun, Paul Katz, John Kieschnick, Lin Fu-shih, Liu Shu-fen, Poo Mu-chou, and Xu Pingfang, as well as the members of the History of Health and Healing Research Group who let me attend their meetings. Hwang Ming-chorng shared both his considerable knowledge of Chinese traditional architecture, and also his skill with the Adobe Suite, going beyond the call of duty in providing aid in both intellectual and technical areas. Nixi Cura, Jenny Liu, Gil Raz, Ken Swope, Tseng Lan-ying, Michael Walsh were all forced into discussions with me about Jinci, temple architecture, and local religion (Michael at numerous dinners in Nan-kang). I thank them all for their comments and advice. Chang Che-chia deserves particular thanks for his help with this project, beginning in graduate school and continuing at Academia Sinica. Thanks also to Ma Meng-ching and Lin Lina for their help in navigating the unique bureaucracy of the National Palace Museum. Lina's exhibit on *jiehua* was the inspiration for much useful discussion, and she is a fabulous travel companion.

I would like to thank Yang Youwei for sharing his knowledge of Chinese thought, for his tutelage, and for invaluable help in translating the stele inscriptions that appear in the text. Many thanks also to Sukhee Lee for detailed comments on the final translations. Ron Knapp and anonymous readers for Harvard University Asia Center and *The Art Bulletin* offered helpful suggestions on both translations and the overall project. Paul Goldin and Ruth Rogaski were kind enough to read and comment on later drafts of the manuscript, and I thank them for their insights and valuable time. Thanks to Min-min Liang for her help in the early stages of the project. Virginia Bower and Cary Liu both commented on the dissertation; their suggestions made for a much better book, and I am grateful. I am indebted to Kalliopi Nikolopoulou and John Janusek for their individual insights on the central thesis of this book, and for encouraging me to consider larger contexts. My thanks to Amy Kirschke and Leonard Folgarait for advice on the organization of the manuscript, one that was further improved with the editorial skills of Edward Batchelder. And a very, very special thanks to Freda Murck, who made me a member of her Beijing family. I will never be able to repay her for her kindness and support of my work.

I have benefited also from correspondence with many scholars. I would especially like to thank Patrica Ebrey for sending me a draft article on ancestral portraits, Henrietta Harrison for her insights into the work of Liu Dapeng and water management at Jinci, Amy McNair for encouraging me to pursue this topic from the beginning, Ruth Mostern for allowing me use of a draft article on garrison/settlement patterns, Raul Birnbaum and William Powell for their insights on approaches to sacred sites, and Jae-hoon Shim for advice regarding Shang and Zhou archaeology.

Photographs for this book have been significantly improved with the help of our digital photographer in Vanderbilt's Visual Resources Center, Kirvin Hodges, and the whole slide room staff of Vanderbilt helped me catalog and database those images. My thanks for your continued help.

It is my family who deserves the greatest thanks of all. I would like to thank Mary Jo and Michael for their help getting me to China in the first place. Thanks to my parents, who never lost faith in me; Nathan, Alan, and David, who supported me even when their faith might have wavered; and Aileen and Lindsay, who remind me that so much of life (past and present) is about the next generation. And of course, to my husband, Peter Lorge, who carried my camera equipment for a year of travel in North China, read and commented on both the dissertation and manuscript, participated in endless discussions of Chinese art history and archaeology, and who is always in my heart.

T.M.

Song, Xi Xia, and
Liao Empires ca. 1100
Showing major cities
and locations of extant
Northern Song buildings
outside Hedong (Shanxi)
LIAO
XI XIA
GOBI DESERT
Western C.
(Datong)
Southern C. (Beijing)
Xingqing Fu
Zhending
(Zhengding)
Jinci
Taiyuan
Fen R.
Yellow R.
TIBET
AMDO
Bian Canal
Dengfeng
Kaifeng
SONG
Chengdu
Hangzhou
Yuyao
Yangzi R.
Dali
DALI
KINGDOM
Fuzhou
Putian
Guangzhou (Canton)
0
500 km.
0
500 mi.

numerous other temple buildings dedicated to a variety of divinities—some canonized as Daoist and others who had a following conventionally considered to be Confucian—have been added within the walls of the Jinci compound. Yet all were organized to face toward the center of the compound, confirming physically the centrality of the three springs, and the irrigation canals that they fill, to belief regarding the spirituality of the place. Thus, the name Jinci, which may have originally signified a single worship hall, came to refer to the larger site of the sacred springs and was eventually extended even to the surrounding community.

The ambiguity of the name allowed for a contest of patronage, with the largely itinerant literate elite focusing on Shu Yu of Tang and the local population on the Spirit of the Jin Springs. In fact, a detailed description of the site as it appeared at the end of the eighteenth century—the point of our earliest pictorial evidence of its overall layout—highlights the contrasting images of the shrine dedicated to Shu Yu and the buildings used for veneration of the Sage Mother (Figs. 1.3, 7.5).[2] The offering and main worship halls of the ancestral figure are contained within a standard walled courtyard, but those same ritual structures used for the worship of the Sage Mother are open to the local topography of the site. This distinction shows clearly that different types of deities were expected to occupy different types of structures or groups of structures. Thus, the choice of building and complex was made in order to express an understanding of the identity of the divinity housed within it.

The Pattern of Heaven and Principles of Earth

We are taught to believe that the Chinese built environment—whether it is a palace, temple, or city—is composed of rectilinear complexes of buildings all cardinally oriented to the south.[3] The Jinci compound provides a contrasting picture with its seemingly random distribution of buildings. As in the case of the Shu Yu Shrine, the traditional courtyard complex can be found, but only as one of the temple types within the larger compound. The difference between these shrine or temple complexes within the walls of Jinci reflects a difference between topographical and cosmological organizations, and thus points to an essential conceptual difference in the religious environment of the two divinities.

In the topographical configuration, major landscape features such as mountains, rivers, or oceans were not necessarily delineated from the individual temple buildings but instead sometimes served as the focal point for their orientation.[4] By imperial times, however, the construction of rectilinear, walled courtyard complexes created a standardized space that could be transplanted into any environment as a generic ritual complex, the organization of the buildings itself communicating that those worshiped within—whether deities, emperors, or officials—had a high degree of status within

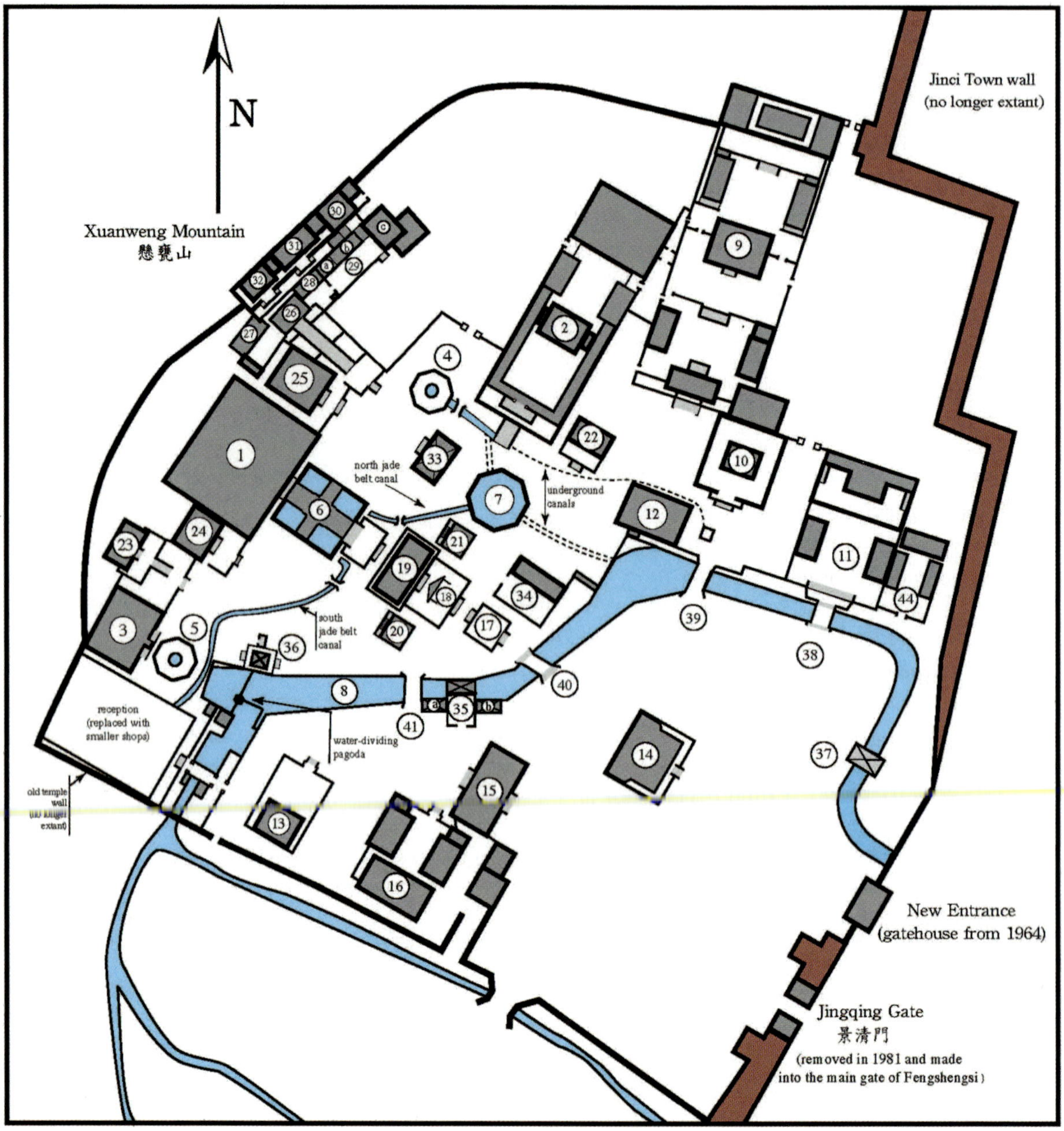

Fig. 1.2 Plan of Jinci (R. and T. Miller, adapted from Chai, *Jinci*). The overall plan of the site displays the emphasis on the topographical over cosmological orientation of the buildings. Because all of the worship halls face inward toward the springs and canals, this plan displays how the relationship to the water was a dominant factor in deciding building orientation.

Key to Fig. 1.2

1. Sage Mother Hall 聖母殿, 1038–87
2. Shu Yu of Tang Shrine Complex 唐叔虞祠, 1770–71
3. Dressing Tower 梳妝樓/梳洗樓 (present Water Mother Tower 水母樓), 1563
4. Perfect Benefit Spring *Ting*-gazebo 善利泉亭, 16th century
5. Eternal Youth Spring *Ting*-gazebo 難老泉亭, 16th century
6. Spirit Bridge 神橋 or Flying Bridge 飛梁, 11th century
7. Octagonal Pool 八角池, pre-1551
8. Earl of Zhi Canal 智伯渠, Han dynasty, with later modifications
9. Haotianshen Shrine Complex 昊天神祠, 1795
10. Temple/Shrine Complex to the Eastern Peak 東嶽祠, 16th–18th centuries?
11. Wenchang Temple Palace 文昌宮 and Jin River Seven Worthies Shrine 晉水七賢祠, 1773

Key to Fig. 1.2, cont.

12. Juntianyue Terrace 鈞天樂臺, 1795
13. Three Sages Shrine Complex 三聖祠, 1737?
14. Water Mirror Terrace 水鏡臺, Ming dynasty (16th century?)
15. Tower of the Beautiful Ying Island 勝瀛樓, 17th–18th centuries
16. Unified Rejoicing *Ting* Complex 同樂亭; Fu Shan Memorial 傅山紀年館
17. Iron Man Terrace 鐵人臺 or Lotus Terrace 蓮花臺, late 11th century
18. Duiyue Memorial Gateway 對越坊, 1576–1606
19. Offering Hall 獻殿, 1168
20. Drum Tower 鼓樓, 1606
21. Bell Tower 鐘樓, 1606s
22. Tang Taizong Stele *Ting*-gazebo (Zhenguan Baohan ting 貞觀寶翰亭), 1770
23. Gong Shuzi Shrine Complex 公輸子祠, 17th–18th centuries?
24. Tai Tai Temple 臺駘廟, 1533, with later repairs
25. Descendants' *Tang*-hall 苗裔堂 (also called Descendants' Temple 苗裔廟), 1511?
26. Fangzhang Cavern 方丈洞 (also called Laojun Shrine 老君祠), pre-17th century?
27. Chaoyang Cavern 朝陽洞 and Lingguan Hall 靈官殿, 17th century?
28. Tea Smoke Cavern 茶煙洞, 17th century?
29. (a) God of Wealth Shrine 財神祠 (also called Open Spring Cavern 開源洞), 17th century?
29. (b) Awaiting the Phoenix *Xuan*-pavilion 待鳳軒, 1718
30. Triple-Terrace *Ge*-pavilion 三臺閣, 17th–18th centuries?
31. Reading Terrace 讀書臺 (also called Bantongting 伴桐亭), 1785
32. Ancestor Lü *Ge*-pavilion 呂祖閣, 17th–18th centuries
33. Pine River *Ting*-gazebo 松水亭, late 18th century
34. Qinghua *Tang*-pavilion 清華堂
35. White Crane *Ting*-gazebo 白鶴亭, 16th–19th centurie
36. Genuinely Wonderful *Ting*-gazebo 眞趣亭, 1916–17
37. Sluice-Gate *Ting*-gazebo 水閘亭, 1953
38. Lock Rainbow Bridge (鎖虹橋; also called Wenchang Stone Bridge 文昌石橋), 1773
39. Mt. Tai Bridge 泰山橋 (also called Emerald Wave Bridge 碧瀾橋)
40. Meeting Transcendents Bridge 會仙橋
41. Suspended Snow Bridge 掛雪橋 (also called Double Bridge 雙橋)
44. Five(-Colored) Clouds *Ting* Complex 五雲亭, 1773

---

the Chinese empire. These courtyard complexes were typically oriented cosmologically—to the cardinal directions and usually facing south—and generally consisted of main buildings arranged on a central axis, surrounded by a rectilinear wall or series of subsidiary buildings placed along the wall.

Evidence that the courtyard complex came to signify official sanction in a generic way is found in its use for major temple and shrine complexes regardless of sectarian affiliation from the middle imperial period. Modern archaeology has shown that this configuration has a long history and was used in palace complexes of the pre-dynastic Zhou elite dating roughly to the eleventh century BCE (Fig. 1.4).[5] The *Kaogongji* 考工記 or "Record of an Examination of Craft," a text dating from the late Warring States Period (480–221 BCE) and incorporated into the *Rites of Zhou* during the Western Han dynasty (202 BCE–9 CE), describes the process of orienting to the cardinal directions using the sun and stars as the first step in Chinese city planning.[6] The cardinally oriented courtyard complex was adopted for Buddhist monasteries as early as the Northern Wei dynasty (386–534 CE), where it not only recalled the original bureaucratic buildings Buddhist monks first occupied when they entered China,[7] but also dovetailed with theological interests of Buddhism, which deemphasized this world so that acolytes could focus on becoming one with the universe.[8]

So, although the name "Jinci" suggests that the shrine complex would take the form of the standard Chinese ritual complex used for veneration of historical figures, the actual site defies this expectation. Courtyard complexes are mixed with other individual temple buildings and viewing pavilions, and all of them are arranged so that they face the three springs,

Fig. 1.3 Shu Yu of Tang Shrine Complex, 1770–71, view of gatehouse from the bridge in front of the Sage Mother Hall. The eighteenth-century reconstruction of this complex, in this location from at least the thirteenth century, emphasized the raised elevation as a means to show that Shu Yu was the primary divinity with power over the site, including the spring water.

canals, and ponds filled by the water of the Jin (Jinshui 晉水). In other words, they are not oriented cosmologically (to the cardinal directions) but rather topographically (to face the flow of water through the site). While early textual evidence on the worship of Shu Yu—a deity with power and significance for members of the government, be they emperors or officials—states that by the thirteenth century (and very likely before) he had been provided with the courtyard complex of the Zhou dynasty tradition, it was subordinated to the overriding topographical plan of the larger compound.

For this reason, twentieth-century architectural historians Liang Sicheng and Lin Huiyin reported being surprised by this configuration because it was so unusual for a ritual complex that was enclosed by a wall and entered through a standard *sanmen* 三門 gatehouse holding guardian deities (Fig. 1.5). They described it as looking like a private garden, but the gardens that came to look like Jinci were ultimately based on similar sacred sites where deities were known to take up residence.[9] In this paradigm, buildings were placed with respect to the features of the landscape that were most important for a particular circumstance. This kind of placement was subsumed within the purview of what would come to be known as *fengshui* 風水, but at Jinci it seems to be used in contradistinction to the more rigid, cosmological

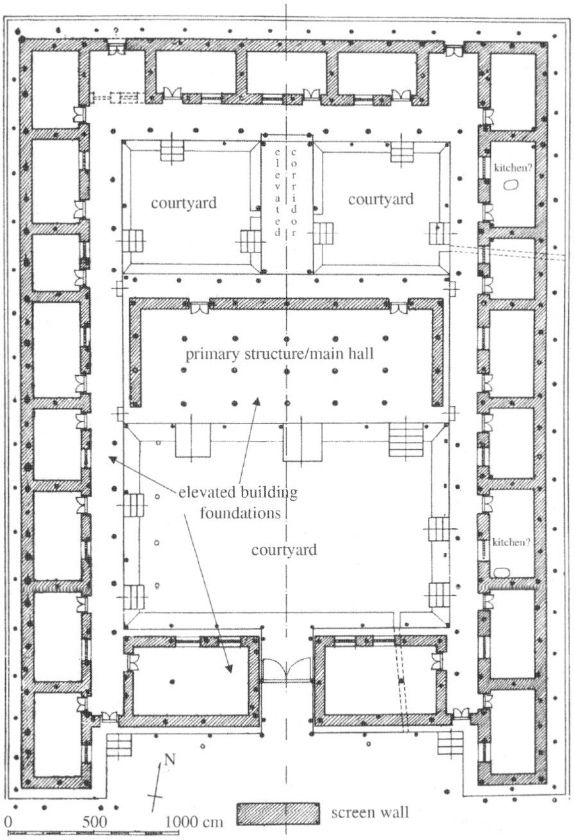

Fig. 1.4 Pre-dynastic Zhou palace-temple complex at Qishan, ca. 1050 CE. This architectural complex excavated at Qishan, near the ancestral home of the Zhou-dynasty kings, has critical features that come to characterize elite temple and palace complexes in imperial China, including an enclosed rectilinear compound, buildings elevated on raised platforms, principal buildings on the central axis, and overall bilateral symmetry. Reconstruction drawing (after Yang Hongxun, *Jianzhu kaoguxue*, 96).

Fig. 1.5 Jingqing Gatehouse in the 1930s (Mizuno, *Sansei kosekishi*, Courtesy Kyoto University, Institute for Research in Humanities). This image shows the main gatehouse into the complex during late imperial times. Guardian figures were located in the secondary bays framing the entrance.

organization of the courtyard complex that signified the order of empire across Asia during Chinese imperial times.[10]

Although the name of Jinci does not clearly denote the object of worship at the site, the distinction between the two types of compounds reiterates the differing nature of the two spirits of Jin, Shu Yu of Tang and the Sage Mother, and their patrons. The issue of the name of Jinci, its effect on our understanding of the identity of the main divinities there, and the physical layout of the complex are the subject of Chapter 2. Chapters 3 and 4 focus on the changing significance of Shu Yu across time and the impact that had on the shrine complex built for him. Chapters 5 and 6 turn to the worship of the Spirit of the Jin Springs, including the importance of the springs to the local agrarian community and the purpose for building a temple at the site of the Jin Springs—to provide shelter for human encounters with the nature spirit resident there. In Chapter 7, I discuss the changes in the interpretation of the Sage Mother's identity within the context of transformations in Chinese society during the sixteenth and seventeenth centuries when popular religion and Neo-Confucian ideology began to develop differences that were exacerbated by the loss of China to the Manchurian invaders of the Qing dynasty.

Shu Yu and the Cult of a State Founder

Although I will argue that the presence of the Jin Springs was the impetus to build a temple at Jinci and thus, given the pattern of temple building and nature spirit worship in Shanxi province, a temple dedicated to a spring spirit likely antedated any other worship hall at that location, the earliest positive identification of the main deity at Jinci was Shu Yu of Tang. Because of the early textual documentation and the significance of Shu Yu's place in the historical canon to later interpretations of the site, reconstructing the cult of this figure with respect to his changing patronage base over the course of the middle imperial period is vital for understanding his changing position vis-à-vis the Spirit of the Jin Springs.

Early records of the site itself and of individuals worshiping Shu Yu indicate that his cult was of vital, if not primary, importance to Jinci. Yet his power was fundamentally tied to imperial sovereignty over the Taiyuan basin. As the first of the Zhou dynasty to rule an area known for its mixing of cultures with the "barbarian" Rong 戎 and Di 狄 peoples, Shu Yu was important for would-be emperors seeking to appropriate his power for conquest or imperial legitimacy over the Taiyuan basin. From the Period of Disunion (220–589 CE) through the beginning of the Northern Song dynasty (960–1127), standard histories and geographic texts are either ambiguous as to the clear identity of the Jinci deities or indicate that the primary deity of Jinci was the state founder Shu Yu of Tang. Modern archaeology suggests that Shu Yu's fief of Tang was actually located not at Jinyang/Taiyuan but rather in the vicinity of modern Quwo 曲沃, over 240 kilometers (150 miles) to its south, yet the tradition of Jinyang/Taiyuan as the center of the Tang fief was included in the Standard Histories beginning in the Han dynasty. Worship of Shu Yu of Tang was first documented in Li Daoyuan's (d. 527) *Shuijing zhu* (Commentary on the Classic of Waterways), where he emphasized his role in the Zhou royal family and his place as the first Zhou ruler over the newly conquered Taiyuan basin. We have documentation of Shu Yu's continued patronage through the beginning of the Northern Song dynasty, while the memory of Jinyang as a regional power base remained strong. But after the second emperor of the Song dynasty succeeded in conquering and destroying the Northern Han and its capital of Taiyuan at Jinyang in 979, the administrative capital Taiyuan was moved from its location at Jinyang, at most five kilometers (three miles) north of the temple complex, to Sanjiaozhai 三交寨 in Yangqu county, another sixteen kilometers (ten miles) further north. The movement of the capital away from Jinci saw the waning of his cult there, so that by the end of the Northern Song, worship of Shu Yu was eclipsed by that of the Sage Mother. After the fall of the Northern Song to the Jin in 1127, Taiyuan was no longer a border region, and Shu Yu never again enjoyed the imperial patronage he had held through the twelfth century.

Shu Yu was still in the official sacrificial statutes (*sidian* 祀典), however. Consequently, the local officials still worshiped him, and his temple buildings continued to be the responsibility of the state. Late imperial patronage shifted from emperors to local literati, men who were interested not in the power or legitimacy he could give a newly created empire but in the moral value of worshiping the correct deities. Patronage of Shu Yu from the thirteenth through the eighteenth centuries reflects the interests of this new group of elites. During this time, local officials were frustrated by the need to keep rebuilding the temple complex due to lack of donations by the local populace, but their reasons for doing so were not always the same. In the sixteenth century, the time of our first extant local gazetteer for Taiyuan county, we can get a clear picture of one purpose for rebuilding the temple to Shu Yu—the interest of local elites in performing revived sacrificial rites to the founding deity. Early in the seventeenth century, another county magistrate, again disgusted at the condition of Shu Yu's temple, desired to move Shu Yu into the grandiose Sage Mother Hall in order to be consistent with the rites and to steer the people to worship the more proper historical figure. By the eighteenth century, the rationale for rebuilding the complex to its current form was to prove that Shu Yu was the master of the whole site, including the springs. Here we see that competition with the Sage Mother over dominance of the irrigation water was of primary concern. Overall, worship of Shu Yu during the late imperial period was always in frustrated response to the strong local patronage of the less-appropriate Sage Mother.

As a result, his shrine complex—more than any other within the Jinci compound—conforms to the Chinese imperial model, with its near-southern orientation, steep stair up to the gatehouse, covered corridors surrounding the front courtyard, and timber-frame buildings throughout. But this arrangement too may be the result of late imperial distinctions between temple types. Across the imperial period we see an increasing interest in creating a visually appropriate home for Shu Yu. Because of the lack of archaeology on the Jinci site, determining precisely the location for Shu Yu's shrine complex over the course of history is quite difficult. However, early descriptions of the complex from the sixth through the tenth centuries emphasize the location of his shrine, or at least its main offering hall, as part of a larger complex of buildings near the source of the Jin River. By the thirteenth century, the present complex was oriented on a north-south axis, and by the time of our first pictorial evidence of the Shu Yu shrine, we know that his complex was surrounded by regular, rectilinear, enclosing walls. His official-style courtyard complex was delineated as such in marked contrast to the Sage Mother Hall, which, at the same time, was completely open to the springs and canals of the larger site.

The Significance of the Jin Springs and the Temple to Its Spirit

The power of the site of Jinci is manifest in the water emerging here and its genius loci, the Spirit of the Jin Springs. Jinci is located at the site of three springs that originally fed the Jin River (Jinshui) between Xuanweng (literally Suspended Vat or Well Bucket) Mountain and the Fen River in the Taiyuan basin (Fig. 1.6). Poetry and prose written by travelers to the Taiyuan area describe Jinci as a necessary destination, primarily because of the beauty of the place. In contrast to the relatively dry surrounding community, which today receives on average twenty inches of rain a year,[11] the site of the Jin Springs is a verdant oasis with willow trees lining the banks of clear, bubbling waterways. Road-weary tourists and pilgrims remarked that the place looked magical, as green as the Yangzi delta region and completely out of keeping with the landscape in China's more arid north. In this area, spring sites were highly prized and typically had a temple to the spirit of the spring in residence. Through a close reading of the physical evidence of the temple compound as a whole, in conjunction with stele inscriptions and standard historical sources, the Sage Mother emerges not as an adjunct to the state founder but as the central figure of the Jinci cult site, whose primary power lay in delivering much-needed water to an agrarian community.

Although China's earliest geographic text, the *Classic of Mountains and Seas*, identified the Jin River as emerging from springs at the base of Xuanweng Mountain, in the Han dynasty we first have information that a system of irrigation canals was created to channel the flow of the Jin Springs. Over the course of imperial Chinese history, a canal network was created and expanded so that by the middle imperial period, the surrounding community was dependent on the flow of the Jin Springs for crop irrigation and milling.

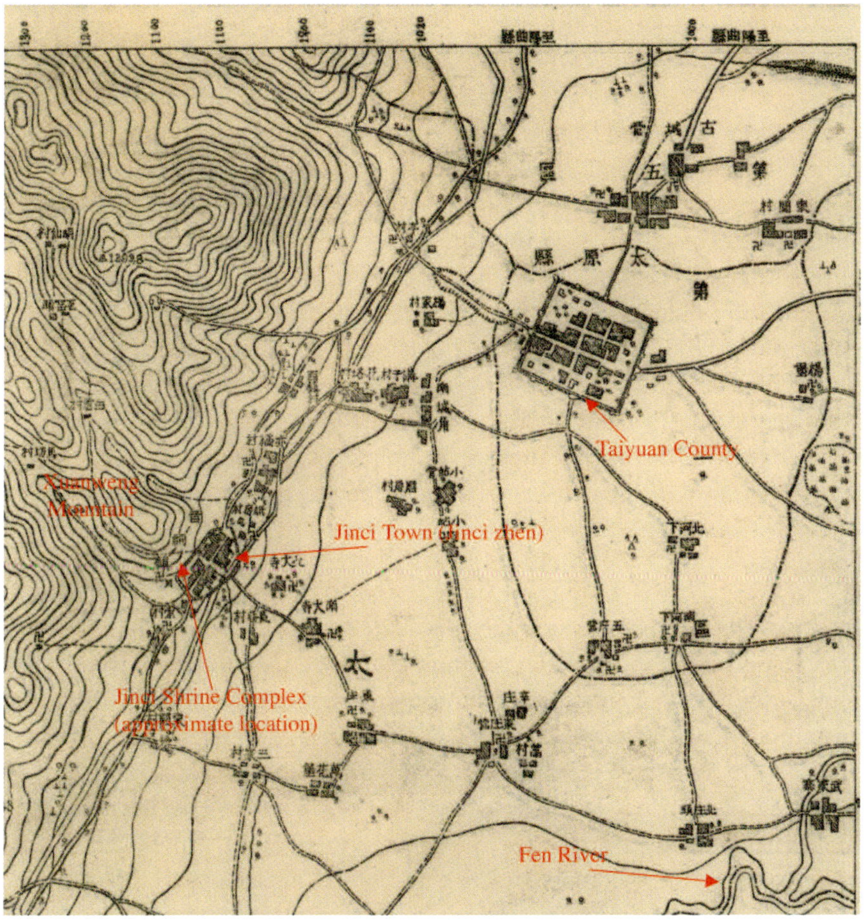

Fig. 1.6 Topographical map of the Jinci area, ca. 1921–34 (Detail of *Shanxisheng Qingyuanxian ditu* P04-B-0920, courtesy Academia Sinica, Institute of Modern History Archives) showing the location of the Jinci complex between the Xuanweng mountain range to the west and the Fen River to its east.

The increase in the prominence of the Spirit of the Jin Springs during the Song dynasty may be tied to a canal expansion that doubled the amount of acreage that the water from the Jin Springs could reach. However, her title increases, including her promotion to Sage Mother of Manifest Aid, and the change in the name of the temple from the Memorial Shrines of Jin (Jinci) to the Temple of Far-reaching Benevolence (Huiyuanmiao 惠遠廟) were in gratitude for miracles in delivering rain that were documented by local authorities. Her significance in the Ming dynasty lay in the authority her cult held for the network of canal heads who physically distributed water to noble and private landholders according to a set schedule. Even into the twentieth century, canal heads were expected to pay homage to the Sage Mother annually, village by village. Chapter 5 also describes the history of the Jin River canal network and the centrality of Jinci in the distribution of water to the surrounding community from the Eastern Han through the Ming dynasties (25–1644 CE).

An understanding of the popular voice at Jinci is possible primarily because of the publication of the *Jincizhi* (Jinci gazetteer) in 1986. Compiled and annotated by the classically trained Liu Dapeng (1857–1942), the *Jincizhi* contains transcriptions of stele inscriptions extant at the site, as well as material relating to the shrine complex and the surrounding community available from the Standard Histories and geographic texts. Yoshinami Takashi was able to make use of this work in manuscript form in his examination of issues of water management in north China; access to it has now been much facilitated by the regular typesetting and distribution of modern presses. Since the publication of Liu Dapeng's work, scholars such as Peng Hai (1997) and Henrietta Harrison (2002) have also been able to provide a much clearer picture both of the local culture in the community surrounding the Jinci Shrine Complex and of the significance of the Spirit of the Jin Springs to the agrarian society of the Taiyuan basin—both elite and common.

Methodology and Approach

As a historian of art and architecture, I am seeking the motivation behind the creation of art in the form of temple buildings, sculpture, and wall paintings. My interests necessitate a fundamentally interdisciplinary approach, and throughout this book I draw on the research of archaeologists, anthropologists, historians of religion, and social historians, in addition to that of historians of art. By focusing on the way in which the temple buildings and the deities worshiped within them were used to act out the political and social history of the region across time, and how competing patronage groups used temple architecture to serve their specific interests, I seek to understand the underlying connotation of buildings placed in a sacred landscape, both in terms of choices made when selecting the size and style of structure to be added to a larger complex and the way in which those buildings were organized with respect to preexisting landscape and the earlier buildings and complexes.

The basis for my approach is a close reading of available textual evidence and comparison of that evidence with the physical remains of the site. Examining the inscriptions written about Jinci across time, one can see that their creation, and ultimately the creation of the temple complex itself, was based in a genuine belief in the existence and power of the Spirit of the Jin Springs and Shu Yu of Tang. As I detail in Chapter 6, the Sage Mother Hall itself was originally constructed to honor an increasingly important divinity in the middle of the eleventh century and became an iconic symbol of her continued power through the beginning of the Qing dynasty (1644–1911). Although we do not know the location or appearance of the original worship hall dedicated to Shu Yu of Tang, or any other pre-eleventh-century building at Jinci, we can be relatively certain that the Sage Mother Hall was constructed between 1038 and 1087 CE. During this time, the Spirit of the Jin Springs was canonized through her entry into the official sacrificial statutes, and she was promoted from a Gentlewoman (*nülang* 女郎) to Sage Mother. The building was constructed in the official imperial style of Chinese ritual architecture, so much so that it was a primary source of information in the study of the Northern Song dynasty government building standards, the *Yingzao fashi* (published in 1103). The forty-one works of Song-period sculpture within the hall are so fine that, even with limited preservation and later repainting, they are still considered to be hallmarks of the Song dynasty, a period known for the quality of its artistic production. Indeed, the combination of the fine temple building and the sculpture within it has been the primary reason for modern scholars of Chinese art and architecture to believe that the Sage Mother was actually the mother of Shu Yu. To our eyes, with our necessarily limited access to the sculpture and architecture of the eleventh century, it is easy to believe that it must have been imperially sponsored and dedicated to a member of the Zhou royal clan, as Yan Ruoqu 閻若璩 (1636–1704) suggested at the end of the seventeenth century.[12]

But all of the documentation we have indicates that the building was the creation of a devoted constituency of local patrons, people who believed that the landscape around the Jin Springs was inhabited by "efficacious transcendents," who had the power to bring irrigation water and rain. This is most evident in the topographical orientation of the building and the lack of a rectilinear wall to enclose it from the springs. Perhaps, as Walter F. Otto has suggested in the case of Greek art and architecture, the quality of the building and sculpture was the product of divine inspiration on the part of the craftsmen and artists involved, and it is that passion we respond to as observers.[13]

The preservation of the Sage Mother Hall and the sculpture within it was unlikely to have been a mere accident of history. Although the temple hall, with a body of water and canal at its entrance, was perhaps easier than others to save from the ravages of the wars taking place from 1125 to 1368, wars that destroyed much of north China, it and its offering hall of 1168 are the only pre-Yuan dynasty buildings in the complex. That they were preserved bespeaks a strong and continuous patronage for the local water spirit, a hypothesis confirmed by the lamentations of local officials who wished that more of the offerings made at Jinci were directed toward their charge, Shu Yu of Tang. At the same time, the scale and grandeur of this building remains an indication of the power of the deity. Like modern visitors to the site, the elite of late imperial China had difficulty believing that this building was an appropriate temple hall for a local water spirit.

Confronting Late Imperial Reinterpretations

The late imperial interpretation of Jinci transformed our understanding of its origin and history, and a central part of this project is to contextualize, as much as is possible, the purpose behind new construction at various points in time and the influence of physical remains, the ancient architecture, on later interpretations of the site. Jinci and the Sage Mother Hall appear frequently in surveys of Chinese art, architecture, and sculpture, though the Sage Mother is not usually described as the Spirit of the Jin Springs. She is more commonly identified as the mother of Shu Yu, the historical Western Zhou queen Yi Jiang 邑姜. Scholars who have favored this interpretation recognize the Sage Mother's history as a water spirit, but consider this a secondary identity, one constructed by local farmers unfamiliar with the classical sources of her origin. Chapter 7 is dedicated to putting the Jinci site and the activities of worship that took place there into the historical and intellectual context of the Ming-Qing transition in order to elucidate reasons for the interpretation of the Sage Mother as Yi Jiang. The original source of this interpretation can be traced to the seventeenth-century prefect of Taiyuan Zhou Lingshu 周令樹 and the literatus Yan Ruoqu, the latter of whom had a very personal agenda in constructing the Sage Mother's identity in this way. Because Yan's family name can be traced back to Shu Yu of Tang, his making the most powerful local divinity into the mother of Shu Yu worked to appropriate her into his own ancestry and thus made the whole of Jinci a lineage temple to his family. Further, the iconoclasm ushered into China, first by efforts at modernization and then with the Communist and Cultural Revolutions, has caused most scholars of local religion in pre-Mao-era China to depend almost exclusively on local gazetteers that were written by and for the elite—people like Yan Ruoqu. Consequently, our understanding of Jinci has inherited a specific early-Qing-dynasty elite bias.

Because the Jinci ritual complex, while unusual for a single, walled building complex, is similar in its accretion of buildings to larger sacred sites in China, and because the interpretation of the Sage Mother as a local nature spirit for one constituency and a deified historical figure for another is also not without precedent in the history of Chinese popular religion, I have used several methodological perspectives to flesh out the multiple meanings communicated through the form of individual buildings and their arrangement within the natural landscape. Scholars of anthropology, history, religious studies, and art history have researched the accretion of identities for local spirits in China and their work forms the background of this study.

Perhaps the best-known scholar to employ the anthropological approach to the study of Chinese popular religion is James Watson. In his 1985 study of the modern cult of the Empress of Heaven (Tianhou 天后, also known as Mazu 媽祖) in southeastern China, Watson addresses the role of the state in the promotion of popular divinities. Arguing for the imperial use of religion to create a common culture, Watson intended in this study to determine whether the state was leading or following the masses in its promotion of specific divinities. His conclusion was that the state both led *and* followed. Deities could not have become part of the official pantheon without state support, but the state was unable to impose a deity on the masses. The state's role in standardizing gods came only after the deity was recognized by local officials and recommended for promotion. Once deities were recognized by the court and entered into the sacrificial statutes, they often "enjoyed special privileges, including the construction—at state expense—of elaborate temples in centers of government throughout the empire."[14] Because the promotion of the Tianhou cult along the southeast coast was paralleled by the rise in state authority over the region, Watson asserts a mutual cause-and-effect relationship between the two.

The "state-sponsorship" discussed in Watson's study of Tianhou was carried out by the literate men of a community as a way to assert their gentry identity. Local divinities were moved aside as nationally recognized cults were installed by the state-empowered elite.

> The unsanctioned, purely local deities gradually disappeared as new, recognized ones were installed in these temples. Local gods were never completely eradicated, of course, and it is still possible to find cults dedicated to deities known only to the residents of one or two communities. Nevertheless, the promotion of state-approved cults in South China was so successful that, by the mid-Qing, local gods had been effectively superseded by a handful of approved deities.[15]

This conclusion assumes that the gazetteers written by the literati are an accurate and complete representation of the religious landscape. Although regional differences may account for some of the disparity between Watson's study of Tianhou and my own presentation of the cult of the Sage Mother, these two cults would not appear to be so different without the stele inscriptions and the physical evidence of the temple site.[16] After the Sage Mother was incorporated into the sacrificial statutes in the Song, she began to take precedence over Shu Yu of Tang, but only in stele inscriptions. General histories of the site emphasized its long history as the location of the sacrificial temple to the Marquis of Jin, Shu Yu. However, in the sixteenth century, there was a move to re-identify the Sage Mother, to replace her traditional role as the Spirit of the Jin Springs with that of the mother of Shu Yu, Yi Jiang. Unable to change either belief or practice (the Sage Mother was still the undisputed powerhouse of Jinci, and the state authorities were unwilling or unable to interrupt her patronage), the literati integrated her into the cult of Shu Yu, at least in textual studies. By the end of the eighteenth century, the site was occupied by temples to nationally venerated divinities such as Guan Yu 關羽 (ca. 162–220; also known as Guandi 關帝), the Three Pure Ones (*Sanqing* 三清), and Wenchang 文昌.[17] Yet the evidence of the site itself shows how little the impact of the textual reinterpretations and additions of nationally venerated deities affected the cult of the local water goddess. To this day, the Sage Mother Hall and the spring water she embodies are the focus of all the temple buildings within the larger precinct.

The more relevant point addressed by Watson in his study of Tianhou is how a single divinity can mean different things to different people, depending on their own position in the social hierarchy and how "people align themselves with temples that best represent their own interests."[18] Because Jinci contains cults to disparate divinities, these two aspects are much more separated than in the case of multiple temples to the single goddess Tianhou. There is evidence to show, however, that from at least the mid-Ming, different interpretations of the Sage Mother's identity began to emerge and take on a factional character. For example, there is documentation by the sixteenth century of members from all classes patronizing the Sage Mother as the Spirit of the Jin Springs by burning incense and candles and maintaining the Sage Mother Hall. Additionally, private local farmers from a village on the northernmost end of the Jin River canal system used an earlier interpretation of the Sage Mother as having originally been a local girl from that village to justify their claim to a greater share of the water. A different interpretation was promoted during the sixteenth and seventeenth centuries by the Confucianized elite who had larger social as well as personal motivations for insisting that the Sage Mother was Yi Jiang, thereby elevating a local water goddess to a devoted ancestral mother and a famous Western Zhou queen.

Historians including Prasanjit Duara, Timothy Brook, and Kenneth Pomeranz have all incorporated these examples of local religious activities into their work on historical developments. Duara uses the cult of Guandi, the patron saint of war, in his examination of the local history of north China in the nineteenth and twentieth centuries, approaching local religion from an anthropological perspective with an interest in how deities and temple networks were used in political struggles. He calls this accretion of varying identities the "superscription of symbols." In his 1988 article on the cult of Guandi, Duara discusses the "interpretive arena of myth" where different levels of society vie for power. Because no new interpretation of a deity completely displaces older conceptions of the deity's identity, complete state hegemony over a local population through superscription is not possible. Yet the assimilation of pre-existing cults to new ends by reinterpreting old legends can succeed to a certain extent because it uses the cultural legitimacy of a pre-established divinity.[19]

At Jinci, and elsewhere, I would propose, the interpretive arena of myth is the temple complex. Following Duara's model, at this temple complex the state (through officials), farmers, local nobility, and literati all built on the identity of the Sage Mother as the Spirit of the Jin Springs in order to assert their own control over the wealth of the Jin River. By using the temple site as a primary source, it is possible to approach the immediate effectiveness of interpretive superscription. In this case, although all interpretations of the divinity's identity were eventually entered into the record of the site's textual history, the individual participants were less successful at gaining power through superscription than they might have liked. For example, although the farmers from the Sage Mother's original "hometown" were able to convince the nobility to give them a bit more water, when the case was officially assessed, the farmers were imprisoned and flogged. Ultimately people with other, arguably more tangible, means (state-empowered authority, land, and troops) were able to control the distribution of water, regardless of these spiritual claims. Additionally, the history of the temple buildings also shows that a textual record of superscription may be only that. Although the new interpretation of the Sage Mother as Yi Jiang by late Ming and early Qing literati occurs in texts of the sixteenth and seventeenth centuries, it did not affect the Sage Mother's dominance over the site or her local identity as the Spirit of the Jin Springs. One is left to wonder if there was ever really a superscription at all.

While these two models are helpful in understanding the deities at Jinci, the influence of the state in this local cult was not as dominant as it would appear to have been in the cases of Tianhou and Guandi. This may be due to her lack of widespread popularity, or is perhaps indicative of differences between the Ming and the Qing. Timothy Brook's research on gentry patronage of Buddhism in the Ming has shown that the Ming state was not interested in using Buddhism to heighten its power.[20] This also appears to have been the case at Jinci. Although the early Ming court recognized the Sage Mother, the state did not sponsor temple-building activities in her honor. Official participation in temple rituals was focused on seeking rain, but when miracles were granted, officials needed to gather funds for the reward—repairing the temple—from the local population.

Kenneth Pomeranz has documented the increasing Confucian interest in controlling local ritual activities in the Qing. In the case of the Handan Rain Shrine, this included the transformation of the Mother of the Dragon God into the Dragon God himself in the nineteenth century.[21] Additionally, because it represented a female identity outside traditional family roles, an increasingly rigid Confucian literati considered the worship of Bixia Yuanjun 碧霞元君 to be inappropriate.[22] It may be possible, therefore, that the interpretation of the Spirit of the Jin Springs as the mother of Shu Yu was accepted late in the Qing as a method of reconciling the dominant position of the Sage Mother Hall at the location of the ancestral shrine to Shu Yu of Tang with the increasingly conservative Confucian orthodoxy. Ultimately, the dominant physical presence and antiquity of the Sage Mother Hall itself was the source of this new interpretation of the deity's identity.

By researching Chinese popular religion in modern Taiwan, the religious historian Daniel Overmyer and ethnographer David Jordan have been able to take full advantage of both their methodologies to address the issue of belief in agents who were directly involved in miraculous events. They discovered that engagement in the production of miracles did not undermine the faith of believers in popular sects.[23] In his work on the painting program of the water spirit temple and Buddhist monastery at Guangshengsi 廣勝寺, roughly 175 kilometers (108 miles) south of Jinci, Anning Jing has shown that painting programs both reflected the rituals that took place at the site and were magically charged to bring rain and subdue earthquakes.[24] Within this paradigm, the educated elite of premodern China were capable of genuinely believing that their prayers for rain to the Sage Mother were being answered by her, even if they exaggerated the connection between the ritual they performed and the subsequent rainfall, which was documented in the accompanying inscription recording that ritual. Even the most skeptical of inscriptions about the deities at Jinci, written at the end of the sixteenth century, indicated that local elites *believed* in the Sage Mother but thought the local people gave her too much attention.

If the quality and grandeur of a temple building, then, are not only a reflection of a local patronage base but also evidence of the existence—the reality—of divinity and divine power, we can see the concerns of local officials about the shrine to Shu Yu of Tang in a new light. Given their education and responsibility, it is natural that they would consider the spirit of a member of the Zhou royal family to be of primary importance at the site. Usually this would be understood as Confucian morality—officials were responsible for making sure that they and the local population were worshiping the most appropriate deities within the context of official Chinese culture. But the perennial disrepair of the shrine to Shu Yu reflected more than the immorality of local society; it indicated that the Spirit of Shu Yu was no longer resident at the site—his divine presence had abandoned the Jin River and was perhaps never really there. This sense of urgency, increasing as evidential scholars argued in the seventeenth century about the location of Shu Yu's original fief, may have been the inspiration necessary for them to make their own miracle and rebuild the shrine of Shu Yu. This study of the art and architecture of Jinci is thus about creations for the divine and their power to create divinity.

Chapter Two
Jinci: Place and Name

Shu Yu of Tang and the Sage Mother are both spirits of Jin; one is the spirit of the political unit that became the Jin state, the other the spirit of the Jin Springs. Yet, primarily because of late imperial connotations of the word *ci*, at this time a memorial/ancestral shrine, Qing dynasty elites insisted on interpreting Jinci as a shrine to the Jin state founder—either Shu Yu or his mother—and not as a place to worship water spirits. By understanding both the shape and the name of the place within a larger historical context, however, we see that Jinci was a contested site with the two Jin spirits, ancestral and water, competing for patronage for most of the history of the place. The worship of Shu Yu has always been acceptable for the literati elite who documented China's past. He is a deified historical figure, the second son of King Wu of Zhou, whose life is documented in canonical histories such as the *Zuozhuan* and *Lüshi chunqiu*. Furthermore, as the first Zhou-dynasty official to rule the territory of Tang, later renamed Jin because of the river that flows through it, Shu Yu is the first ancestor of the Jin state. As early as the sixth century, the textual history of the site emphasized that Jinci was first and foremost a shrine dedicated to the worship of the Jin state founder. But casual visitors, including poets and traveling literati, wrote instead about the springs of Jinci, and by the thirteenth century they also made note of the dominance of the Sage Mother, the Spirit of the Jin Springs, and her Song dynasty worship hall. As the divinity of the water source that became increasingly important across the imperial period as a source for irrigation, the goddess of the Jin Springs was entered into the official court sacrificial statutes in the eleventh century as the Sage Mother of Manifest Aid (Zhaoji shengmu 昭濟聖母) and was later reinterpreted by Qing-dynasty literati as the mother of Shu Yu, Yi Jiang 邑姜.

Because the interpretation and reinterpretation of the identities of these divinities relied on expectations developed from the name of the complex and were played out through the traditional language of Chinese temple architecture, I begin this chapter with a description of a typically large-scale, imperially sponsored nature-spirit temple as a way of outlining the major structures of that language. I then compare that complex to the present state of Jinci to determine precisely how Jinci falls outside that model and how it was made to conform, at least superficially, to patrons' desire to present the Spirit of the Jin Springs as a Confucianized divinity, if not also the mother of Shu Yu. Finally, I examine the name of the shrine and explore how that, perhaps most profoundly, influenced the written record and the later elite interpretations of the identities of divinities worshiped there.

The Modern Site of Jinci as Shrine and Sacred Landscape

Jinci is located at the site of a set of springs that feeds the Jin River, the eponym of the Warring States Period Jin state. The significance of the Jin River to the local agrarian population, and of the Jin state to the national elite, resulted in two groups of patrons who competed with each other for dominance over the site. Evidence from the Warring States Period indicates that the location was famous first for its springs and then became a nexus of temple complexes organized according to the variation of the unique topography of the place, rather than following the cosmological orientation toward the south that was standard for ritual complexes in China of the Zhou dynastic tradition.[1] Although it is possible to describe this as being influenced by *fengshui,* Jinci's variation from the basic *fengshui* principles allows us to learn about the significance of China's sacred landscape to building orientation without dismissing it as resulting from a single overriding *fengshui*, which never existed as a complete, unified system.

Entering the shrine complex today, one finds that it is nothing like the usual large courtyard-style building complexes employed in most Chinese ritual sites, be they large shrines dedicated to nature spirits, monastic complexes constructed for Buddhists or Daoists, or palatial complexes such as the Forbidden City.[2] The temple complex of the Earth Queen at Fenyin 汾陰 (modern Wanrong 萬榮 county), Shanxi province (Fig. 2.1), a major imperially patronized temple to a nature spirit, shows how the courtyard complex common to Buddhist, Daoist, and palatial compounds was also used for nationally known female nature spirits. The stele inscription is twelfth century but shows the site as it would have stood in the eleventh century. Typically, large-scale courtyard complexes such as this communicated at a fundamental level the divinity's official high status, despite being outside any particular sectarian tradition. The buildings inside the complex varied according to the needs of the specific sect, but the organization and structure of most of them followed the format of the courtyard complex described above, so much so that different sects could reuse them with only minimal adjustments.[3]

This basic format was used for all major ritual complexes during the middle imperial period (tenth–sixteenth centuries), regardless of their sectarian affiliation. The feature most representative of Chinese ritual architecture in this context is its cardinal, southward orientation, clearly shown in the 1137 CE relief carving of the Northern Song dynasty plan of the site. It is

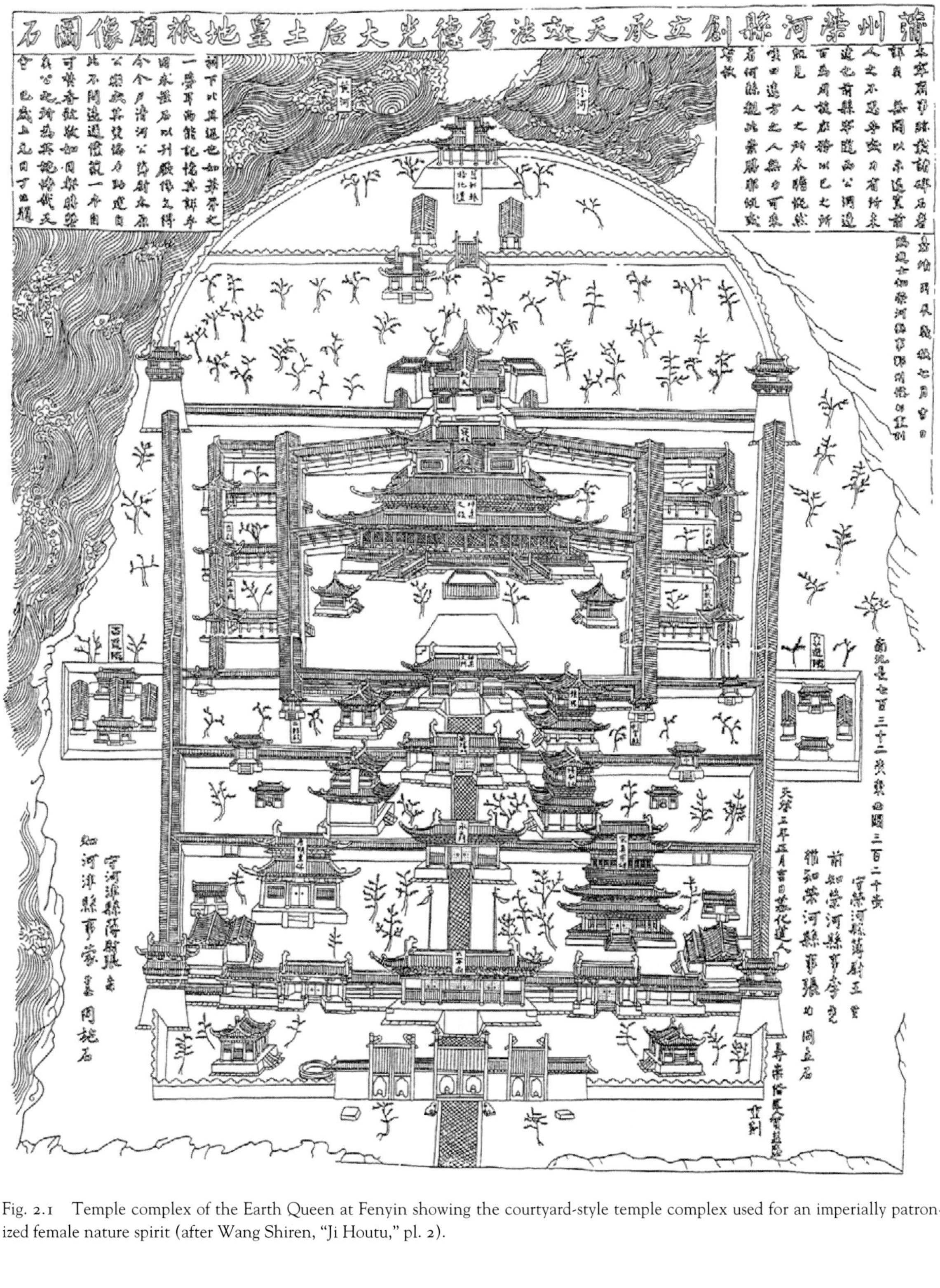

Fig. 2.1 Temple complex of the Earth Queen at Fenyin showing the courtyard-style temple complex used for an imperially patronized female nature spirit (after Wang Shiren, "Ji Houtu," pl. 2).

indicated first through the inclusion of basic geographical features—the Fen River (at the top of the rendering) flows into the Yellow River (on the left side of the rendering), indicating that the top is north and the left is west. Additionally, two subsidiary courtyards on the left and right are labeled west and east respectively.

The next apparent feature is the front gateway and enclosing walls. After entering through the first gateway, one would progress through four more gatehouses distributed along a central axis. The first of these gatehouses is joined on either side by a roofed gallery that encircles the larger complex. The second and third gatehouses also join with walls that extend to the larger enclosing wall on the left and right. The fourth gatehouse joins with another inner enclosing gallery that appears to extend from the gatehouse to the back hall of this inner complex. The main hall of this complex is located behind an axial altar/stage platform. This small square platform, called a *lutai* 路臺 at the Temple to the Central Peak, could be either an altar, a worship platform, a theatrical stage, or conceivably all three depending on the occasion.[4] The hall is linked to a smaller vestry (*qindian* 寢殿) by a covered platform, creating a capital-I-shaped main hall combination.[5] A central back gate behind this hall leads to a set of northern altars in a rounded enclosure separated by a single wall and gateway. Notably, all of the subsidiary buildings and courtyards in this carving are positioned either parallel or perpendicular to the central axis.

Although some details of this complex are not widely seen in the majority of extant ritual complexes in the Chinese sphere, the basic features of southern orientation, main halls on central axis, and surrounding galleries, are not constrained by sectarian divisions.[6] Indeed, even the capital-I-style main hall, which is specified for an ancestral complex in the fifteenth-century carpentry manual *Lu Ban jing*, can be seen in Buddhist complexes in Shanxi from the twelfth to fifteenth centuries.[7] The walls of the courtyard itself isolate both the divinity and the devoted from the immediate surroundings and provide a familiar atmosphere that transcends any specific location.

The organization of Jinci does not follow this pattern (Fig. 1.2). The most prominent feature of the complex is that it is not oriented cardinally. The Sage Mother Hall and the Shu Yu of Tang Shrine complex are described as facing east and south respectively, but modern measurements of these structures, shown in the plan in Fig. 1.2, show that the Sage Mother Hall is oriented 48° east of south and the Shu Yu of Tang Shrine complex is oriented 30° west of south.[8] The variation is not due to a lack of technology by early Chinese builders. Extant crafts manuals, specifically the late Warring States period *Kaogongji*, describe techniques for orienting cities north/south using the path of the sun and alignment with the North Star.[9] Even given the consideration to differences in orientation to true north rather than magnetic north and the possibility of polar wandering, the

Fig. 2.2 Water Mirror Terrace (Ming dynasty), used for celebrations associated with the worship of the Spirit of the Jin Springs; a stage has been in this location since the early sixteenth century. Because of the addition of a new entry gate in the mid-twentieth century, this stage has become part of a central axis of buildings leading to the Sage Mother Hall.

variation should not be more than seven degrees from present magnetic cardinal directions, rather than the thirty- to forty-eight-degree variance in the two main buildings. Closer inspection of the site plan shows that all the buildings face onto springs and canals that flow through the site, thereby emphasizing water as the *raison d'être* for building worship halls at this location.

Although the new entrance is placed east of the roughly eastward-oriented Sage Mother Hall, it is not directly on axis with this building.[10] Wandering along the concrete path leading from the new entrance, the modern tourist first arrives at the Water Mirror Terrace (Shuijingtai 水鏡臺, #14 on the plan in Fig. 1.2, pre-1551, repairs in 1573 and 1844). From the front, this late Ming-dynasty stage appears to be a temple hall (Fig. 2.2).[11] But, after stepping up onto the building platform, one discovers there was no original staircase down on the west side of the building. This hall was never part of a ritual axis along which the devotee would have progressed.

As experienced temple-goers, most modern tourists in China find their way to what is today called the Meeting Transcendents Bridge (Huixianqiao 會仙橋, plan #40),[12] leading across the Earl of Zhi Canal (Zhibo qu 智伯渠,

Fig. 2.3 Meeting Transcendents Bridge, n.d. This bridge is the primary point of crossing over the Jin River canal system when approaching the complex from the east.

plan #8), because it appears to lead to a gateway in the distance. It would thus seem to mark the path of progression to a main worship hall (Fig 2.3). Yet, as one can see from photographs, this is not squarely on a central axis. After crossing over the bridge, the next raised platform is the Lotus Terrace (Lianhuatai 蓮花臺), which was also called the Iron Man Terrace (Jinrentai 金人臺) because of the cast-iron statues of warriors, or guardian divinities, occupying its four corners (Fig. 2.4, plan #17, 1094–98 CE).[13] A miniature pavilion crowned in glazed tiles, which Liu Yongde believes is from the Ming dynasty, stands in its center.[14] After passing over the Lotus Terrace, the visitor arrives at the Duiyue Memorial Gateway (Duiyuefang 對越坊, Fig. 2.5, plan #18, 1576, rebuilt 1606). This gateway is flanked by a drum tower on the south and bell tower on the north (Plan #20 and #21, 1606 CE), giving the viewer the sense of having arrived at a recognizable temple complex.[15] Crossing through the open Offering Hall (Xiandian 獻殿, Fig. 2.6, plan #19, 1168 CE), the visitor steps onto a small platform and then crosses a stone bridge, called the Spirit Bridge (Shenqiao 神橋) or Flying Bridge (Feiliang 飛梁, Fig. 2.7, plan #6, ca. eleventh century), to reach the majestic Sage Mother Hall (Fig. 1.1, plan #1, 1038–87 CE). Within the hall, the image of the Sage Mother sits on a phoenix throne surrounded by forty-two female attendants (Fig. 2.8). The statue of the Sage Mother and forty of the attendant figures are thought to be original works of the eleventh century.[16]

Fig. 2.4 Iron Man Terrace, 1094–98, with later additions. This structure was likely originally intended as a stage for ritual dancing involved with rain spirit worship.

Fig. 2.5 Duiyue Memorial Gateway, 1576–1606. The plaque presently on the west façade was calligraphed in 1576, providing the date for the structure. The literate would have understood this quote from the *Book of Odes* as an allusion to the Western Zhou–dynasty ancestral temple. The location of this structure on axis with the Sage Mother Hall contributed significantly to the late imperial interpretation of the Sage Mother's identity as the Western Zhou queen Yi Jiang.

Fig. 2.6 Offering Hall, 1168. An inscription on an interior timber dates this building to Western equivalent of 1168. The bracketing of the hall was made to match the Sage Mother Hall, leading scholars of the early twentieth century to conclude that the buildings were constructed at the same time.

Fig. 2.7 Spirit Bridge (Flying Bridge), eleventh century. This bridge, called Flying Bridge (Feiliang 飛梁) today in reference to the discussion of Jinci in the sixth-century *Shuijingzhu*, stands directly in front of the Sage Mother Hall and was originally filled by one of the three springs on the site.

Fig. 2.8 Sage Mother of Manifest Aid with Attendants, painted clay, h. 110 cm; h. with chair 228 cm, eleventh century (Shi Yan, *Wudai, Song diaosu*, 92). The image of the Sage Mother is shown on a wooden chair dated 1087, framed by a wooden screen also thought to be of the Song period. She is further contained within a wooden statuary niche from the Ming period, all of which is elevated on a brick plinth with a glazed tile panel on the front. This image shows four attendant figures, the two closest to the Sage Mother are Ming dynasty additions and the outer two are contemporary with the image of the Sage Mother. The inscription on the Sage Mother's chair states that it was donated along with six carved wooden dragons for the front columns of the building. The front apron area of the chair is carved with six dragons, echoing the building itself, and may have been an allusion to the chariot of the famous goddess, the Spirit of the Luo River. (Courtesy Wenwu chubanshe.)

Looking back on the complex from the broad veranda of the Sage Mother Hall, the visitor can see the larger complex that has developed since the thirteenth century around the springs, the Sage Mother Hall, and the Sage Mother's offering hall. Because the temple buildings were placed along the base of the mountain and around the springs and canals, the Sage Mother Hall (and thus the Sage Mother) seems to reign over the location of the Jin Springs. Since the end of the Song dynasty, none have questioned her power or dominion over the complex. This was made clear to the devoted through the size and magnificence of the temple that housed her image. From the Yuan dynasty until today, her temple not only was the largest in the complex but also was not partitioned off from the springs and temple buildings of the larger precinct. Although the building clearly dominates the site, from this perspective it is difficult to understand the relationship of

Fig. 2.9 Dressing Tower (Water Mother Tower), 1563, front façade with Eternal Youth Spring. This two-story structure, a dressing tower for the Sage Mother until the late nineteenth century, stands directly behind the Eternal Youth Spring, the most productive spring at the site. Statuary inside asserts the local legend that the Sage Mother was originally a village girl from the nearby Jinshengcun.

the rest of the buildings to this later central axis. They seem to be scattered at random.

North and south of the Sage Mother Hall are the Descendants' Hall (plan #25, first built in 1111, rebuilt in 1511), holding images of child-giving female deities, and a worship hall to the ancient god of the Fen River, Tai Tai 臺駘 (plan #24, 1267, rebuilt in 1533), respectively. On a steep slope rising southwest of the Tai Tai Temple is the Gong Shuzi Shrine Complex 公輸子祠 dedicated to the patron saint of carpentry, Lu Ban 魯班 (plan #23, ca. seventeenth to eighteenth century). The recently traversed Flying Bridge spans a pool originally filled by a spring that originated underneath the Sage Mother Hall and was probably called the Sage Mother Pool in the eleventh century.[17] Two more springs to its north and south, the Perfect Benefit Spring (Shanliquan 善利泉, plan #4) and the Eternal Youth Spring (Nanlaoquan 難老泉, plan #5) form the core of the complex and are said to have been first covered with pavilions in the sixth century.[18] To the west of the Eternal Youth Spring is a Water Mother Tower (Shuimulou 水母樓), originally conceived as a Dressing Tower (Shuxilou 梳洗樓) for the Sage Mother (Fig 2.9, plan #3, 1563). The western side of the site on the north holds Facing the Sun Cavern (Chaoyangdong 朝陽洞, plans #26–30),[19] a series of religious structures built into the side of Xuanweng mountain that served as the residence of monks put in charge of the complex (both Daoist and Buddhist) at different times in its history. All of these buildings follow stereotypical *fengshui* practice in that they have a mountain to their backs and waterways in front of them.[20] Yet while the buildings within the Jinci complex are not oriented cardinally, they are also not restricted to this basic siting principle. Though still a topographical orientation, what is important to the organization of the totality of the complex as it presently stands is that the buildings face onto the water emerging from the Jin Springs.

We see this in practice with the other complexes to the north and south of the Earl of Zhi Canal. On the southern side, two ritual complexes and two viewing pavilions frame the leg of the Earl of Zhi canal that first extends from the Eternal Youth Spring. The Three Sages Shrine Complex (Sanshengci 三聖祠, plan #13, 1737, with later restoration) was originally two temples dedicated to the Medicine King (Yaowang 藥王) and the True Lord (Zhenjun 真君), which were combined into a single complex with a main hall and entry gateway in 1737. At this time a third deity, a Dragon King (Longwang 龍王) was added. Notably, the complex was first called the Shrine of the Three Kings, or Sanwangci 三王祠, only to be given the title Three Sages at a later point. To the southeast of this complex is an expansion of the original United Rejoicing *Ting* Complex (Tongleting 同樂亭, plan #16, expanded in the eighteenth century and again in 1963), which is today a museum commemorating the works of the calligrapher Fu Shan 傅山 (1607–84/85).[21] Slightly to the north of this complex are the Tower of the Beautiful Ying Island (Shengyinglou 勝瀛樓, plan #15, ca. eighteenth century) and the White Crane *Ting*-gazebo (Baiheting 白鶴亭, plan #35, sixteenth century, with repairs and expansions in 1778 and 1822). The buildings contain this corner of the complex and return the visitors back across the canal to the buildings dedicated to the Sage Mother.

On the northern side of the compound, the complexes are also organized to frame the flow of water from the springs. Facing southward here stand four temple complexes, three of which are completely walled-off from the site with only entry gateways visible from the openness of the temple complex's interior. The shrine complex to Shu Yu of Tang is the westernmost of these (Fig. 1.3, plan #2, thirteenth century, with the latest complete rebuilding in 1770–71). The Shrine to the Jade Emperor (Haotianshenci 昊天神祠, Fig. 7.11, plan #9, 1795), which includes worship halls to the Three Pure Ones and to Guandi, the deified Guan Yu, sits slightly north and east of the Shu Yu of Tang Complex and faces both its own stage (plan #12, eighteenth century) and a sharp turn in the Earl of Zhi Canal. Further to its southeast is the Shrine to the Eastern Peak (Dongyueci 東嶽祠, plan #10, pre-1551, repaired nineteenth century). In the southeastern-most location of the site stand the Wenchang Temple Palace and its ritual preparation complex (Wenchanggong 文昌宮, Fig. 7.10, plan #11, 1773). Although the Shu Yu Shrine has a stele pavilion on a parallel axis beside it to contain the Jinciming bingxu 晉祠銘並序 stele inscription of the second Tang dynasty emperor written in 646 CE (plan #22, 1770), it still reads as only one of the northern complexes and not the focus of the site as a whole. Yet, according to the textual tradition, as the Jin state founder he, not the Sage Mother, should dominate the site of Jinci.

The modern central axis onto which the visitor is guided makes this place understandable as a temple complex in the Chinese tradition. But the creation of this axis is the result of a historical process, the last addition of which occurred in 1964 when the main Jinci gatehouse was built at a location on axis with the Water Mirror Terrace, approximately twenty-five meters north of the previous main gatehouse. Construction of ritual buildings at Jinci to conform ever closer to a preconceived notion of the imperial Chinese tradition is based in the desire to homogenize elite Chinese worship into one of the three traditions of Buddhism, Daoism, or Confucianism and to allow other practices to be explained as popular misunderstandings of proper religion. This began with a narrowing of the meanings understood for deity and temple names.

The Significance of the Term "Jinci"

The ambiguity of the name Jinci had significant consequences—it allowed the site to be interpreted both as a temple to a local state founder as well as a water spirit, depending on the interest of the patron. The names of shrines to individual divinities within the complex changed over time, but from as early as the sixth century, the whole was referred to as Jinci.[22] By the Ming and Qing dynasties, public *ci* were usually shrines dedicated to the spirits of historical personages, and in that sense, too, the word has been translated as "ancestral shrine."[23] But the name was used long before the word *ci* came to imply a building in which to worship a deceased individual. Evidence from the Northern Song dynasty and before indicates that *ci*, used nominally, denoted a shrine or temple to a deity. Because of the powerful influence of Neo-Confucianism, the late imperial/modern understanding of the name Jinci is an ancestral shrine to the historical founders of the Jin state. The change in meaning contributed to modern historians' willingness to favor the interpretation that the main deities of Jinci, both Shu Yu of Tang and the Sage Mother, were originally historical individuals. The following examination of naming practice for temple and shrine complexes during China's early and medieval periods shows that the term Jinci could refer to a shrine dedicated to a local nature spirit (the Spirit of the Jin Springs), as well as to the historical founder of the Jin state (Shu Yu of Tang). Given the age of the name, which can be traced back to the Northern Wei period, we must understand *ci* here in its earlier and much broader usage. My inquiry into the meaning of the word Jinci aims to transcend a strictly philological analysis of the origin of the characters Jin 晉 and *ci* 祠 and to focus instead on how they were understood across time by those reading about or visiting the site.

Before we have any evidence of a shrine or temple dedicated to Jin, textual sources describe the springs at the foot of Xuanweng Mountain that were the fountainhead for the Jin River. In the relatively dry region of Shanxi, springs were highly valued, and temples or shrines were frequently placed near them for sacrifices to the spirit of the spring.[24] Yet it is fully 700 years after the earliest record of the Jin Springs that we first have a description of a religious building at the site. Although this shrine has been interpreted as a memorial to Shu Yu, the ambiguity of naming practices leaves open the possibility that this earliest shrine was dedicated to either Shu Yu or the Spirit of the Jin Springs. We can be certain, however, that this early religious site was not dedicated originally to the mother of Shu Yu, Yi Jiang.

As mentioned above, the earliest geographic work that discusses the existence of a spring in the location of the Jin Springs today is the *Shanhaijing* (Classic of Mountains and Seas). As with most pre-Qin texts, its dating is problematic and disputed, but it is probably from no later than the Warring States period.[25] The Jin Springs appear in the entry on Xuanweng Mountain (Xuanwengshan 縣雍山, now Xuanwengshan 懸甕山), with the Jin River having its origin in this mountain and flowing east into the Fen River.[26] The next piece of evidence about the Jin Springs comes from the geographic sections of early standard histories. The Jin Springs or River is found under the "Treatise on Geography" in the *Hanshu* (Standard history of the Han), which states that the spring of the Jin River is at Dragon Mountain, northwest of Jinyang (Qin-Han Taiyuan commandery) and that it flows eastward into the Fen River.[27] The "Treatise on Geography" in the *Hou Hanshu* (Standard history of the Later Han) follows the *Hanshu* description.[28] From an additional record documenting the repair to the canals around Taiyuan in 116 CE, we learn that the canals leading from the Jin Springs were used to irrigate both government and private lands. Later commentary on this passage suggests that the canals repaired in the Han dynasty were the same as those discussed in the sixth-century *Shuijingzhu* (see Chapter 5), where the shrine of Jinci is also described in great detail.[29] The first definite reference to the Jin Springs, the Jin River south of Taiyuan, and a temple at the site appears in the "Treatise on Geography" in the *Weishu*, the standard history of the Northern Wei dynasty covering the years 386–550. Similar to the earlier standard history geographic treatises, the account is brief: "Southwest [of Jinyang] is Xuanweng Mountain, which is also called Dragon Mountain. The Jin River originates here and flows east into the Fen River. There is a Jinwangci 晉王祠 (Shrine to the King of Jin) [here]."[30]

The description of the mountain as the location of a "King of Jin Shrine" is the first mention of a shrine that could be attributed to Shu Yu of Tang near Jinyang. Yet Shu Yu of Tang never held the title of king, nor did anyone within the Jin state.[31] As I will discuss in the next chapter, the Spirit of Shu Yu of Tang was first invested as King of Arising Peace in 941 CE. Like the name Jinci, Jinwangci is also ambiguous.

An examination of the possible meanings of Jinwangci shows that the shrine at the Jin Springs was, even at this early period, dedicated either to Shu Yu of Tang or the Spirit of the Springs, or to both of them. However, the tendency of later historical sources in Chinese and English to regard the *Weishu* quote as firm evidence of early Shu Yu of Tang worship at the Jin Springs is the result of late imperial Confucianism, where *ci* would be most frequently understood as a worship hall dedicated to a historical ancestor. English translations for Chinese religious structures are not consistent, nor do they reflect the variety or deeper meaning of the original Chinese word. Although I have chosen to translate *ci* as shrine for the purposes of this book, it could be (and has also been) translated as hall or temple.[32] Yet other terms for religious structures in China are also translated as temple, including *miao* 廟, *gong* 宮, *guan* 觀, *si* 寺, and *tang* 堂, leaving one to speculate that some differentiation existed in their application to specific sites of worship. An etymological inquiry into these terms reveals that naming practices were not rigid; however, the relationship between the terms *ci* and *miao*, terms used to refer to the religious structures at the Jin Springs at one time or another, is significant for understanding the expectations of readers about Jinci.

At root, the terms *ci* and *miao* are very different, but by the time we have historical documentation about the temple at the Jin Springs, an ancestral figure or a nature spirit could equally have been worshiped in a structure or complex under either name. The greatest distinction between them can be seen in the characters themselves. Early dictionaries such as the *Er Ya* and the *Shuo Wen* describe *ci* as a sacrifice, specifically the annual Vernal Sacrifice, a ritual in which the standard ritual animals were not offered, but rather consisted primarily of spoken liturgy and gifts of jade tablets, *bi* rings, leather, and silk.[33] The meaning is carried by the character *shi* 示 that serves as its radical and means a communication between Heaven and people.[34] In the Zhou dynasty, the *ci* was the spring ancestral sacrifice for the king, which took place in the *zongmiao* 宗廟, or ancestral temple.[35] Early historical sources such as the *Book of Documents* (*Shangshu*), also use *ci* verbally, in this case meaning to sacrifice to a spirit or former king (*ji* 祭), but not necessarily one's own ancestor.[36] In a broader context, the neighborhood (*li* 里) Vernal Sacrifice was a rite of thanks, and the term *ci* could also be used verbally as an act of worship giving thanks for favors granted by divinities more generally. By extension, it could also be used to refer to the building or complex used to venerate *shen* 神 spirits, as in the compound *shenci* 神祠, an abbreviation for *shen citang* 神祠堂 or a hall for venerating *shen*. While *shen* can refer to the spirits of humans, they were also nature spirits—entities considered to be the source of all life, with Heaven and Earth being the most important.[37] But while in the pre-imperial period the *ci* was a ritual honoring noble as well as nature-spirit ancestors, by the Han dynasty small structures placed at tombs for the purpose of venerating the dead of the elite were also called *cishi* 祠室 or *citang* 祠堂.[38]

A synonym for the *shen citang* given in encyclopedic dictionaries is *miao*. A *miao* differs from a *ci* in that it is fundamentally a structure, a place to hold spirit tablets, audiences, or rituals, rather than a ritual or sacrifice itself. This, too, is expressed in the composition of the character *miao*, where *yan* 广, meaning roof or room, is its radical. During the Zhou dynasty, *miao* held the ancestral tablets for worship by kings and feudal nobles, and in that sense a place inhabited by ghosts and spirits could also be called a *miao*. Depending on the context, a *miao* could furthermore be the front hall in the palace of a king. In the *Er Ya* definition of the term, the *miao* is said to be a large hall within the larger palace complex, having two side halls, in contrast to the back hall/vestry, or *qin*, which would consist of only one main chamber.[39] Although the imperial ancestral temple was called the Grand Temple, or Taimiao 太廟, by the Zhou, the term *miao* was not limited to ancestral temples for the nobility, and buildings called by this name were used for the veneration of a variety of spirits.[40]

Thus, by the sixth century CE, when the entry in the *Weishu* was written, *ci* and *miao* were both associated with the worship of royal ancestors and nature spirits, the latter of which were considered to be, at least in some sense, ancestors in and of themselves. Although *ci* was a ritual and *miao* a building, *ci* was also used as an abbreviation for the building in which *ci* sacrifices took place.

By the Han dynasty *ci* had also been appropriated by the elite as the term used to refer to halls for venerating deceased ancestors at their tombs, yet there is reason to believe that the widespread understanding of *ci* primarily as a shrine to a family ancestor did not occur until after the Song dynasty. According to Patricia Ebrey, the Song dynasty Neo-Confucian philosopher Zhu Xi 朱熹 (1130–1200) was the first to use the word *citang* 祠堂 to refer to the ancestral shrine, or "offering hall" as Ebrey translates the term, found within the home in his *Family Rituals*. This book was extremely popular from the thirteenth century throughout the late imperial period. But in the eleventh-century writings of both Sima Guang 司馬光 (1019–86) and Cheng Yi 程頤 (1033–1107), the home ancestral hall was called an "image hall" (*yingtang* 影堂), reflecting the widespread practice of worshiping images rather than tablets of the ancestors in such places.[41] Thus our modern understanding of *ci* as being first and foremost an ancestral hall dedicated to a deceased human is something that developed long after Jinci had been established as a ritual site where both Shu Yu of Tang and the Spirit of the Jin Springs received offerings. The social context of this late imperial understanding of the site is discussed further in Chapter 7.

The two other terms mentioned in this first source on Jinci are *jin* and *wang*. The term *jin* comes first from the Jin River, which ultimately served as the eponym for the later Jin state. Although *jin* can mean to enter, as in the entry of the myriad things after the first sunrise, in the context of the Taiyuan region during the imperial period, *jin* would certainly refer to the

Warring States Period Jin state.[42] As I discuss in greater detail in the next chapter, Han dynasty sources attribute the change in the name of Shu Yu's original fief of Tang to Jin to a decision made by Shu Yu's son Xie Fu 燮父. According to these sources, Xie Fu moved his capital to the banks of the Jin River and took the name of the river as the name of his state. This city, named Jinyang 晉陽 because of its location north of the Jin River (*yang* means the north side of a river or the south side of a mountain), held the administrative bureaucracy of the Taiyuan commandery and was a major military and political center until the fall of the Northern Han dynasty in 979 CE.

The term *wang* is, in this book and most commonly elsewhere, translated as "king," but it was a title given to spirits as well as humans. *Wang* was used through the Western Zhou dynasty to refer to the temporal ruler, but because the ruler was also considered to be the son of heaven, the implication is that a *wang* has a spiritual as well as a political right to rule. During the Eastern Zhou, leaders of smaller states began to refer to themselves using *wang* as an expression of their superiority, and although the Eastern Zhou kings did not approve of this activity, local lords were able to do so because the central government was too weak to stop them. The broad use of *wang* to refer to local feudal lords led to the creation of the new title "emperor" (*huangdi* 皇帝) by Ying Zheng 嬴政 (b. 259 BCE) of Qin after his conquest of Zhou territory to indicate his position as supreme ruler. As a consequence, *Jinwang* has often been interpreted as referring to Shu Yu. However, the Jin state was historically a marquisate and Shu Yu a marquis (*hou* 侯) until his first posthumous elevation in 941 CE.[43] In a separate use of the term, *wang* could also refer to popular deities as well as the spirits of deceased humans. In a recent article on the name of the popular goddess Xiwangmu 西王母, Paul Goldin has discussed the various meanings of *wang*, including its use in the sense of "an attribute of a satiated spirit" or a "numinous" spirit.[44]

The term *Jinwangci* could therefore mean an ancestral temple to the Jin rulers or a temple dedicated to a powerful Jin nature spirit. The preference for interpreting the earliest reference in the *Weishu* to a temple at the Jin Springs exclusively as a temple to Shu Yu may be related to a particular Confucianized understanding of temple and spirit nomenclature. For the interpreters of late imperial religion, the Sage Mother Hall at Jinci was in the wrong type of religious complex and the wrong scale to be dedicated to a water spirit. In Susan Naquin's study of temples in Beijing during the Ming and Qing, she observes that a *ci* was usually dedicated to a historical individual, whereas the term *miao* was applied more broadly and was used not only for deified people (including Confucius) but also for nature spirits, divinities of canonical Daoism, and the imperial ancestral temple. From this perspective, a *ci* was not for a female nature spirit. Additionally, we have evidence that the elite authors of the standard histories tended to obscure the gender or status of powerful female spirits. In his book *Divine Woman*,

Edward Schafer has shown that throughout the imperial period, female water spirits were given titles that implied male gender and temporal status, such as *wang*, effectively masking their femininity and spiritual power.[45] During the Tang dynasty, even the Luo River goddess, a famous divinity from the pre-imperial period rendered in the image of a classical queen or empress in poetry from the third century CE, was given the noble title Marquis of Clear Sagacity (Xiansheng hou 顯聖侯).[46] Thus, if *wang* were used in the *Weishu* as an honorific title, or a title that indicated the power of a deceased ancestor or nature spirit, then *Jinwangci* could mean a temple to the spirit of Shu Yu of Tang, but it could equally refer to a shrine dedicated to the Jin Springs water spirit, or a sacred site that included both divinities.

Another factor in the interpretation of Jinci as dedicated primarily to ancestral rather than feminine water spirits was the large physical size of the Sage Mother Hall. While water spirit temples were frequently located at spring sites and often dedicated to female spirits, they tended to be small. Rolf Stein describes the commonality of small temples to female divinities at "meeting places" near pools, waterways, and crossroads in southeastern China and Vietnam. These deities were "often anonymous, being designated only by vague terms like *thanh-mâu* ([sage] mother), *ba* (lady), *durc-ba* (noble lady), or *chua-ngoc* (jade princess)."[47] In Shanxi, as early as the Tang dynasty (and probably before), temples to spring spirits such as that dedicated to the King of Broad Benevolence (Guangrenwang 廣仁王) in Ruicheng 芮城, Shanxi, were placed on land directly above the site of the spring. The Yuan dynasty Water God's Temple (Shuishenmiao 水神廟), next to the Lower Guangsheng Monastery (Guangshengxiasi 廣勝下寺) in Hongtong 洪洞, Shanxi, also stands before the emerging Huo Spring (Huoquan 霍泉). Only the latter of these, which is dedicated to the male Spirit of the Huo Spring, the King of Righteous Response (Mingyingwang 明應王), approaches the size of the Sage Mother Hall. Even the architectural historians Liang Sicheng and Lin Huiyin were surprised that this local water spirit temple was built at such a grand scale.[48] Because the Sage Mother Hall is the largest building in the Jinci complex and appears to preside over the whole compound, the Sage Mother is clearly the most dominant deity of Jinci. The local population, which was dependent on the spring for irrigation water and had built and sustained the Sage Mother Hall over the centuries, knew that the name Jinci referred to the Spirit of the Jin Springs and River. However, the late imperial interpreters of a historical record that first documented Jinci as *Jinwangci* and understood *ci* to mean ancestral temple, knew local water spirit temples to be small, and were aware of the significance of Shu Yu of Tang to the history of the Taiyuan/Jinyang region. For these men the authority of the canonical Chinese textual tradition was pre-eminent. Consequently, the worship of a local water spirit should *not* supersede the worship of historical Jin state ancestors at a place called Jinci, and it was in their power to reinterpret the identity of the Sage Mother of Manifest Aid from the Spirit of the Jin Springs to the mother of Shu Yu, Yi Jiang, at least for the textual record. Before turning to the worship of the Spirit of the Jin Springs, it is important to contextualize the worship of the ancestor of the Jin state, Shu Yu of Tang, at the site of the Jin Springs. This is the subject of the next two chapters.

tion of the Shang fief of Tang, and subsequently the first fief of Shu Yu, more extensive excavation of the Fen River valley is needed. Until then, we must base our conclusions on a combination of textual sources and what archaeology has been done. We can see, however, that the Taiyuan basin contained a mixture of Central Plains and Northern Steppe cultures from at least Shang times.

The most probable locations for the Shang state of Tang, as understood from the textual tradition, are Jinyang and the Quwo-Yicheng 翼城 area to its south.[30] Early sources such as the *Book of Documents* or the *Zuozhuan* provide some general information about the location of the Jin territory. As stated above, these sources describe Tang/Jin as a border region of the Zhou in the Fen River valley. Later commentaries on these texts have provided multiple interpretations of late Shang and early Zhou geography.[31]

Zhang Youchun 張友椿 (1896–1966) concisely summarized the commentarial debate over the location of the Tang fief in a short essay published in 1983.[32] As Zhang points out, those who believe that the Yicheng vicinity was the original site of enfeoffment include and follow the arguments of: *Shiji zhengyi* 史記正義 (Orthodox interpretation of the *Shiji*) by Zhang Shoujie 張守節 (Tang dynasty); the *Guadizhi* 括地志 by Xiao Deyan 蕭德言, Gu Yin 顧胤 et al. (Tang dynasty); Gu Yanwu's 顧炎武 (1613–82) "Tang-Jin bian 唐晉辨" (Analysis of Tang and Jin); and Xu Jiyu's 徐繼畬 (1795–1883) "Jinguo chufengkao 晉國初封考" (Research into the original enfeoffment of the Jin state).[33] These people largely focus on the passage in the "Jinshijia" 晉世家 section of the *Shiji* in which Sima Qian explains the "Tang" in Shu Yu of Tang as being a territory of about one hundred square *li* located east of the Yellow and Fen Rivers. Because Jinyang was located west of the Fen River, it could not have been the state of Tang.[34]

Those who have suggested that Jinyang was the original location of the Tang state include Ban Gu (32–92) in his *Hanshu*;[35] Zheng Xuan 鄭玄 (127–200) in the *Maoshipu* 毛詩譜;[36] Du Yu 杜預 (222–84[?]) in his *Zuozhuan zhu*;[37] Li Daoyuan in his *Shuijingzhu*;[38] the "Maoshizhuan" 毛詩傳 by Zhu Xi;[39] and Yan Ruoqu's "Shidi yulun" 釋地余論.[40] Their arguments revolve around the title held by the son of Shu Yu, "Marquis of Jin," and its ultimate derivation. Although Sima Qian gives no reason for this title, Ban Gu and Zheng Xuan state that it was given to the son because the Jin River flowed through the territory of Tang.[41] Thus, we can know that from at least the Han dynasty, the Jin River was believed to be the eponym for the state of Jin.

As Zhang Youchun informs us, the tradition of Yu the Great having one of three capitals at Jinyang allows Jinyang to be a possible ancient Xia site (Xia *xu*). Furthermore, the tradition of Jinyang being only the first capital of the newly formed Jin state, after which it was moved to more southern areas, also supports the possibility of the original Tang fief being located, at least temporarily, at Jinyang. Unfortunately, the textual evidence for a clear relationship between the location of Western Zhou (or Shang) Tang and modern Jinyang is limited to sources from the Han dynasty and after.[42] Yet, many archaeologists believe that recent finds around Yicheng have provided sufficient evidence to prove that Shu Yu of Tang's fief was actually located further down the Fen River valley, approximately 250 kilometers (over 150 miles) south of Jinyang.

Archaeologists of Shang and Zhou China (see below) have devoted much effort to correlating textual place-names with their locations on the ground. Although Tang appears as a place-name in oracle bone inscriptions found at Xiaotun, Anyang 小屯安陽, Henan province, no archaeological discovery of the so-named "Tang" ruins has been made to date. Much has been done to identify different cultures within Shanxi according to the characteristics of excavated material, however. Speculation about the possible original names of excavated sites is usually based on correlating archaeology, traditional and modern place-names, and textual information. Because only a small percentage of extant early textual sources (other than oracle bones and bronze inscriptions) can be dated to the Western Zhou, most of the information on this period published in book form is considered anachronistic in any discussion of Shang and Western Zhou.[43] Although a convenient exact match between the archaeological and published historical traditions is not yet completely available, excavation in Shanxi province has far toward proving that the original enfeoffment of Shu Yu of Tang was in the Yicheng area.

Shanxi province has been divided into four distinctive groups of Shang archaeology (Fig. 3.1): (1) *The Western Shanxi Plateau—the area occupied primarily by the Lüliang Mountains (Lüliangshan 呂梁山) reaching south to near the lower Fen River and including the mountainous area of eastern Shaanxi.* This area contains many late Shang bronzes that share distinctive stylistic features but show the influence of more southern Yinxu culture.[44] (2) *The Jinnan 晉南 Basin—primarily the southwestern section of Shanxi extending southeast to the Zhongtiao Mountains (Zhongtiaoshan 中條山), northwest to the Lüliang Range, and north to the Linfen 臨汾 area.* Although Erligang-style (early Shang, ca. 1500–1400 BCE) bronzes have been excavated in this area, late Shang bronzes are noticeably lacking, which may indicate that the area was occupied by semi-nomadic steppe peoples rather than agrarian Shang at the time of the Zhou conquest.[45] (3) *The Southeastern Shanxi Plateau—extending from modern Lucheng 潞城 in the north, the Taihang Mountains (Taihangshan 太行山) in the east, the Lüliang Mountains in the northwest, and the Zhongtiao Mountains to the southwest.* Here the archaeological record shows a clear stylistic relationship to Yinxu style bronzes, and it is believed to have been under direct control of Shang kings toward the end of the dynasty. (4) *The Jinzhong 晉中 Area—defined roughly as the Taiyuan basin extending from Yanmenguan 雁門關 in the north to Lingshi 靈石 in the south.* Pottery related stylistically to Yinxu material was excavated at the site of Baiyan 白燕 near Taigu 太谷, but many objects also appear to have developed from the Longshan culture of the area independently of southern influence. Thus, though communication with the

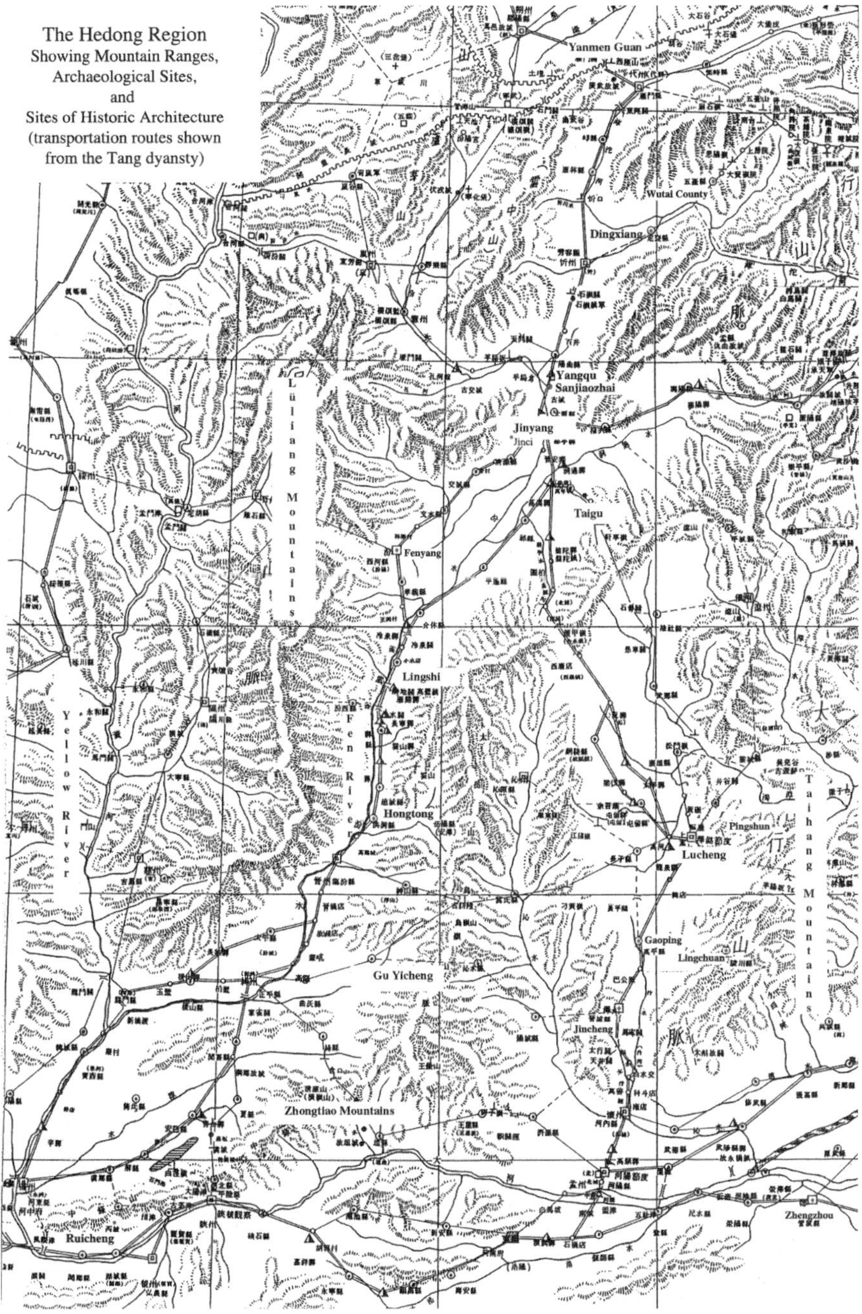

Fig. 3.1 Topographical map of the Hedong region (modern Shanxi province) showing major archaeological regions and locations of historic architecture discussed in the text, adapted from Yan Gengwang, *Tangdai jiaotong tukao*, vol. 5, pl. 19.

Shang is in evidence, the Jinzhong area is considered an independent archaeological culture.[46]

Because the textual tradition links the first capital of the future Jin state with either Xia or Shang cultures and identifies it as bordering Rong territory,[47] these archaeological divisions of Shang remains do not conclusively prove any specific location for the city in question. But the archaeological distinction between Jinzhong and the Jinnan Basin supports the hypothesis that Jin culture was not centered in Jinzhong. The hypothesis is further supported by the lack of early Western Zhou remains near Jinyang, and the abundance of Western Zhou material found in the vicinity of Yicheng. One is hesitant to conclude anything regarding archaeology based on negative evidence alone, and Jinyang has not been fully excavated. Yet, what little archaeology has been done suggests that Jinyang became a capital city associated with Central Plains culture only during the Warring States Period.

Tang as Jinyang

The archaeology done at Jinyang has yet to reveal strong evidence that the site was a Western Zhou regional capital and that its connection with the Central Plains is strongest from the Warring States Period and after. Of the eight textual/traditional place-name possibilities, Jinyang has been one of the most compelling because of its eponymous relationship with the state in question.[48] As Edward Shaughnessy has stated, one of the fundamental principles of historical geography is that rivers and mountains retain their names better than cities and states,[49] and the Jin River is the only natural landmark bearing the Jin name. However, there has been no full excavation of ancient Jinyang. The town of Jinyuan 晉源, also the seat of Taiyuan county from 1372 through the twentieth century, lies east of Jinci on the banks of the Fen River (Fig 3.2). In 1961, a team lead by Xie Yuanlu 謝元璐, a member of the national cultural relics office, began an initial survey of city-wall remains located around the periphery of this town with the hope of identifying early evidence of a late Shang or Western Zhou city that would have been the capital of Shu Yu's fief. Although they did find aboveground remains of walls appearing to date from the Warring States Period through the Five Dynasties, they were unable to excavate or investigate them more thoroughly because a large percentage of the area in question was covered with paddy fields. Zou Heng undertook another exploratory investigation of these ruins in the 1970s, but it found only shards of Eastern Zhou roof tiles. Later investigations did reveal some material that may have been from the Western Zhou period, but it differed dramatically in style from objects in the Central Plains.[50]

There was one other possibility of ruins that could be explored. From the Tang dynasty onward, Shu Yu of Tang's tomb is occasionally mentioned in gazetteers of Taiyuan, and a "King" of Jin tomb (*Jinwangmu* 晉王墓) appears on the 1551 map of the site published in Gao Ruxing's *Taiyuan xianzhi* (Fig. 3.3).[51] Perhaps owing to its compact size, this tomb location was excavated in 1979, but the material found was not earlier than the Tang

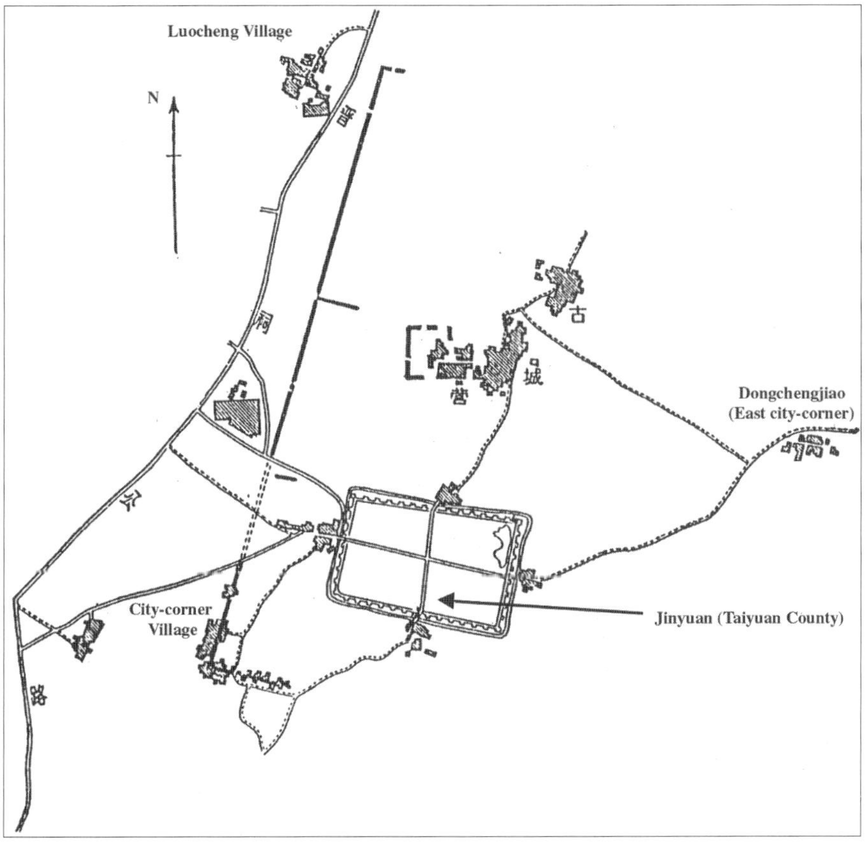

Fig. 3.2 Map of Jinyuan county showing the location of Warring States Period city walls (after Xie, "Jinyang gucheng," 56).

dynasty.[52] Because of the lack of evidence, archaeologists of this area have rejected Jinyang as a possible location of Shu Yu's investiture.

Tang as Yicheng

That is not to say that other areas traditionally believed to be Jin state capitals have been left untouched. In 1962, Xie Yuanlu and his colleagues also surveyed the area around Houma 侯馬 to find the remains of a city wall in the northeastern area of the Quwo county, which similarly appeared to date from as early as the Warring States Period to as late as the Han. That September, members of the cultural relics office at Yicheng discovered bronze vessels in an early Western Zhou tomb about ten kilometers (just over six miles) northeast of the city wall. The following year, a team from the graduating class of the Peking University archaeology department did an experimental excavation under the supervision of the Shanxi Cultural Commission (Wengonghui 文工會), the results of which verified the existence of Western Zhou remains. Although other corroborative discoveries of Early Zhou tombs and cities were made over the following decade, it was not until

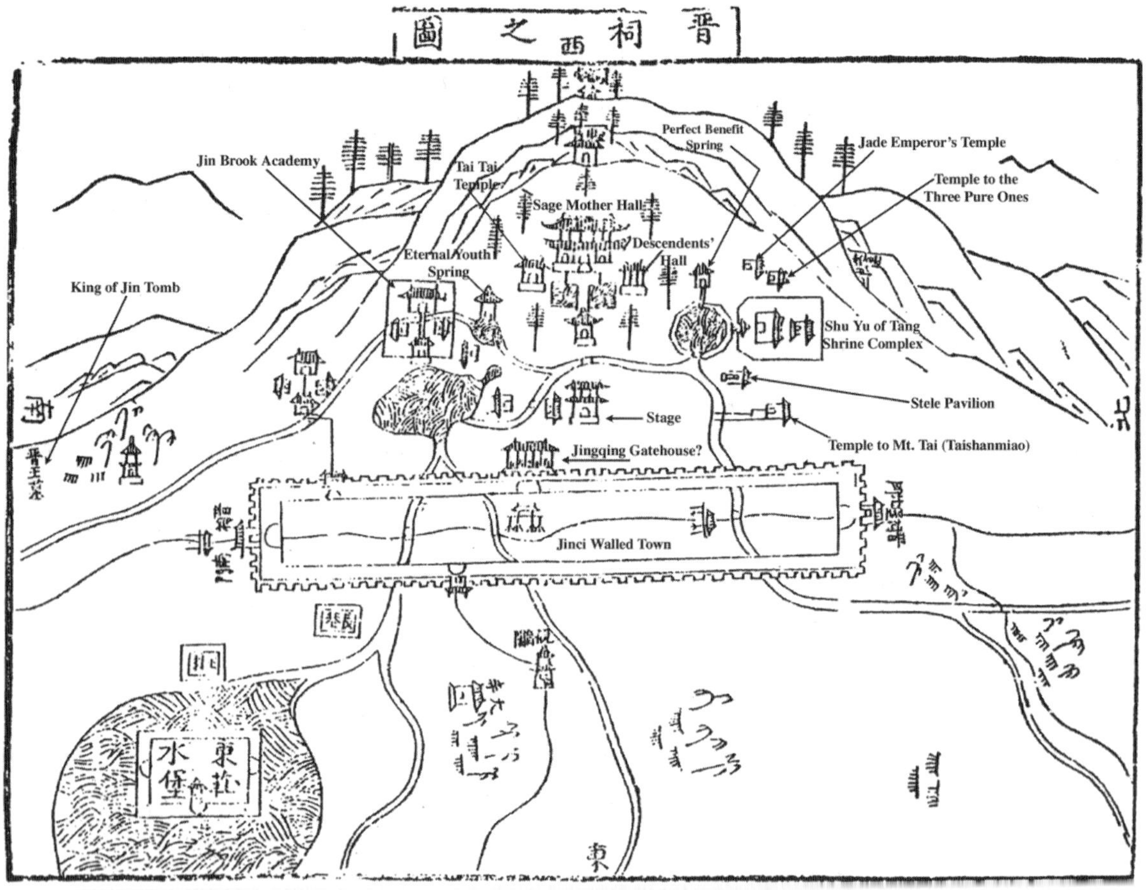

Fig. 3.3 *Jinci zhitu* (Diagram of Jinci), after Gao Ruxing, *Taiyuan xianzhi*, 322. This diagram shows the major features of the site, including springs, canals, the Sage Mother Hall, and Shu Yu of Tang complex in the locations we find them today.

1979 that a formal excavation began in the Tianma 天馬–Qucun 曲村 area.

The area was more fully explored over the next three years.[53] During this time, the site expanded to encompass 3.8 × 2.8 kilometers (2.4 × 1.7 miles) in the vicinity of Tianma-Qucun, including burial grounds and ultimately would exceed that of the Houma excavations.[54] Excavators found a large number of objects dating from the middle to late Western Zhou, periods 3–5, but very few from period 6 and after. This links nicely with the Jin site near Houma that flourished beginning from period 6. This investigation concluded that the Tianma-Qucun area was the old Jin city of Jiang (*Gu Jiangdu* 古絳都). It was made a capital by Marquis Mu of Jin (Jin Muhou 晉穆侯) but was abandoned in favor of the area near Houma called Xintian 新田 (also Xinjiang 新絳) sometime around the beginning of the Eastern Zhou (Fig. 3.4).[55]

In 1984, several early tomb sites were discovered in the area, but archaeologists were unable to excavate. It was not until 1992, after it became known that the tombs were being robbed and bronzes began appearing on

Chapter Four
The Shrine of Shu Yu of Tang

Because modern archaeology confirms that Shu Yu's and Yao's original fief of Tang was located in the Yicheng-Quwo area, far south of the Taiyuan basin, Shu Yu's significance as the primary deity of Jinci appears to be due more to his role in the historical canon as the first Zhou dynasty ruler over Taiyuan at Jinyang, rather than to any continuously maintained temple to him at the Jin Springs from the first millennium BCE. The reason for building a shrine to Shu Yu at the site of Jinci was most likely because the Jin River was the eponym for the Jin state, there was a pre-existing patronage base for the nature spirits who were thought to reside at the springs. Patronage of the Shu Yu Shrine Complex across the imperial period reflects the changing significance of the Zhou-dynasty feudal system for ruling the territory of the Taiyuan basin, as described in the Chinese historical canon. The cult of Shu Yu emerged in the historical record during the time of turmoil after the Han, when Taiyuan played an important role as a power base for warlords and future emperors. Positive textual evidence of a shrine at the site of the Jin Springs begins from the Northern Wei, and even at this time there was likely a ritual complex with multiple worship halls.[1] But in the sixth century CE, Li Daoyuan describes Jinci only as the Shrine of Shu Yu, implying that it was the Jin state ancestral temple. Although the emphasis on Shu Yu at Jinci waned after the capital of Taiyuan was moved from Jinyang and the Jin River, he was still in the sacrificial statutes, and, consequently, a local official was responsible for maintaining his temple and making sacrifices to him. This responsibility became even more important to the local elite during the Ming-Qing transition, when Confucian ritualism and lineage temples began to become an important part of the gentry's agenda for reinvigorating the Confucian tradition and the Zhou-dynasty feudal system. This chapter will first establish the form and significance of the Western Zhou ancestral temple to show that although Shu Yu's shrine is more consistent with those of more generalized, nationally venerated deities, its location at the Jin Springs falls outside of the canonical ancestral temple model. I will then show how Jinyang's loss of status during the Song dynasty resulted in a patronage shift from emperors to local elites, along with a dramatic reduction in the scale and importance of the Jinci shrine and the deity within it.

The Form of Ancestral and Founders' Temples

The ancestral temple was a central part of Zhou dynasty royal ritual, and its construction took precedence in the establishment of capital cities. In this system, the capital city and ancestral temple of a feudal lord would have served to bind the surrounding territory of the fief to the Zhou central government. Scholars of early China believe that the earliest Zhou dynasty temples were dedicated to the royal ancestors, and all extant archaeological and textual evidence suggests that these palace/temple complexes were rectilinear, south-oriented building compounds surrounded by an enclosing wall.

The Zhou dynasty was structured on a feudal system in which the kingdom was ruled through the allocation of states (*guo* 國) to members of the Zhou royal family. Because King Wu died shortly after conquering the Shang royal house, King Wu's younger brother, the Duke of Zhou, and King Cheng, the minor heir to the throne and older brother of Shu Yu, were responsible for conquering the outlying Shang territories. King Cheng established the capital of the Zhou dynasty at Chengzhou 成周 near modern Luoyang, and ritual texts inform us that an ancestral temple to the Zhou founders was constructed at its center.[2] Sixteen descendents of King Wen, four descendents of King Wu, and six descendents of the Duke of Zhou were enfeoffed in the larger region surrounding the Zhou capital, including Shu Yu in the former Shang fief of Tang.[3]

Each of these vassal states under the authority of a Zhou clan member would theoretically have followed the model of the Zhou royal capital by establishing capital cities (also called *guo*) with appropriate temples at their centers, thus creating a system in which members of the Zhou royal house were worshiped across the kingdom. The location and primacy of the ancestral temple in this system follow the well-known description of the establishment of a state capital city found in the *Kaogongji* (ca. fourth–third centuries BCE):

> The builder builds the capital city (*guo*).
> It is nine-*li* square, with each side [of its outer wall] having three gates.
> Within the city there are nine longitudinal streets and nine latitudinal streets.
> The longitudinal streets are nine carriage-widths across.
> On the left [of the ruler/palace] is the Ancestral Temple.
> On the right [of the ruler/palace] is the Altar to Soil.
> In front [of the ruler/palace] is the court.
> Behind [the ruler/palace] is the market.[4]

> 匠人營國。方九里，旁三門。國中九經九緯，經涂九軌。左祖右社，面朝後市。

This scheme has been understood as making the state capital city a ritual center, thereby linking the whole country within both a ritual and a familial network that would function on temporal and supernatural levels.[5] Although the shrine to Shu Yu of Tang at Jinci was in a suburban location outside the city walls, and so was never an official ancestral complex, the concept of binding the local society to the larger state through lineage temples had great appeal in late imperial times. I will return to this theme at the end of the chapter.

Because of its importance in understanding the structure of early Chinese society and culture, the form of the Western Zhou ancestral temple has been the subject of much archaeological and scholarly inquiry. Descriptions in early texts are extremely vague, but if we combine these with archaeological discoveries, we can say that Zhou dynasty palaces and temples appear to be the model of cardinally oriented, rectilinear courtyard complexes on which later, official ritual complexes were based.[6] As discussed by Wu Hung, descriptions of the Zhou building projects in the *Shijing* (*Book of Odes*) emphasize walls and multiple gates rather than the space within the sacrificial halls:

He called his superintendent of works;
He called his minister of instruction; and charged them with the building
of the houses.
With the [plumb] line they made everything straight;
They bound the frame-boards tight, so that they should rise regularly.
Up rose the ancestral temple (*miao*) in its solemn grandeur.
. . . .
They set up the gate of the enceinte;
And the gate of the enceinte stood high.
They set up the court gate;
And the court gate stood grand
They reared the great altar [to the Spirits of the land],
From which all great movements should proceed.[7]

Exactly what the gates in this hymn enclosed is not made clear in the text itself; they may refer to enclosures for a separate ancestral temple complex or a palace complex within which the ancestral temple was one of many buildings.[8] In either case, the emphasis of this passage on the construction of walled compounds with gates is notable, as it becomes a fundamental feature of the imperial ancestral hall.

The foremost example of an excavated palace-temple complex similar to that described in the *Shijing* is the pre-dynastic Zhou site of Fengchu in modern Qishan, Shaanxi province (Fig. 1.4). The complex consists of two large buildings separated by open courtyards and entered through a gatehouse at the southern end. Surrounded by covered corridors extending from subsidiary side halls, the entire complex is symmetrical across a central north-south axis, elevated on a tamped-earth platform forty-five meters north-south by thirty-two meters east-west, and oriented facing southward at 350°.[9] Approximately four meters south of the main entryway, a five-meter-wide screen wall hinders casual viewing into the first courtyard yet still allows ease of entry. This organization of main halls on the central axis with the larger building in front of a smaller structure (*qianmiao houqin* 前廟後寢 or *qianchao houqin* 前朝後寢) became a formula for those wishing to invoke the authority of ancient ritual in later times.[10]

Because the architecture of the Western Zhou kingdom had been lost due to the elements and extensive warfare by the time of the Warring States Period, later Chinese ancestral temples were modeled on a schematic understanding of Zhou precedent recreated from classical textual sources. The enclosing walls, axial symmetry, and southern orientation became the defining characteristics of official ancestral temples. We can see this clearly in the description of the *zongmiao* used in the institutional histories written during the Song dynasty, when the second Song emperor Zhao Kuangyi sponsored the rebuilding of the temple complex to Shu Yu some two thousand years after the building of the Fengchu palace-temple.[11] In his *Wenxian tongkao*, Ma Duanlin (1254–1323) describes the ancestral temple system from the Xia dynasty (2100–1600 BCE) through the beginning of the thirteenth century CE. His schematic diagram of this system emphasizes the organization of the complex rather than detailing the size and shape of individual structures within it. In Fig. 4.1, the ancestral temple complex is located within the larger palace walls. Beginning from Zhou times, the number of ancestors worshiped depended on the status of the individual—the emperor sacrificed to seven, nobility to five, mid-ranking officials (*dishi* 適士) to two, and lower officials (*guanshi* 官師) to one.[12] Each of the temples within the compound would also be oriented southward, with a front hall and back chamber separated by courtyards, and be completely enclosed within a rectilinear wall (Fig. 4.2). Access to the complex would again come from a gateway on the south side.

Temples dedicated to deified historical figures came to follow the courtyard-complex format, with the local deeds that made the deity famous emphasized by means of plaques placed on the individual buildings and/or gateways leading up to those buildings. The primary means of giving respect to and displaying the status of the deity within that building would be to add additional buildings on axis with the main hall or layers of walls and gateways leading up to it.[13] These temples tended to be established in the traditional hometowns of the individuals to whom they were dedicated or in a place where they had performed a particularly worthy deed.[14] It is therefore very likely that the Jin Springs was chosen as a location for a shrine to Shu Yu because of the eponymous relationship between the Jin River and the Jin state, as interpreted by scholars of the Han dynasty and later.

Thus, although official ancestral temples were originally established as a means to bind the vassal states to the royal center, the temple complexes would have been located in the capital city, to the east of the royal palace, within a rectilinear enclosing wall oriented southward. Although Shu Yu of Tang was placed in Tang, part of this original Western Zhou feudal system, and though his enfeoffment was intended to establish a Zhou lineage on the

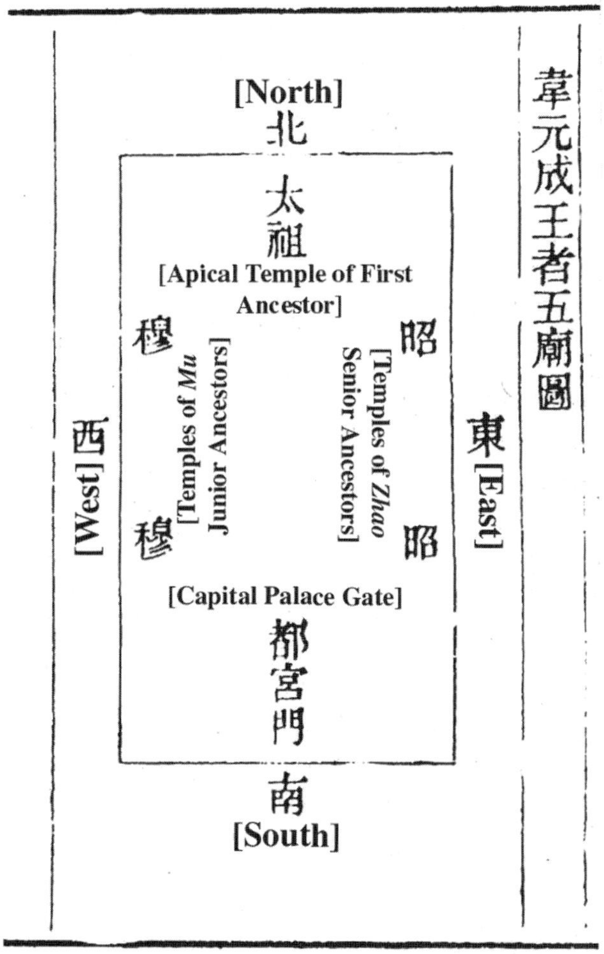

Fig. 4.1 *Wumiaotu* (Five Temples diagram), from the *Wenxian tongkao*, 91/827. This diagram shows the organization of ancestral temples within the larger palace walls. Multiple ancestors were worshiped in their own temples (or temple compounds), each facing south.

northern edge of the kingdom's territory, the shrine to Shu Yu at Jinci did not follow the temple system of placement within the capital city of Jinyang. Furthermore, given that Jinyang was unlikely to have been the original capital of the Tang/Jin state, as seen from the modern archaeological evidence discussed in the previous chapter, it was equally unlikely to have originally been part of this network. But textual documentation of the shrine indicates that the pre-Yuan dynasty complex, and very likely the tenth-century complex, did conform to the walled-courtyard format that was used for individual ancestral temples within this system, as well as for larger temples and shrines dedicated to other deified historical figures.[15] Rather than a change in *organization*, shifts in patronage resulted in a change in *scale*, from the grand shrine patronized by local warlords and emperors through the beginning of the Song dynasty, to a much smaller courtyard complex that required repeated rebuilding by local officials in the Yuan, Ming, and Qing dynasties.

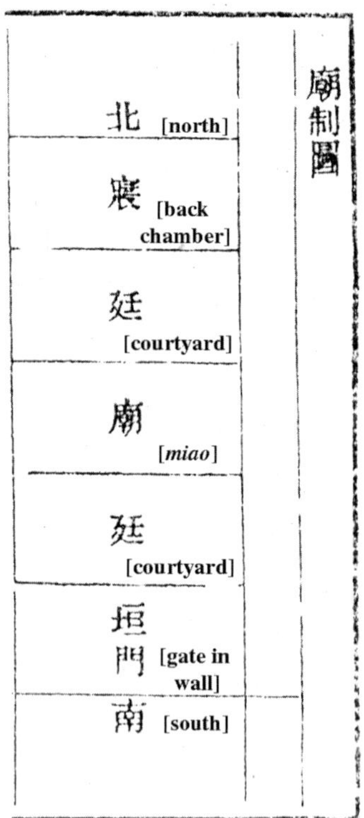

Fig. 4.2 *Miaozhitu* (Diagram of the temple system), from the *Wenxian tongkao* 91/828. This would be the organization of an individual temple within the larger ancestral temple compound. Importantly, this shows a front audience hall and a back hall or vestry (*qin*).

Shu Yu and Imperial Legitimacy: The Founder's Shrine from the Sixth Century Through the Northern Song Dynasty

The location of Shu Yu's shrine at Jinci by the Jin Springs at the foot of Xuanweng Mountain, southwest of the capital city, thus differs fundamentally from the official model as described in classical ritual texts.[16] His identity as a representative of the Zhou royal family in the border region of Taiyuan required that he be given a minimum official ritual complex, but its location at the Jin Springs suggests this was a later addition to a pre-existing site of water-spirit worship. Descriptions of the ritual complex at the Jin Springs written during the time Jinyang was still the location of the regional capital emphasized the overall impact of the shrine complex as a place of spiritual power dominated by a Zhou feudal lord. Documentation of repairs made by local officials beginning in the thirteenth century are more generally descriptive and focus on the cosmological orientation of the complex—that is, on the consistency with which the complex followed the official model.

The appearance of Jinci in Li Daoyuan's *Shuijingzhu* dramatically influenced the elite understanding of divinity worship there. The first definite reference to the Jin Springs, the Jin River south of Taiyuan, and a temple at the site was the *Weishu* entry mentioned in Chapter 2, which tells of a Jinwangci 晉王祠 located at the site of the springs. But Li Daoyuan is the first to describe a shrine complex to Shu Yu of Tang in this location, and it becomes the standard reference for Jinci from this point forward. Reading the passage in full, the springs themselves seem insignificant when compared to the worship of Shu Yu, a historical personage of remarkably esteemed pedigree. Li was clearly impressed that a member of the Zhou royal family could be worshiped here, and his shrine seems to confirm for him that the Taiyuan basin was the original fief of Tang. By describing the history of the place as being Shu Yu of Tang's fief before discussing any other aspect of it, Li Daoyuan implies that Jinci is an official ancestral shrine. Furthermore, because he included Shu Yu's mother Yi Jiang in his quote from the *Zuozhuan*, he opened the door for late imperial historians to equate a female divinity at this site with her historical personage.

[Jinyang] county is the ancient Tang state. According to the *Zuozhuan*, before the birth of Shu Yu of Tang, his mother, Yi Jiang, dreamt of the Thearch, who addressed her saying, "I name your son calling [him] Yu. In the future I will give Tang to him, which is under the constellation Shen." Upon his birth he was named Yu. In the *Lüshi chunqiu* it says, "Shu Yu lived with King Cheng. The king took a paulownia leaf as a *gui* 珪-tablet and gave it to him saying, 'I enfeoff you with this.' [Shu] Yu told the Duke of Zhou this. The Duke of Zhou asked [King Cheng], 'Did the Son of Heaven enfeoff [Shu] Yu?' The king replied, 'I was only jesting.' The Duke said, 'The Son of Heaven has no "jesting" words.'" At that time Tang had been taken [by the Zhou], and Shu Yu was enfeoffed in Tang county. [Within this county] is the Jin River. Later the name was changed to Jin. That is why Zi Xia's[17] "Preface to the [Mao version of the] *Shi[jing]*" said, "This [book is about] the Jin, which is called Tang, because [the people] . . . in their economy regulated by propriety, exemplified the manners which had come down to them from the example of Yao."[18] The Record of Lands and Roads in the *Jinshu* and the *Shisanzhou zhi* both state that "the Jin River emerges from Dragon Mountain, which is also called Jiechu Mountain. It is located northwest of the county seat." This is false. The *Shanhaijing* says, "Xuanweng Mountain . . . the Jin River emerges from it." It is located southwest of the present county seat. In ancient times there was [the event of] the Earl of Zhi damming the Jin River in order to flood Jinyang. [At the spring] in the upper reaches of the river, later people used [the canal's] ruins to create a pool by collecting water [in it]. West of the pool a border of mountains faces the river. There is a shrine to Shu Yu of Tang. Beside the river there is an open-hall, and cantilevered bridge(s) (*feiliang*) are joined over the river. On the left and right various trees interlock to provide shade; rarely do you see the light. Intimate friends and traveling officials go there; none among them does not seek the bridge(s) so as to amuse and console each other. It is the most marvelous place to entertain on the Jin River.[19]

晉水出晉陽縣西懸壅山。

【注】

縣故唐國也。春秋左傳稱叔虞未生。其母邑姜「夢帝謂己【曰】余名而子曰虞。將與之唐。屬之[20]參。」及生。名之曰虞。呂氏春秋曰：叔虞與成王居。王援桐葉爲珪以授之曰。吾以此封汝。虞以告周公。周公請曰。天子封虞乎。王曰。余戲耳。公曰。天子無戲言。時唐滅。乃封之於唐。縣有晉水後改名爲晉。故子夏敘詩稱：「此晉也。而謂之唐。。。。。。。儉而用禮，【乃】有堯之遺風也。」晉書地道記及十三州志並言晉水出龍山以名結絀山。在縣西北，非也。山海經曰。懸甕之山。晉水出焉。今在縣之西南。昔智伯之遏晉水以灌晉陽。其川上溯。後人踵其遺跡。蓄以爲沼。沼西際山枕水。有唐叔虞祠。水側有涼堂。結飛梁於水上。左右雜樹交蔭。希見曦景。至有淫朋密友。羈遊宦子。莫不尋梁契集。用相娛慰於晉川之中最爲勝處。

In this earliest description of the temple complex at the Jin Springs, we gain an image of the place, yet the orientation and detailed placement of the shrine is ambiguous. Li Daoyuan describes the building or buildings wherein Shu Yu was venerated as being located near a pool. Depending on the interpretation of the passage, the shrine may have been located west of the pool with a mountain at its back—that is, in a location very much like that of the Sage Mother Hall's today. A bridge or bridges over the river were emphasized as a popular site for rendezvous.[21] Notably, while describing the site as a destination for travelers to the area, Li does not mention any other spirits being venerated here. Of primary importance was the eponymous relationship between the Jin River and the Zhou period Jin state.

Research on developments in popular religion during the early imperial period suggests that the Shu Yu shrine may have been added to the site of the Jin Springs to take advantage of a pre-existing numinous location and its cult patronage. In his 1985 article on city god cults, David Johnson provides an example of the Dragon Mother of Dragon Mother Mountain near Taizhou 台州, in modern Zhejiang province. As early as the fourth century, legends of a dragon and his numinous mother resident in the mountains near Jiushui Pool (Jiushuitan 湫水潭) had been given historical pedigrees making the dragon king the historical ancestor of a powerful local clan. Following the argument of Edward Schafer discussed in Chapter 2, Johnson suggests that the inclusion of a mother figure in this way is an example of the incorporation and masculinization of an earlier female water spirit into the ancestral cult of the local clan to enhance their power by claiming descent from acknowledged powerful divinities. By the eleventh century the Dragon King had become the city god of Taizhou.[22] Unlike the Taizhou city god, Shu Yu was not identified in the textual record for power over water; rather his significance lay in giving the border region of the Taiyuan basin an intrinsic connection to the Jin state and the Zhou heartland. This relationship would have been graphically displayed by placing his shrine by that of the spirit of the eponymous Jin Springs and River. This would also serve to masculinize and Confucianize the worship that was already taking place there, thereby making it a more legitimate destination for aspiring emperors.

Li Daoyuan's account of the Jin Springs as a popular place for young lords to travel is further supported by a story from the Northern dynasties. Around 534, at the time when the Northern Wei was splitting to become eventually the Eastern and Western Wei, and not long after Li Daoyuan went to the Jin Springs, a group of men including Gao Huan (496–547), the military ruler of the Eastern Wei, went to Jinci. The whole party, except Bi

Xiaotong 薛孝通, kneeled, completely fulfilling the rite of worship. Bi Xiaotong only raised his hands in respect saying, "This is the demesne of the feudal lords, who are removed from me by a great distance (time). To show respect which does not accord with the rites would cause the spirits to laugh." All of those who had fully worshiped were ashamed of their actions.[23] This story is of interest for two reasons. First, Bi Xiaotong did not refer to Shu Yu as a "king," as would have been expected if his shrine were a *wangci* but instead used the term "feudal lords" (*zhuhou* 諸侯). This is an accurate representation of Shu Yu's title during his lifetime and suggests that he had not been elevated during the Northern Wei. Second, aspiring rulers worshiped at Shu Yu's shrine outside official ritual prescriptions, most likely to request his help in their efforts to take the territory for themselves. Again, Shu Yu's power seems to be tied to rights of legitimate sovereignty over the Taiyuan region.

During the Northern Qi Tianbao reign period (550–60), the temple complex at the Jin Springs was greatly expanded with an increase in towering buildings and waterways.[24] According to Tang sources, it was from this time that the complex became a not-to-be-missed tourist attraction (*jieyou jiyan* 皆遊集焉).[25] In 569, the complex was changed from Jinci to Da Chonghuangsi 大崇皇寺, the name of which suggests that it had been changed to a Buddhist institution.[26] This name did not hold for long (although it is unclear for how long it was under Buddhist management) as there is a record of the Northern Qi ruler Houzhu 後主 (r. 576–77) gathering his troops at "Jinci" in 576.[27]

In addition to the worship of Shu Yu, beginning from the seventh century there is textual evidence to support the worship of water-giving spirits at the Jin Springs. Although I will expand upon evidence for early water-spirit worship in Chapter 5, the following event shows the significance of Jinci to rulers stationed at Taiyuan. In 617, when Li Yuan (Tang Gaozu) was the regent (*liushou* 留守) of Taiyuan commandery and planned to overthrow the Sui government, two of his officials, Wang Wei 王威 (the vice-regent) and Gao Junya 高君雅, conspired to assassinate him. Their plan was to convince him to go to Jinci to pray for rain and then ambush him when he arrived. The mayor (*xiangzhang* 鄉長) of Jinyang, Liu Shilong 劉世龍, discovered the plot and warned Li Yuan, who was then able to escape the conspiracy.[28] While this source does not document Li Yuan venerating Shu Yu, it does verify that the first emperor of the Tang dynasty was familiar with the shrine and that spirits with power to bring rain were worshiped there.

In 646, twenty-nine years after the assassination attempt and thirty years after the Tang dynasty was established, Li Shimin 李世民 (r. 626–49), the second Tang emperor and Li Yuan's second son, returned to Jinci and composed the "Jinciming" stele inscription ("Jinciming bing xu" 晉祠銘並序). Although his father traced the origins of his dynasty back to the legendary ruler Yao (traditional ascension date: 2356 BCE) and the traditional belief that the territory of Tang in the Taiyuan basin was his fief,[29] his son focused on the significance of Shu Yu as the first Zhou dynasty ruler of the region. The following are excerpts from Li Shimin's introduction to the "Jinciming," in which he lays out the importance of Shu Yu's support for the Tang dynasty founding.

In beginning a country and establishing a state, one relies on one's closest relatives for assistance. Flourishing virtue (*de*) actually resides in [the act of] dividing the *gui* and bestowing the altar (territory). If not for close relatives then there is nothing by which to establish a full foundation; if not for virtue there is nothing by which it can be transformed. . . .

夫興邦建國，資懿親以作輔。分珪錫社，實茂德之攸居。非親無以隆基，非德無以啓化。。。。。。

Only the spirit of the one who was born efficacious in the Zhou house, descends his virtue on Fengdu, spreading through the branches of the imperial family, multiplies the jade extremes (the power of the north star, i.e., the imperial family); with a warp of benevolence and a woof of righteousness, he walked the path of prosperity and dwelled in correctness. . . .

惟神誕靈周室，降德酆都，疏派天潢，分枝璇極；經仁緯義，履順居貞。。。。。。。

Virtue is that which people honor, [and the people] looked upon [virtue] as the principle of the country. Thereby [the Zhou royal family] was able to unify the [people, which was the] magnificent destiny of the state, guiding in the great foundation of 700 years [of Zhou rule]. . . .

德乃民宗，望爲國範。故能協隆鼎祚，贊七百之洪基。。。。。。

Although the [Jin] territory was split into three parts, the remaining [Zhou] influence was not eliminated, time underwent a millennium of constant change, but the remaining merit is still extant. . . .

雖地盡三分而餘風未泯，世移千祀而遺烈猶存。。。。。。。

It is like the soaring mountains that forever rise, the great fortifications in the territory of San; the border stations surround the strategically important area, representing the nearness of the northern regions. . . .

若夫崇山亙峙，巨鎮參墟；襟帶邊亭，標臨朔土。。。。。。

[Shu Yu] only assists the worthy, it is not the offerings that are considered fragrant [influencing his decision]; [Shu Yu] only relies on virtue, how could containers of sacrificial articles be considered favor. . . .

惟賢是輔，非黍稷之爲馨；惟德是依，豈筐篚之爲惠。。。。。。

Our late emperor inherited a dynastic title that will last for a millennium and gained the expectation of 800 years of endurance. He exhausted the sincerity of his heart to pray for good fortune. When [Li Yuan] first led his troops, he began his success [in creating the Tang dynasty] in this spiritual shrine. He launched [his campaign] swiftly like wind and lightning; rolling [across a] great distance [it] covered heaven and earth. In one war the empire was settled, and all in the six directions became one family. . . .

先皇襲千齡之徽號，膺八百之先期，用竭誠心，以祈嘉福。爰初鞠旅，發跡神祠。舉風電以長驅，籠天地而遐捲。一戎大定，六合爲家。。。。。。

As an emperor, Li Shimin venerated Shu Yu as an act of respect to the Zhou dynasty ruler of the territory. Li Shimin refers to the length of Zhou rule with the wish that his own Tang dynasty supersede it through Shu Yu's support of a worthy ruler. Thirty years after the dynasty had been established, this reference indicated that the Spirit of Shu Yu considered both him and his father virtuous emperors. Perhaps most importantly for those travelers to the area reading the stele inscription, Li Shimin overtly connected the initiation of the dynasty to Jinci. It may not have been the original feudal ancestral temple, but with this act, Li Shimin tied Jinci and the worship of Shu Yu to the founding of the most influential dynasty in Chinese history.

As a younger brother of the previous heir to Li Yuan's throne, Li Shimin may have also felt a personal connection to Shu Yu, the younger brother of King Cheng, which would account for the emphasis he puts on family connections. This link appears again in the Northern Song when the second emperor, also a younger brother, had the Jinci Shrine Complex rebuilt following his conquest of Taiyuan in 979 CE.

Shu Yu continued to be important in legitimizing rule over the region of Taiyuan while the northern provinces of China were again under dispute during the Five Dynasties period. As mentioned in Chapter 3, the first Later Jin dynasty ruler, Shi Jingtang, elevated Shu Yu to King of Arising Peace (Xing'anwang 興安王) and Tai Tai, the Spirit of the Fen River mentioned as a Jin state tutelary divinity in the *Zuozhuan*, to Duke of Flourishing Tranquility (Changninggong 昌寧公) in 941 CE.[30] Shi Jingtang's act of enfeoffment may have been an effort to derive legitimacy from the Zhou rather than the Tang dynasty, thereby superseding his Later Tang predecessors. By 951, the Turkic Northern Han held Taiyuan as their capital and were supported by the Kitan Liao dynasty. Taiyuan was an intermediary step to the northern territories held by the Tang dynasty—territories necessary for the Song to restore the empire to its full form. When the second Song emperor finally conquered Taiyuan in 979, he sponsored a complete rebuilding of the Jinci complex. Upon its completion in 984, the official Zhao Changyan wrote an essay and poem describing the significance of the emperor's conquest and the importance of rebuilding the shrine of Shu Yu of Tang:

> To become unified through pacifying the rebellious, this signifies the emperor's merit. Attaining peace through receiving [divine] mysterious support, [for this] we should honor the way of the spirits. . . .
>
> 除厲階而成混一，式顯帝功。資幽贊而致和平，必宗神道。。。。。。
>
> After viewing the marvelous landscape of the mountains and rivers and inquiring about worthy and dignified personalities at historic sites, his majesty turned to his officials saying, "Jinci is [for sacrifices to] the spirit of Shu Yu of Tang." Shu Yu inherited the great virtue of Hou Ji[31] and continued the great foundation of King Wu of Zhou. Embodying spiritual force and concentrated strangeness, he had the

pattern (character) on his hand, his naming matched the portent of Shangdi (the Thearch). Sharing the fief he was enfeoffed by cutting the *tong* branch, initiating the state he received the position bestowed by King Cheng. . . .

覽形勝於山川，訪賢穆於古昔。顧謂群臣曰：晉祠者，唐叔虞之神也。 叔虞承后稷之洪德，衍周武之丕基。炳靈鍾異，則有文在掌，命名符上帝之言。胙土分茅，則剪桐爲封，開國荷成王之業。。。。。。。

In the beginning, he offered a tribute of Excellent Sheaves of Grain, the Duke of Zhou made public the evidence of his virtue. Afterwards, treading upon his territory in search for allies, [his descendant] Duke Wen became one of the Five Hegemons.[32] This is what is called merit continuing generation after generation, [it is] his favor reaching to the people.

His jade-like virtue is signified to infinity; his fragrant wind (influence) is from the distant [antiquity].

Then [his majesty] noticed that the previous system of the temple was in a state of decline. It was appropriate to order a managing official so that they could enlarge and renew it. . . .

其始也，嘉禾人貢，周公明一德之徵。其後也，踐土尋盟，文公成五霸之業。所謂功垂奕世，澤及生民，昭玉德於靡窮，藹芳風而自遠。乃眷靈祠，舊制仍陋，宜命有司，俾新大之。。。。。。。

Looking at the completed main hall, the galleries surrounding it, the interlocking rafters cover [us from] the sun, flying with [text lost].

Hanging in the sky the great roof-ridges [text lost] in tangled undulation.

The hall and veranda extends and; [text lost].

The myriad brackets gather like constellations; the chiliad pillars shimmer like *zao* aquatic plants.[33]

Bright walls, brilliant and crystalline as the autumn moon; jade lintels, colorful and dazzling as morning clouds.

The lofty [timbers] and radiant [decoration] are now completed on a grand scale.[34]

Furthermore, in front it faces onto an angular pool (*quzhao*), the spring is so deep one can fathom hundreds of feet. At the rear it embraces the steep hill, the mountains and hills, like a screen, reveal heights of ten thousand yards.

It is exactly [this kind of] marvelous site that encourages the residence of the spirits. . . .

觀夫正殿中啓，長廊周布。連甍蓋日，□□而翬飛。巨棟横空，蜿蜒而虬□。欄堂延而□□□□□□□萬拱星攢，千楹藻耀。皓壁光凝於秋月，璇題色晃於朝霞。輪焉奐焉，於茲大備。況復前臨曲沼，泉源鑑澈於百尋。後擁危峰，山岫屏開於萬仞。實惟勝槪，允助神居。。。。。。。

The emperor promulgated an edict to the managing official, that he offer a timely sacrifice.

Having formal and subsidiary [halls], the [shrine is] beautiful and great.

A commentator said, “How great our lord is! Editing the imperial map and coming to the great treasure (sovereignty) which is the foundation of royal ruling.”

Through coming to the ancestral temple to make a (bloodless) offering of timely food, this is to enlarge the ruling in accordance with filial piety.

Encouraging teaching through opening a national academy, this is to develop the teachings of Confucianism.

制命有司，以時致享。有嚴有翼，美矣盛矣。論者曰：大哉我后[35]。纂皇圖而臨大寶，御丕基也。來宗廟以薦時食[36]，廣孝治也。開成均以勸講學，興需教也。

Furthermore, in the Jinyang expedition we have pacified this dark rebelliousness.

Afterwards, we built this temple and courtyard, how could it not be for honoring that outstanding person.

而又晉陽之役，靖茲亂畝。搆此祠庭，豈不以旌彼哲人。

How could this be compared to [the first] emperor of Qin setting out an [imperial] tour to sacrifice to the eight deities on the seashore?

The Han emperors preferred strangeness; they sacrificed to the Earth Queen at Fenyin.

This matter came without historical precedence; none among their government reached to their people.

豈比秦帝浪遊，祀八神於海上。漢皇尚異，祀后土於汾陰。事出不經，政無及物者哉。

The actual poem that makes up the body of the inscription reiterates many of the above sentiments but emphasizes the recent conquest of the Taiyuan region. In this text, Zhao Kuangyi is shown to have saved the local people by eliminating a Turkic warlord and establishing rule from the Yellow River Valley, just as King Cheng and Shu Yu would have done at Tang. The appropriate way for the new ruler to pay respect to and thank the ancient worthies in the region was to rebuild their temples and reinstate sacrifices appropriate to the ancients' status. By re-establishing the proper rites of worship, the power of Shu Yu would allow the region to prosper—proving that the new emperor had the spiritual right to rule.

All barbarian's lands
have entered the imperial territory
None among the rebels in Zhang, Quan, Jiang, or Zhe
was not pacified.

. . . .

四夷百蠻，咸入版圖， 漳泉江浙，罔不盪除。

○ ○ ○ ○ ○ ○

Only at Bingmen
do the people dare to become rebels
they disturbed our boundary
and consolidated their base

. . . .

惟此幷門，敢爲鶩桀，擾我邊陲，固其巢穴。

○ ○ ○ ○ ○ ○

Beginning from this military expedition
[the emperor] enlarged the territory and [text lost] the world
pardoning that leading rebel

[the emperor] avoided polluting our execution tools

興茲戎務，廓萬宇□，捨彼元元，免污鑕斧。

Stabilizing the good people
favor was then distributed
after eliminating the rebellion
[the emperor] then visited [temples of] the ancient worthies

安其良善，惠澤斯布，既除亂畝，乃訪古賢。

Saying, Shu Yu,
who was the descendant of King Wu of Zhou
[that] conferred on [him] by the Thearch in a dream
the character on his hand [text lost]

曰茲叔虞，周武胤傳，夢帝錫兮，掌文□□

He was enfeoffed here by means of cutting the paulownia branch
his transformation was announced [text lost]
prospering and [enjoying] longevity generation after generation
the peace was continued [text lost]

. . . .

剪桐封兮，化宣□□，世榮壽兮，安連□□。

○ ○ ○ ○ ○ ○

[We] order the managing official
to protect this temple
shining the pillars to make [the shrine] worthy of sacrifice
changing (renewing) its dilapidated system

式命有司兮，攸徒是庇，刮楹達享兮，撼其舊制。

The stele inscriptions commemorating the two imperially sponsored reconstructions of the site show that the official reason Li Shimin and Zhao Kuangyi patronized Jinci was to pay homage to the state founder venerated at the site. Like Li Shimin, Zhao Kuangyi was a younger brother who could also have felt a connection to Shu Yu because of his familial position. There are indications even within the inscriptions of the significance of the spring to the people and the site as a whole (which I will discuss at length in Chapters 5 and 6), but overall the focus of the text is to legitimate sovereignty over the strategically important border region of the Taiyuan basin through the power of the Zhou royal family member.

Although he was a younger brother, Zhao Kuangyi did not have the same understanding as Li Shimin of Taiyuan as the origin of his dynasty; rather, he seemed to have considered it a threat to his rule. The first two emperors of the Song had worked as generals in the army of Guo Wei, the founding emperor of the Later Zhou whose power base was in Henan province. Zhao Kuangyin named the Song dynasty after Songzhou, Henan, where he had been appointed military governor under Guo Wei's son Guo Rong.[37] As discussed in Chapter 3, Taiyuan had defied the conquest of Zhao Kuangyin in 969, and as the above inscription makes clear, at Taiyuan the people of Bing stood in strong opposition to the Song. Thus, by rebuilding Jinci, Zhao

Kuangyi made an appeal to the local deities to support his sovereignty over the region while at the same time working to completely dismantle it as a power base.[38] By 982 CE, Zhao Kuangyi had the administrative capital of Taiyuan moved from Jinyang to Yangqu. What was left in its stead was Pacifying Jin county, which was relocated, along with the new administrative capital, away from the Jin Springs on the east side of the Fen River.

Across the Northern Song, extant textual sources document continuous, if sporadic, imperial attention given to the shrine, showing that Shu Yu of Tang continued to be worshiped as a Zhou feudal lord whose power lay in supporting virtuous rulers. By 1011, the buildings and pools of the complex were in a state of disrepair, and because people from outside Pacifying Jin county regularly performed spring and autumn sacrifices there, an imperial decree was sent out ordering the prefectural government to repair the shrine. In 1017, an additional decree was made for the establishment of an official to oversee temple funds and ensure that they were going toward the upkeep of the shrine and sacrifices.[39] Further, in 1070, the shrine, here called the Temple to the King of Arising Peace (Xing'anwang miao 興安王廟) was added to the expanded list of temples used for sinecures when Wang Anshi 王安石 (1021–86) began to use the sinecure system to provide alternative means of employment for officials who disagreed with him at court.[40] In 1104, Emperor Huizong's court changed Shu Yu's title from King of Arising Peace to King of the East of the Fen River (Fendongwang 汾東王),[41] reiterating the connection between Shu Yu and the management of the territory.[42]

The final Northern Song document mentioning Shu Yu of Tang and his shrine confirms the importance of this deity for imperial control over Bing prefecture. This text, dated June 2, 1123, and, from at least the Ming dynasty called the "Text Giving Thanks for Rain" ("Xieyuwen" 謝雨文), goes one step further to attach Shu Yu's power to that of the water goddess also enshrined at Jinci. As I will discuss in much greater detail in Chapter 6, during this same period, in particular during the late eleventh and early twelfth centuries, the Spirit of the Jin Springs became officially recognized for providing rain and received several title increases from the central government. A drought in the Taiyuan area during the 1120s required that the local official take action by worshiping efficacious rain deities; here, that meant the Sage Mother of Clear Efficacy and Manifest Aid, the Jin Springs water spirit who had been first officially recognized in 1077 at a time when water spirits across the empire were receiving noble titles from the Song court.[43] Because this text is vital for understanding late imperial interpretations of the identities of and relationship between these two divinities, I have quoted significant sections of it for discussion below:

> Then the sacrifice was made at the Shrine of the Sage Mother of Clear Efficacy and Manifest Aid and the King of the East of the Fen:
>
> Hereby, I received an edict to serve as the Pacification commissioner [of this region], both Yan and Jin are under my control. . . .

致祭于顯靈昭濟聖母汾東王之祠：兹啣命而出使兮，總燕晉之撫綏。。。。。。。。。

When Yun[zhong] (modern Datong) and Shuo[zhou] first came to belong to us, our heavenly majesty impressed the distant barbarians.

惟雲朔之初附兮，震天聲於遠夷。

I believe, if it were not for the secret assistance of the divinities, by what means could we have prevented these vermin from pilfering from our borders?

. . .

諒非神之隱相兮，何以杜鼠竊於藩籬？

。。。。。。

In speaking of the origin of the Sage Mother's fortune, she originated the House of Jin by establishing its foundation.

惟聖母之發祥兮，肇晉室而開基。

The king had the manuscript on his hand,[44] from this his spiritual efficacy could be known.

王有文之在手兮，其神靈之可知。

We see the forest's band of reflection (in the stream), the cliffs and rockeries manifest an outstanding nature.

顧林薄之映帶兮，發嚴岫之英奇。

The spring(s) emit from beneath the hall(s), providing for the 10,000 *qing* within their magnificent slopes.

泉一出於堂下兮，作萬頃之宏陂。

Surely this is the cave residence of efficacious transcendents, and thus it is appropriate to have a temple and sacrifices for them here.

信靈仙之窟宅兮，宜廟食之在兹。

How do we know the abundant favor in the story "Bestowing the Cereal?"[45] It is undoubtedly to favor the homeland.[46]

矧歸禾之盛德兮，惠故土而不疑。

Judging from the evidence we have, only the Sage Mother, and not Shu Yu, was known for being a rain spirit, making the inclusion of Shu Yu in the text extraordinary. But the timing of the text is crucial for understanding its significance. The document was written only ten days after the return of the Sixteen Prefectures from the Liao to the Song on May 22, 1123. Although the Song received the maps for Yunzhong and Shuozhou (and nine other prefectures in northern Shanxi), Shuozhou was held only for a short period before the Jin dynasty retook the territory.[47] Jiang Zhongqian mentions this event twice in the "Xieyuwen." I suggest that the primary reason Shu Yu of Tang is mentioned in this document is the overwhelming importance of the moment when the full empire was finally unified under Chinese rule. Jiang Zhongqian believed that the Sixteen Prefectures had been given to the Song through the help of that member of the Zhou royal family who ruled over the northern borderland, Shu Yu.

The Shape of the Pre-Yuan Shu Yu Shrine Complex

It is impossible to determine the precise location of Shu Yu's shrine complex during the Song-Jin period, since the only pre-Yuan buildings that survive to the present are the Sage Mother Hall and the Offering Hall. Yet, some information exists in Yi Gou's "Record of the King of the East of the Fen Temple Complex Repair" from 1267. One purpose of the repair project and establishment of the stele was to define the extent of the compound both before and after the destruction of the area during the Jin-Yuan wars. The site before the rebuilding was described thus:

> More than 100 paces south (in front) of the King's hall was the *sanmen*, further south (forward) 200 paces was Jingqing Gatehouse. Outside Jingqing Gatehouse turning east several tens of paces it connects with a north/south postal road. In this sense the scale of the temple was quite magnificent. Furthermore, to convenience swift entry and exit, the inhabitants there also constructed a road east of the Sage Mother Hall and established a *sanmen* (gatehouse) there.[48]

> 王殿南百於步爲三門，又南二百步許爲景清門。門之外東折數十步合南北驛路。則廟之制又甚雄且壯矣。居民利其出入之便又當聖母殿開道而東制三門焉。

If one pace was approximately 1.56 meters, then the distance between the hall dedicated to Shu Yu and his own entry gatehouse (*sanmen*) would have been more than 156 meters.[49] There would have been another 312 meters between the *sanmen* and the Jingqing Gatehouse (景清門), which appears from the description to be the main entry to the whole complex.[50] By comparison, the outer wall of the eighteenth-century Shu Yu of Tang complex is less than 57 meters total from the gatehouse to the back of the Main Hall. Furthermore, the main gatehouse to the Jinci complex in late imperial times (approximately located) was less than 190 meters southeast of the Sage Mother Hall.[51] If Yi Gou's measurements were accurate, then the scale of the Song-Jin dynasty complex would have been half again the size of Jinci during the Qing and twentieth century.

In addition to the vast difference in scale between what is presently the core of the Jinci temple complex and the pre-Yuan site, the location of the main gatehouse also appears to be different. If the Shu Yu shrine were in the vicinity of the present complex, the Jingqing Gatehouse would have been at least 150–200 meters south of the Sage Mother's offering hall, and 75–125 meters south of the nineteenth-century complex wall. Most importantly, it would have been south of the Sage Mother Hall rather than southeast of it. Thus, the larger pre-Yuan complex, of which the Sage Mother Hall was only part, was likely oriented north-south, or at least considered such by the local inhabitants consulted during the survey of the site. This supposition is supported by two lines within the 1267 inscription. The first is quoted above: "For the sake of convenience, the inhabitants there constructed a road east of the Sage Mother Hall and established a *sanmen* gatehouse there." This gateway east of the Sage Mother Hall was built in addition to the Jingqing Gatehouse to facilitate entrance to the site by the local population, who by now was primarily interested in the Sage Mother rather than Shu Yu. The location of the Qing/twentieth-century Jingqing Gatehouse was also east of the Sage Mother Hall, but this transposition of names must have occurred after the thirteenth-century survey.[52]

The second piece of evidence comes from a different section of the inscription, which describes the beauty of the pavilions and lakes on the site. After this description, Yi Gou states, "*[N]orth* of the Jingqing Gatehouse is a place for sightseeing which is extremely beautiful, quiet, and vast" (emphasis mine). Taken together, it is clear that the main gatehouse of the pre-Yuan Jinci temple complex was located to the south, and it was only in response to the demands of the local population that the temple-complex began to be reoriented with the addition of a secondary *sanmen* on the east side of the complex.

Local Officials and the Shu Yu Cult

Local officials from the Yuan through the Qing dynasties found it difficult to maintain the Shrine to Shu Yu at its Song-dynasty scale without imperial patronage. Beginning from the thirteenth century, documentation of repairs to Jinci describe the periodic rebuilding of the Shu Yu complex necessitated by the lack of local interest in continued upkeep. At the same time, locals were supporting the Sage Mother Hall and the water-providing deity housed within it. When rebuilding did take place, an effort was made to construct the shrine in accord with official shrine buildings wherever possible.

The detailed description of Jinci recorded in "A Record of the King of the East of the Fen Temple Complex Repair" provides most of the information for the site during the eleventh to twelfth centuries. The Yuan dynasty had conquered the Jin in 1234, and the operation of the complex was given to the official Master of Untraditional Religious Communities (*zhangjiao* 掌教), the Perfect Realization (*Quanzhen* 全真) Daoist master Zhang Zhijing 張志敬 (who held the position from 1257 to 1270).[53] Because the pre-Yuan site was quite vast, funds enabled the local officials to rebuild Shu Yu's complex according to the "rites of a king," but they were insufficient to rebuild the rest of the complex at its previous scale.

> The king's temple deteriorated daily without being repaired; as a result the matter of sacrifice disintegrated without being reestablished. This continued through repeated administrations after the war, therefore [the people and administrators of the region] only required of it the pleasure of visiting the mountains and rivers. They did not remotely know how to take care of the intention of venerating a king of previous times; how could one sigh enough? . . .
>
> 王之祠日就頹圮而弗修，祀事廢墜而弗舉。因循逮於兵後累政，惟求山水遊觀之樂。而向之尊王之意邈不知省，可勝歎哉？。。。。。。

Prior to this, the buildings were destroyed, the location of his spirit tablet was too narrow; now all destroyed parts were replaced and renewed. Both the inside and the outside were lined with [statues of] palace attendants, high-ranking officials, and guards in accordance with a king's rites. Further a new vestry (*qindian*) was built behind [the main hall] and many pines and cedars were planted. The only worry of the inhabitants who participated in raising funds to help the temple was to be behind [in terms of the quantity of donations]. . . .

先是殿宇摧毀，神位迫窄，廢壞皆補完而更新之。内外列以宮侍，卿大夫，武衛如王者儀。又創寢殿於其後，多植松柏。里人化之樂助用者，惟恐其後。。。。。。

Presently, other than the king's hall, although it is not able to be completely like the original scale, [people] are actually following the intention of Mr. Li by ceaselessly building; it is adequate to be a blueprint for a complete restoration [in the future].[54]

今王殿之外，雖未能盡如舊制，誠能纘承公意營葺不已，足爲他日完復張本。

By 1267, the local inhabitants had forgotten about the historical significance of Shu Yu to Jinci, and it had become a water-spirit shrine. The officials felt it their responsibility to renew the rites and rebuild Shu Yu's temple complex according to the rites of his title, King of the East of the Fen River. This included a series of attendants as well as a new vestry (*qindian*) behind the main hall, causing the shrine to conform more fully to the *qianmiao houqin* arrangement of ancestral temples standard from the Period of Disunion.[55]

The whole Jinci complex was repaired again in 1342, and the description of the complex in the memorial inscription of the project by Wang Sicheng 王思誠 is the first that states that the Shu Yu Shrine Complex was oriented north-south. Significantly, according to this gentry author in the late Yuan, the site was named Jinci because of the shrine's location near the riverside and was commonly visited by people of the region (Bingzhou) in order to pray for rain.[56] At this time the importance of Shu Yu was lost even on the local officials.

In 1370, the first Ming dynasty emperor stripped all noble titles from spirits across the empire,[57] and by the next year Shu Yu was known as the Spirit of Shu Yu, rather than King of the East of the Fen River, thereby ending his association with political power over that territory.[58] During the late Ming, Shu Yu began to gain the attention of the gentry beyond the local magistrate. Their efforts to rebuild his shrine and re-establish proper rites of worship appear to be part of a larger effort by late Ming gentry to restore local order. This rebuilding is also significant because we have for the first time pictorial evidence of the shape of the complex and can see the similarities between the Shu Yu shrine and the official temple system described in the classics.

Shu Yu's shrine complex was repaired in 1548 by a group of administrative officials and local literati.[59] The map of the area from 1551, only three years after this restoration, shows the Shu Yu Shrine Complex as a standard walled-courtyard format with the main buildings on axis (see Fig. 3.3).[60] Cardinal directions are indicated on the outer edge of the drawing and show that the shrine to Shu Yu was oriented southward, behind the Octagonal Pool. The configuration of the buildings is consistent with that described in the 1267 commemorative stele by Yi Gou, with the larger main hall in front and a smaller back hall or vestry behind, in the *qianmiao houqin* arrangement. Although not shown in detail on this map, the individual buildings were made to conform to the *Erya* definition of *miao* and *qin,* as the new construction also included the addition of "wing halls" on either side of the main hall.[61]

The rebuilding of the Shu Yu Shrine Complex was intended to remind the people of the importance of this historical figure. As at the end of the Song, this effort became necessary because money and attention were being lavished on the water-giving Sage Mother while Shu Yu was being ignored. The desire of the local gentry to renew the rites of worship to Shu Yu is manifest in the inscription documenting this repair:

Shu Yu of Tang was the son of King Wu of Zhou and the younger brother of King Cheng. . . .

唐叔虞，周武王子，成王弟也。。。。。。。

Annually on the twenty-fifth day of the third month there is a local executive who supervises the sacrifice, which was recorded in the sacrificial statutes. From the Zhiyuan period[62] to the present it has been more than 200 years; the beams are broken, and it cannot provide shelter from the wind and rain. Consequently, the spirit has lost his residence, and the sacrifices are no longer sincere.

歲以三月二十五日有司致祭，載在祀典。自至元迄今二百餘年，棟梁摧折不蔽風雨，神失所棲，祀事弗虔。

Beside [the King of Jin Shrine] is the Sage Mother Shrine. Every day the candles and incense are offered in large quantities. But Shu Yu of Tang's shrine is alone by the water; people do not even know that he is the proper divinity.

其旁有所謂聖母祠者，香火日極崇奉，而唐叔虞之祠，顧寂寞水濱，不知爲正神。

How could that which is involved with [the shrine of Shu Yu] merely be reduced to the offering of incense and wine? In the winter of the twenty-sixth year of the Jiajing reign period (1547), Vice Censor Li Chengyun (Su Wei's deputy) and Assistant Censor Zhu Zheng, because this matter was related to the sacrificial statutes and the way of transforming local customs lay within it, moreover requested me and the office of the Censorate [to take action].[63] Thereby, [I] issued a document to those officials [who are in charge of this] to remove [the rotten timbers] and renovate [the shrine]. In addition to sculpting images, on the left and right sides of the hall wing halls were built, each being several pillars (bays) [across the front façade]. Then, metal (gold), emerald, cinnabar, and lime plaster completely changed its appearance, which is sufficient to match with the sacrifice.

其所係豈特瓣香酌酹已耶？嘉靖二十六年冬，憲副李君乘雲，憲僉朱君徵，以其事關祀典，而風化之道攸存，具以請於予與巡臺。因檄下所司，撤而新之。復增塑其像，左右各建翼室若干楹。於是金碧丹堊，煥然改觀，足稱報祀矣。

In front of the temple there is an octagonal pool; on the right side of it is the Perfect Benefit Spring; on the mountain are the River View *Ting*-gazebo and Reading Terrace, which we also dredged and repaired with the surplus funds, and the ancient relics were restored. With regard to this action, because the funds were raised through the water conservancy works, the labor was hired (rather than being corvée), the administrator was not burdened and people were not disturbed. Magistrate Hou Lan, County Secretary Li Zhu, Recorder Gao Wei, and Historiographer Zhang Shan supervised with the utmost diligence. Furthermore, the local gentleman (*daifu*) and Vice Censor Gao Ruxing took a lead in righteous action and collaborated with the multitude, making an even greater contribution. . . .

祠前有八角池，右有善利泉，山畔有望川亭，讀書臺，亦以餘力載浚載修，古蹟用復。是舉也，貲因於水利，工出於雇募，官不告勞，民不知擾。之縣侯瀾，縣丞李祝，主薄高巍，典史張珊，供事惟勤。而鄉大夫憲副高汝行實倡義協眾，尤有力焉。。。。。。。

Pan Jiuling told Gao Ruxing, "This [event] cannot be without a carved [inscription] to illuminate it forever." . . .

潘君九齡告高汝行曰：「是不可無刻，以昭永久。」。。。。。。

Thereafter Gao Ruxing wrote about the complete process and begged an essay from me: "I have personally heard that among those that benefit the myriad things, none is greater than water; however among those which inspire the myriad things, none is better than wind. If the [water's] benefit is not guided strictly, then there will be a disaster. If the wind is not dispersed correctly, then it will be perverted. Intending to have them purified and transformed to be appropriate for the people is difficult. Presently the shrine is by the Jin River; its irrigation water benefits the people. They say [they just] go to (focus on) the other sacrificial affairs (worship of the Spirit of the Jin Springs) [in their] prayers. Yet Shu Yu began his enfeoffment from the *wutong* leaf. His descendants survived throughout the Zhou Dynasty; their merit and favor to this land can be researched [in the classics]. However, the devotees have reversed this [and sacrificed to him] last. As a consequence his temple daily fell into disrepair. Under these circumstances, how do we express the proper customs? . . .

而高君因具其始末，乞文於予：竊嘗聞之：利萬物者，莫善於水；而其動萬物也，莫善於風。利匪導以禁之則爭，風匪端以揚之則悖，欲淳化宜民難矣。今祠在晉水上，民之利其潤也，方日諂他祠事報祈，乃叔虞自翦桐啓封，歷世與周久遠，則其功德於斯土可考也。顧祀者反後，而使其祠日頹，曷以示風？

。。。。。。

. . . the [water's] benefit [can be used] to nourish the people and the wind's influence to enlarge the transformation. How could it be that only the people of Jin obtain good fortune and benefit [from the gods]? Those who are in charge of the government also rely on it. Thereby, in order to manifest what is important regarding this shrine, I inscribe it on the Lisheng stone. Furthermore, I wrote three articles to welcome and to see the gods off, to let them ascend in the hymns."[64]

。。。。。。利以滋養，風以宏化。豈惟晉人獲樂利之休？司政紀者亦將可憑藉矣。爰爲著其相關重者，俾刻諸麗牲之石.復爲迎降送神詞三章使登歌焉。

Unlike Yuan-dynasty repairs of Shu Yu's shrine, the late Ming restoration was sponsored by a group of educated elite who pressured the magistrate to order a restoration. Their purpose was both to remind the local people of their cultural heritage dating back to the Zhou dynasty and to provide an acceptable shrine where the deity could dwell. This inclination was part of a trend among the educated gentry elite to reinstate Zhou-dynasty ritual precedents at the local level.[65] This change in attitude accompanied larger societal transformations of the sixteenth century as increasing mercantilism left the Confucian elite anxious about the morals of the local populace. To understand the urgency these men felt, it is necessary to learn about the significance of the spring to the expanding irrigation community surrounding the Jin Springs, the subject of the next chapter.

The Symbolic Value of the Shrine to Shu Yu

The basic features of southern orientation, main halls on a central axis and surrounding walls used in the Shrine to Shu Yu of Tang, derive from Zhou-dynasty precedents of palace-temples, which were most likely used for a system of ancestor worship that functioned to bind the Zhou kingdom to a ritual network. Shu Yu was a feudal lord within that system, but because his shrine at Jinci was not located next to an official residence in his capital city of Jinyang, it was probably never an official ancestral temple. Instead, the location of the hall near the Jin River is consistent with shrines and temples dedicated to deified historical figures separate from an official lineage. Rather than signifying a specific sect, the courtyard complex was used more broadly for high-status or officially sanctioned deities and corresponds with the universal application of belief systems shared by a national culture. One does not have to be trained in how to use this space. The complex is part of a homogenized vocabulary of religious architecture used across the empire in which the ritual progression through buildings is consistent from complex to complex, region to region.[66]

The format of this type of shrine allowed it to be expanded or contracted without compromising the identity of Shu Yu of Tang as an official deity. But changes in patronage were reflected in the size of the shrine. Because of the Taiyuan basin's strategic importance, Shu Yu was significant on an imperial level from the sixth through the tenth centuries when the regional capital was located at Jinyang near the Jin Springs. Before establishing his own rule through the Eastern Wei puppet emperors, Gao Huan performed the full rite of worship to Shu Yu. Li Shimin furthered the fame of Shu Yu's power by stating that the Tang conquest began from Jinci. In 984, Zhao Kuangyi ordered the temple complex of Jinci to be repaired as a way of paying respect to Shu Yu after his own conquest of non-Chinese Turkic rulers. Although imperial patronage of the shrine continued sporadically across the

Northern Song, after the capital was moved north, local interest in water spirits and the cult of the Sage Mother gradually began to take precedence. The Song-dynasty shrine to Shu Yu was also much larger than could be maintained in later periods without continuous imperial support.

The importance of Shu Yu as a Zhou family member was eventually lost on the local officials of the Yuan dynasty, but by the end of the Ming, gentry in the Taiyuan region sought to rediscover the Zhou-dynasty heritage of Shu Yu and Jinci. The trend to re-establish "classical" rites was to take on great fervor during the following century, after another northern steppe people conquered the country in 1644. These men were not just working to restore the cult of Shu Yu, however, their goal was also to restore a proper Confucian social order, one that had no space for an irrigation community focused on a powerful water goddess. It is to this goddess and the ritual complex that developed around her worship hall that we now turn.

Chapter Five
The Jin River and the Emergence of the Spirit of the Jin Springs

A temple to the Spirit of the Jin Springs existed at the site of the springs as an expected part of the religious landscape long before we have positive historical documentation for it. The Spirit of Shu Yu may have been important for those who desired to conquer the area of the Taiyuan basin, but the Spirit of the Jin Springs was central to the agrarian community that likely settled in the region in the first place because of the spring. Prior to her entry into the official sacrificial statutes in the eleventh century, documentation of water-spirit worship was never overt and is nearly unseen in nationally distributed or official histories. This should come as no surprise to us. As discussed in Chapter 2, small temples to spirits of springs were common if not essential elements of a springs setting. By the time clear textual sources on the site are available, however, we only have allusions to a water spirit in stele inscriptions written primarily for local audiences and in poems about visits to the place. These references imply that the spring spirit was always present and so usual at the spring site that she was not worth mentioning in non-local histories. In this chapter I trace the history of the springs and of the canal system that was developed to make broader use of this natural resource. I then discuss the textual evidence for the worship of a female spring spirit, from the early imperial period through her canonization in the eleventh century and consequent inclusion in ritual texts written by local officials in the twelfth century. This canonization and later additions of noble titles to the Spirit of the Jin Springs provide the official, textual basis for later reinterpretations of the divinity as the mother of Shu Yu of Tang. Yet, when examined in the context of documentation (or lack thereof) of other feminine divinities, we see that through the Yuan dynasty and into the Ming, the Sage Mother was a powerful local nature spirit; other, more mundane identities were not necessary to validate her worship.

Springs, River, Canal

Official interest from county and central governments in water management and water-providing deities allowed for the Spirit of the Jin Springs to gain the recognition necessary for her and her temple to attain official sanction and be included in the historical record.[1] Although the Jin Springs and River were important sources of water from as early as the Warring States Period, beginning from the Han dynasty, the canal system was developed to provide irrigation water to an increasing number of people. As the canal system expanded, documentation grew about the importance of the spring, and it is therefore very likely that the expanding canal system resulted in an increased patronage base for the spring spirit. The Spirit of the Jin Springs appears in the historical record in 1077, two years after water-management projects extended the reach of the canal system to more than five times that of the previous century, and two years after the central government announced a new effort to document all rain-providing deities in the empire.

As discussed in Chapter 2, the location of Jinci at the springs of the Jin River allowed for the site to be dedicated to either the Jin Springs spirit or the spirit of the Jin state founder, Shu Yu. Additionally, as spring-spirit temples were common and usually relatively small, they did not always appear in larger geographic works. Where they did, the divinities' female gender was often written out of the text. Although recording the plethora of goddess temples was not given priority by Chinese officials, the documentation of waterways was very important, and the Jin Springs and River were recorded in perhaps the earliest of these sources, the *Shanhaijing*. Like most pre-Qin texts, its dating is problematic and disputed, but it is probably from no later than the Warring States Period.[2] The Jin Springs and River are mentioned in the entry on Xuanweng Mountain contained in the chapter on the northern mountains found in the "Wuzang shanjing" (五臧山經), the oldest portion of the text.[3] This portion is a catalogue of the holy sites inhabited by the multiplicity of divinities (*shen* 神), providing some evidence that nature spirits were worshiped here from the earliest times.[4] The Jin River is described as originating in this mountain and flowing east into the Fen River.[5] Rites of worship to the unspecified divine residents of the mountain follow at the end of the section.

The Treatise on Geography in the *Hanshu* states that the source of the Jin River was at Dragon Mountain, northwest of Jinyang (Qin-Han Taiyuan commandery) and that it flowed eastward into the Fen River.[6] The *Hou Hanshu* follows the earlier *Hanshu* description and further records a repair to the canals around Taiyuan in 116 CE, stating that the canal was used to irrigate both government and private lands.[7] Tang-dynasty commentary on this passage suggests that the canals repaired were the same as those discussed in the later *Shuijingzhu*.[8] We know that the Jin River was south of Jinyang/Taiyuan; thus, later texts regard the description of the Jin Springs being located northwest rather than southwest as a simple transmission error.[9]

The most detailed description of Jinci prior to the Tang dynasty is in Li Daoyuan's Jin River entry in the *Shuijingzhu*, discussed in Chapter 4. Although this quote is the most frequently repeated from the *Shuijingzhu* in later sources about the site, the section following the quote is helpful for understanding the history of the canal system. The *Shuijing* passage states that the river continued east, passed south of the county seat, and then traveled further east to empty into the Fen River. Li Daoyuan's commentary expands on this by adding that two waterways flowed out of the angular pool (*zhao* 沼) mentioned in the first section.[10] The northern canal was the old canal used by the Earl of Zhi in his attack on Jinyang during the Warring States Period. It led to the northeast and into the city of Jinyang in order to irrigate the surrounding gardens, and exited the city on the southeast side, where it emptied into the Fen River. The southern waterway passed through a subterranean channel under a stone tank (*shitang* 石塘)[11] and emerged southeast of the old stream, passing south of the city of Jinyang and emptying into the Fen River to the east.[12] The two major canal branches at the Jin Springs today are split directly in front of the Eternal Youth Spring. Although the water here has been contained in a stone-lined "tank" since the Tang dynasty, this may be the location of the original *zhao* in Li Daoyuan's work.[13]

During the Sui dynasty, there were two Jin River water-management projects. In 584, a third canal was built that flowed southeast into the Fen River. Then, in 586, irrigation canals were built leading off of the southern canal discussed by Li Daoyuan, which would have been the central canal at the time. These canals were used to create the Jin Marsh (Jinze 晉澤) south of the Jinyang county seat and were used for rice farming.[14]

Some fifty-three years later, after the Tang dynasty had been established but before the second Tang dynasty emperor, Li Shimin, returned to Jinci and wrote the famous Jinciming inscription, the canal system was expanded again to meet the needs of the growing urban area. As discussed in Chapter 3, Jinyang had been a capital city during the Northern Qi, and the area remained an important strategic and administrative center through the Tang and Five Dynasties. By the end of the Sui dynasty, three walled enclosures existed within the larger Jinyang city wall located on the west side of the Fen River. In 639, two years after he built the East City (Dongcheng) on the east bank of the Fen River, Administrator Li Ji built an aqueduct called the Jin Canal (Jinqu 晉渠) for the Jin River to cross the Fen and supply its eastern bank with water. The canal then turned westward and drained back into the Fen. Two reasons are given for this expansion. First, Li Ji needed water to fill the eastern moat, presumably necessary since the Fen River was now on the west side of the city wall.[15] Second, the land on the east side of the Fen had a high concentration of salt, making the well water undrinkable. Li Ji built the aqueduct to provide drinking—and probably irrigation—water for those on the east bank of the river.[16] In addition to the aqueduct, the pool in front of the Eternal Youth Spring was faced with stone to create a "tank" in the early Tang dynasty. By the Yuanhe reign period (806–21), three streams extended from this point: the northern Earl of Zhi Canal, the canal extending directly eastward discussed by Li Daoyuan, and the third, southernmost canal, added in 584.[17]

The next documented addition to the Jin River canal system took place more than four hundred years after Li Ji built his aqueduct. In 1060, the magistrate of Pacifying Jin, Chen Zhibai 陳知白 (fl. eleventh century), expanded the canal network both to use in irrigation and to increase the productivity of water milling.[18] This may have been necessitated by severe damage to Taiyuan at Jinyang in 979, when the Song defeated the Northern Han by first flooding and then burning the city. Documentation of the project, dated March 7, 1063, indicates that the farmers were initially resistant to any change. Because of a rumor that an increase in the amount of farmland would result in an increase in taxes, the farmers, who would otherwise have stood to gain much from the expansion, opposed the project. Chen Zhibai announced that those spreading rumors would be punished, thereby assuring the people that their taxes would not increase. After this project, the people's (*min* 民) arable land was increased by 22,170 *mu* 畝, to a new total in excess of 33,459 *mu*.[19] Additionally, the canals powered twelve mills that could be used by private individuals.

The new system divided the water from the Eternal Youth Spring into ten shares. Seven of these shares came from a hole excavated in the temple wall in front of the spring. Those seven were further divided for even distribution. Four of the shares went directly east, and three went north through a "Sage Mother pool" (*shengmuchi* 聖母池) before turning eastward to lead into the old Taiyuan walled city. One-and-a-half shares went directly south past Fengsheng Cloister 奉聖院 and then eastward to Guo Village 郭村. One share went into Jinci Village 晉祠村. The remaining half portion went southeast into the Lubao River 陸堡河.[20] The canal system was repaired again in 1075, expanding the amount of land irrigated to more than 60,000 *mu*.[21]The description of the canal system resulting from the 1060 expansion is similar to the configuration described in the next documented discussion of water management nearly four hundred years later. It seems, therefore, that little change occurred in the canal system of the Jin Springs during the Yuan and early Ming dynasties.

From the earliest history of Xuanweng Mountain and the Jin Springs, the place had been famous for the local nature spirits residing there. After the initial canals were established in the Later Han dynasty, their reach was gradually expanded so that an increasing percentage of the local population was dependent on the springs both to irrigate their farmland and power their mills, reaching a new height in 1060 and 1075 when the canal system was expanded to irrigate more than five times its earlier potential, from 11,289 *mu* to more than 60,000 *mu*. The expanding patronage base across the early imperial period is paralleled by increased discussion of the spring, in addition to the shrine to Shu Yu. And the dramatic development of the canal system in the eleventh century further extended the number of people beholden to the Jin Springs for their livelihoods. These people were responsible for the water spirit's presence in stele inscriptions about the site and her belated entry into the official historical record in 1077, and were the source of the continued patronage necessary to maintain the building constructed for her from the eleventh through the twentieth century. The next section examines the development of the cult to the Spirit of the Jin Springs and of the temple built to her.

The Worship of the Spirit of the Jin Springs

As I suggest above, although we do not know when the first temple to a female water spirit was built at the site of the Jin Springs, documentation of this local divinity indicates that the Spirit of the Jin Springs gradually became more important with the development of the canal system. Spring-spirit worship is discussed at Jinci from as early as the seventh century, but it was only after the political center of the province was moved away from Jinyang that the Spirit of the Jin Springs and her power over water production came to dominate the entire site. Much of the site was destroyed during the wars between the Jurchens and Mongols during the thirteenth century, and as the complex was gradually reconstructed, it was focused on the springs and irrigation canals. In this section, I discuss the evidence for the cult of the Spirit of the Jin Springs prior to her official recognition in the eleventh century, the circumstances for her promotion and entry into the sacrificial statutes in the Northern Song, and the image of the temple buildings associated with her worship during the eleventh and twelfth centuries.

The Early Cult of the Spirit

The *Weishu* entry on Xuanweng Mountain discussed in Chapters 2 and 4 was the first mention of ritual buildings at the site of the Jin Springs. There we read not about Jinci but rather about Jinwangci, a shrine to the King of Jin. Yet, as Paul Goldin has pointed out, *wang* 王 can be more than a noble title; it can also be used adjectivally to mean "numinous" or "powerful," or nominally to refer to local spirits, the *baishen* 百神 that inhabited the landscape of China.[22] Given the significance of springs to the early agrarian people of the Taiyuan basin and to dryer north China more generally, as well as the frequency in which springs spirits were venerated at spring sites in this region, the shrine mentioned in the *Weishu* was very likely dedicated to the Spirit of the Jin Springs. Furthermore, this was likely an ancient practice, as the *Zuozhuan* documents that "the Spirits of hills and streams were sacrificed to in times of flood, drought, and pestilence."[23] Shu Yu's shrine would then have been added to the ritual site at the Jin Springs because of its pre-existing patronage base and acknowledged numinosity, thereby simultaneously Sinifying, masculinizing, and Confucianizing worship otherwise focused on a local water sprite.

We can see part of this process in the earliest firm documentation of spring-spirit worship contained in the Jinciming stele inscription, written by Li Shimin in 646. As discussed in the previous chapter, a large portion of this text is devoted to venerating Shu Yu and the state of Tang as the Zhou-dynasty origin of the Li Tang dynasty. Li Shimin describes Jinci not as a somber shrine exclusively dedicated to the ancestors of the Zhou dynasty but as a transcendents' paradise, a numinous landscape that surpassed the famous goddess temples of history and literature.

The golden *que* gate-towers, nine layers [deep], make [the palaces on] Penglai [seem] quite crude. Its jade towers, eight-thousand feet high, make [the mansions of] Kunlun's Lang peak[24] [seem] hardly unusual. . . .

金闕九層，鄙篷萊之已陋; 玉樓千仞，耻崑閬之非奇。。。。。。。

Regarding [the spring] bestowing favor, harmonious wind and moist dew will be produced by it; dense clouds and enriching rain arise from this. . . .

其施惠也，則和風溽露是生，油雲膏雨斯起。。。。。。。

Regarding its huge capacity, it nourishes the myriad creatures without fatigue; it supplies the four directions (the empire) without exhaustion. . . .

其大量也，則育萬物而不倦，資四方而靡窮。。。。。。。

Daily flowing without cessation, like a fragrant way, which is endless;[25] each year it pours out without overflowing, just as a superior person who avoids becoming full [of awareness] of his virtue. . . .

日注不窮，類芳猷之無絶; 年傾不溢，同上德之誡盈。。。。。。。

Indeed, what is unique about this spring is that it encircles this precinct of immortals as though it were a jewel, so that when we gaze up at the solitude and purity of the divinity's abode, we can still hear its beautiful music as if it were there.

That is why the [carriages of the nobility with] red wheels and ornamented hubs [are lined up] carriage box to carriage box on the lane approaching the altar; and the jade, silk, and rich foods are box by box delivered to the temple's gate-towers. . . .

信乃兹泉之表異，帶仙宇而為珍，仰神居之肅清，想徽音其如在。是以朱輪華轂，接軫於壇衢，玉幣豐粢，連箱於廟闕。。。。。。。

How could it be [considered to be] like the temple of Gao Tang, which had the empty title of Morning Cloud? Or like the shrine to Chen Cang, which had the false legend of evening shadows?[26]

豈若高唐之廟，空號朝雲，陳倉之祠，虛傳夜影？

From this stele it is clear that, by the seventh century, this site was already vital because of the springs. Numerous offerings were made to thank the spirit of the springs for her continuous benevolence in providing water. The experience of the site was heightened by wondrous surroundings more beautiful than the famous magical island of Penglai and Kunlun, the mountain abode of the Spirit Mother of the west (Xiwangmu 西王母). The text of the stele also compares Jinci to the renowned goddess shrine in Song Yu's (active early third century BCE) *Gao Tang Rhapsody* (*Gao Tang fu* 高唐賦)[27] and the cult of Chen Cang 陳倉 (also called Chen Bao 陳寶), who was also considered a female spirit.[28] Yet, Li's text implies that, though the shrine to Gao Tang and the powers of this goddess were fictional, Jinci was by contrast real and the deities worshiped there efficacious. Later scholars have suggested that by making this reference, Li Shimin was venerating a female divinity at the Jin Springs.[29]

But Li Shimin also rendered the spirit of the spring as holding Confucian virtue. By describing the spring's production of water as an endless "fragrant way" who gives of herself in the manner of a "superior person" (*junzi* 君子), readers of his inscription would likely have understood this as a reference to the connection between the superior person and both rivers and springs found in Mencius's interpretation of Confucius.[30]

Across the imperial period, the allure of local female water spirits has been as compelling as it was unseemly to the educated male writers of Chinese history and literature. Although nature spirits were not necessarily always conceived of as anthropomorphic, water spirits had a tradition of appearing to rulers in female form that can be traced to the pre-imperial period, as in the case of the *Gao Tang Rhapsody*, where a king sought a mystic encounter with a beauty that had a moist, feminine nature. Beginning in the early imperial period we have increasing documentation that many local spirits came to be considered human and were represented as members of the imperial court in a manner described as an "imperial metaphor" or a celestial bureaucracy, similar to the government system known in the earthly realm.[31] Access to these deities could be mediated through a religious professional but could also take place as an individual appeal without the trappings of court.[32] By the Song dynasty, local mountain and stream spirits who had not been otherwise documented were commonly entered into the government sacrificial statutes.[33] Many sources of water were considered to be the habitats of male dragon kings, and many more very likely came to be so. However, the "quest of the goddess" found in poetry and cantos from as early as the third century BCE focused on female deities who were conceived as embodying the *yin* 陰 force through their presence as rivers and rain.[34]

We see the poetic allure of the Jin Springs water goddess rendered in a poem about this site by Li Bai 李白 (ca. 701–62), who, unlike the second Tang emperor, focused his remarks about Jinci on the water and natural scenery. Li Bai conceived of the spirit of the river as being female, but the subtlety of the poetic form again falls short of verifying that a water goddess was worshiped at the site. Using established conventions of water goddesses in poetry, he likens the spirit of the river to a beautiful woman:

> Occasionally we went out west of the city, the flowing stream at Jinci was like emerald jade.
> We boated and played in the water accompanied by flute and drum, the minute ripples were like the dragons' scales and the green sedge.[35]

When we were inspired we brought courtesans; weren't they like the floating snow of the poplar blossoms?
Painted faces who enjoy intoxication were appropriate for the evening; the hundred-foot limpid deep streamed like a kingfisher-blue [haired] beauty.
The water spirit and the moon spirit shine under the moonlight; the beauties dance in translucent dresses.
The breeze blows the song into the sky; of itself the music floats into the surrounding clouds.[36]

時時出向城西曲，晉祠流水如碧玉，
浮舟弄水簫鼓鳴，微波龍鱗莎草綠。
興來攜妓恣經過，其若楊花似雪何，
紅妝欲醉宜斜日，百尺清潭瀉翠娥。
翠娥嬋娟初月輝，美人更唱舞羅衣，
清風吹歌入空去，歌曲自繞行雲飛。

The evidence given here for early worship of a female water spirit at the Jin Springs is unsatisfying because the spirit is not addressed by or discussed with a formal name or title. But this is consistent with the manner in which seductive water goddesses were rendered in the poetry of the period. References in this poem are similar to those of *ci* 詞 cantos about goddesses of rivers and rain who embody the *yin* principle. Li Bai was, like Li Shimin before him, undoubtedly familiar with this tradition of erotic poetry venerating goddesses, the origins of which can be traced back to Song Yu's *Gao Tang Rhapsody*. According to Suzanne Cahill, encounters between water goddesses and a king or nobleman took place at the "palace or shrine of the goddess" that stands "beside a river on a famous mountain." The goddesses are further likened to flowers and have blue-black hair the color of kingfisher feathers.[37] Thus, we see in this poem that for Li Bai, too, Jinci was a manifestation of the goddess shrines of literature where temple buildings sat beside waterways embodying divine femininity.

However, Qing-dynasty scholars who searched for the origins of the Spirit of the Jin Springs found more positive textual evidence in the *Songshi* (Standard history of the Song) account of the Song-dynasty siege of Taiyuan in 979. While attacking the city, General Cao Han 曹翰 (924–92) was stationed on the west side of the walls and found himself short of drinking water for his troops. He prayed at a "Damsel's Temple" (Niangzimiao 娘子廟) roughly five kilometers (three miles) west of the city, then constructed a canal leading from the spring and was thereby able to provide enough water for both his men and their horses.[38] The history of the battle between the Northern Song and the Northern Han describes the technique for laying siege to the city of Taiyuan. In this case, as in that of the Earl of Zhi in the Warring States Period and the more recent attempts by the first Song-dynasty emperor in 969, a canal was built to direct water from the Jin Springs to flood the city walls. As the general located on the west side of the city, Cao Han would have known of the methods used in the 969 attack and would therefore have had to have known about the Jin Springs as both a source of drinking water and a siege weapon. Yet, because the complex was completely rebuilt in 984 after the siege and later destruction of Taiyuan, physical evidence for the pre-Song site is no longer extant.[39]

As I have shown in the previous chapter, because of Shu Yu's place in the Zhou-dynasty conquest of the Tang demesne, and because Jinci had been patronized by the second Tang emperor Li Shimin, Zhao Kuangyi rebuilt Jinci after his conquest of the Northern Han in 979 as an expression of Song dynastic legitimacy over the region of the Jin River. We can be reasonably certain that the divinity of the Jin Springs was conceived of as female by this time, but again, the only shrine named in the inscription commemorating the project's completion was that of Shu Yu.[40] Further, I have also discussed the probability that the 984 Jinci complex was much larger than the present site and was oriented north-south rather than east-west—a configuration that would have been more consistent with an official, imperially sponsored temple-complex during the tenth and eleventh centuries, regardless of sectarian affiliation.

Yet, like the Jinciming written by Li Shimin, the inscription documenting the repair of the site written by Zhao Changyan alludes to a more complicated religious system at the Jin Springs than a simple ancestral or founder's shrine. From its unusual phrasing, we can deduce that female nature spirits outside the imperial canon were also worshiped at the Jin Springs during the tenth century. The inscription refers to a previous "crude" (*lou* 陋) system of worship. Furthermore, Zhao Changyan wanted to clearly distinguish the temple-building projects of the Song emperor from those of the Qin and Han:

> How could this be compared to [the first] emperor of Qin setting out an [imperial] tour to sacrifice to the eight deities on the seashore?
>
> The Han emperors preferred strangeness; they sacrificed to the Earth Queen at Fenyin.[41]
>
> 豈比秦帝浪遊，祀八神於海上。漢皇尚異，祀后土於汾陰。

The stories to which Zhao Changyan referred were well known in Chinese history. The First Emperor of Qin and the Han emperors, particularly Han Wudi (Liu Che 劉徹, r. 141–87 BCE), were very concerned with the quest for immortality and the transcendents living on magical isles in the Eastern Sea who could grant eternal life. On one famous occasion, the First Emperor sent out thousands of children to seek these isles and the deities who resided on them.[42] Han Wudi was also responsible for establishing a temple to the Earth Queen at Fenyin in Hedong commandery (modern Wanrong county 萬榮縣, Shanxi), far outside the imperial capital. He personally attended the initial sacrifice in 114 BCE, as well as on five other, later occasions.[43] Zhao Changyan's strong contrast of this project with the Qin and Han emperors' worship of unorthodox nature spirits, including overtly female ones such as the Earth Queen at Fenyin, provides further evidence that Shu Yu was not the sole object of veneration at the Jin Shrines at the time of the Song conquest.

Canonizing the Spirit of the Jin Springs

The promotion of the water spirit at Jinci to Sage Mother follows the pattern of popular spirit elevation across the Song empire at the end of the eleventh century, as documented by Valerie Hansen in *Changing Gods in Medieval China*. Close examination of the evidence dated to the Song period shows that the Song court bestowed noble titles and official plaques on the temple because the local patronage base, which depended on the Sage Mother for water, submitted her name after she provided miracle rains. The titles we have documented for the deity, from Gentlewoman (Nülang 女郎) to Sage Mother, were all commonly used for local spirits in the Song dynasty and before.

While the "Damsel's Temple" from which Cao Han was able to retrieve water for his troops in 979 was not identified in the *Standard History of the Song* as being at Jinci *per se*, beginning in the eleventh century we have positive textual and physical records of a female spirit at the site. Because of the Xi Xia invasion into Song territory at the northwest Song border in 1040, the statesman Fan Zhongyan 范仲淹 (989–1052) was dispatched to the Shaanxi front.[44] In 1044, he was made the pacification commissioner of Shaanxi and Hedong (southern Shanxi) and traveled during this period to Jinci.[45] He marveled at the spiritual quality of the location of Shu Yu's Temple (Shu Yu miao), commenting on the springs emerging from the place:

How spiritual is the Shu Yu Temple!
How marvelous the land [from which] emerges the auspicious springs.
One spring is particularly perspicuous;
[After] several paces it is suddenly a stream.

. . . .

神哉叔虞廟！地勝出嘉泉，一源甚澄澈，數步忽潺湲。

。。。。。。

The brocaded fish are too colorful to fish,
As long-lived as the transcendents of the water (*shuixian*).[46]

錦鱗無敢釣，長生同水仙。

Fan Zhongyan makes a more overt reference to water spirits than we have seen in previous inscriptions, but even by the 1040s, he makes no reference to a Sage Mother.

Although we do not know exactly when the goddess first became known by the name Sage Mother, the 1063 document recording the extension of Jinci waterways referred to a pool located north of Eternal Youth Spring (Nanlaoquan 難老泉) as a "Sage Mother Pool." This was likely the pool located directly in front of the Sage Mother Hall (Fig. 1.2), indicating that the goddess had been elevated to Sage Mother by the time of writing.[47]

The Collected Important Documents of the Song (*Song huiyao*) lists the promotions given to the Sage Mother and her temple, which allowed her name to be included in the official sacrificial statutes for the rest of imperial Chinese history. The first of these was by Emperor Shenzong's (r. 1067–85) court in 1077, when she was given the title Sage Mother of Manifest Aid. The central government bestowed an imperial plaque with the name Temple of Compassionate Aid (Cijimiao 慈濟廟) to the goddess in 1104. In 1111, she was officially elevated to Sage Mother of Clear Efficacy and Manifest Aid (Xianling zhaoji shengmu 顯靈昭濟聖母), and her temple was given a new plaque in 1112, which changed its name to the Temple of Far-Reaching Benevolence (Huiyuanmiao 惠遠廟). This name was used for Jinci through at least the thirteenth century.[48]

Inscriptions within the hall verify that the building was in place and dedicated exclusively to the Sage Mother by the middle of the eleventh century. An inscription on the back of the Sage Mother's seat documents the addition of six dragons to the front columns and a new seat to "Sage Mother Hall at Jinci" (Jinci Shengmudian 晉祠聖母殿) in 1087 (Fig. 5.1), thus the hall must have been built by that time.[49] The patrons were members of a Golden Dragon Society of Taiyuan prefecture who pooled their resources to embellish the building. Additionally, three more inscriptions have been found on roof timbers replaced during a repair after an earthquake in 1102. According to inscriptions on extant roof purlins, this repair was done with official imperial support under the sponsorship of Sun Lu 孫路, the Taiyuan garrison commander of the time.[50]

Perhaps the most important Song-period document for our understanding of late imperial and modern interpretations of the Sage Mother's identity is the "Text Giving Thanks for Rain," dated 1123 and inscribed on a stele still extant at the site, discussed in the previous chapter. The regional commissioner Jiang Zhongqian 姜仲謙 stated that the sacrifice took place in the shrine of the Sage Mother and Shu Yu of Tang rather than in the Temple of Far-Reaching Benevolence, which would have been its official name at the time.[51] It also stated that the Sage Mother was the foundation of the Jin state and that the spiritual power of Shu Yu could be known through the character on his hand at birth. Because of the eponymous relationship between the Jin River and the Jin state, the Sage Mother could be understood in this text as being the mother of the state (and therefore the mother of its first ruler) as well as the goddess of the spring of the Jin River.[52] Although, as I have argued above, the context of this poem at the brief moment in history when the Song dynasty held the Sixteen Prefectures explains why Jiang Zhongqian would include Shu Yu in a prayer about a rain miracle, other lines in the prayer

Fig. 5.1 Sage Mother Hall, detail showing front column dragons added in 1087.

describe the shrine in those terms known from the cantos regarding female divinities:

We see the forest's band of reflection [in the stream]; the cliffs and rockeries manifest an outstanding nature.

The springs emit from beneath the hall, providing for the 10,000 *qing* within their magnificent slopes. Surely this is the cave residence of efficacious transcendents, and, thus, it is appropriate to have a temple and sacrifices for them here.[53]

顧林薄之映帶兮，發巖岫之英奇。泉一出於堂下兮，作萬頃之宏陂。
信靈仙之窟宅兮，宜廟食之在茲。

The life force of the complex is tied to the power of the stream and the spring that comes from beneath the temple. The deities residing here are not the spirits of deceased humans but are *xian* transcendents, similar to the one in the canto "Transcendent Who Presides over the River" ("Linjiang xian" 臨江仙) discussed above, whose temple was placed next to the waterway she embodied.[54]

Other information we have about the eleventh-century history of the site comes from later sources. The most frequently cited is the 1267 stele inscription by Yi Gou documenting the rebuilding of Shu Yu of Tang's shrine complex in that year. According to the inscription, information was gathered from local archives as well as from village elders. The section regarding the tenth- and eleventh-century history of Jinci reads:

> From the sixth year of the [Later] Jin Tianfu reign period [941 CE] [Shu Yu of Tang] was enfeoffed as the King of Arising Peace. It was not until after the Song Tiansheng reign period [1023–32 CE] that his title was changed to King of the East of the Fen River; furthermore, [they] rebuilt the Gentlewoman Shrine (Nülangci) west of the spring facing east. During the Xining reign period [1068–78] the title "Sage Mother of Manifest Aid" was first added; by this time her rank was already clear.[55]
>
> 自晉天福六年封興安王，迨宋天聖後改封汾東王，又復建女郎祠於水源之西東向。熙甯中始加昭濟聖母號，則其品秩既明矣。

The inscription provides the first clear evidence of the Sage Mother Hall being constructed, or at least reconstructed, as an eastward-facing building. Two externally verifiable dates in this inscription—for the elevation of Shu Yu to King of Arising Peace and for the elevation of the Sage Mother to the Sage Mother of Manifest Aid—are accurate. But Yi Gou knew only that Shu Yu's elevation to King of the East of the Fen River and the Gentlewoman Shrine's rebuilding occurred at some point *after* the Tiansheng reign period.[56] Given other textual information preserved in the 1063 stele inscription documenting the waterway expansion and the 1087 inscription giving the date the dragons were added to the front columns of the building, we can conclude that the Spirit of the Jin Springs was worshiped independently in what is now the Sage Mother Hall, beginning at some point between 1032 and 1087. This is further borne out by the style of the building, discussed at length in the next chapter.

The pattern of the Sage Mother's promotion across the eleventh century suggests that local people identified her as being a powerful goddess who controlled the water in their region both in the form of a spring and rain. And, in addition to rebuilding and enhancing the Sage Mother Hall, they petitioned the central government to give her title increases so she would continue acting on their behalf.

The titles given to the Spirit of the Jin Springs show the reverence in which she was held, but in later times they also contributed to the ambiguity of her identity. The water goddess was first called Gentlewoman (Nülang), after which she was promoted to Sage Mother; then, two sets of two-character noble titles were added on separate occasions, a pattern consistent with the canonization of local spirits during the second half of the eleventh century. Although the title Gentlewoman does not specifically denote a water goddess, male water spirits such as the Spirit of the Huo Spring at Guangshengsi in southern Shanxi were called *lang* 郎 prior to the Tang dynasty.[57] The title of Sage Mother indicates a relatively high rank and was associated in medieval China with the mother of the deified Laozi as well as with empresses such as Wu Zetian 武則天 (r. 690–705).[58] Hansen quotes titles for female divinities in the *Song huiyao* as being first mistress (*furen* 夫人) and then promoted consort (*fei* 妃). Her research indicates that titles for female divinities in the *Song huiyao* were listed roughly from highest rank to lowest: 1—consort, 2—mistress, 3—sage mother, 4—mother-in-law (*popo* 婆婆), 5—mother (*mu* 母), 6—matron (*mu* 姥), 7—concubine (*ji* 姬), 8—lady (*nü* 女), 9—gentlewoman, 10—maiden (*gu* 姑), 11—damsel (*niang* 娘). Of the fifty-two overtly female deities with entries in the "Various Shrines" section of the *Song huiyao*, there are four Sage Mothers.[59] Additionally, Hansen states that the character *ji* 濟 was usually used for dragon spirits. Because the second character in the Sage Mother's earliest documented noble title is *ji*, this character may have more broadly applied to water spirits.

Hansen's work also documents a dramatic increase in the official granting of titles to popular deities in the Song, beginning in 1075. At this time, divinities proven to have worked miracles were registered with the government and included in official sacrifices to be undertaken by a local official biannually in the spring and autumn. This was a bottom-up rather than a top-down process as documentation of miracles depended on the local officials to investigate and verify miraculous events related to them by their constituencies.[60]

According to Hansen, the increase in title-granting to popular divinities during the 1070s was the result of the implementation of the New Policies of Wang Anshi, which were aimed at reorganizing and strengthening systems of local authority.[61] Although titles had been granted to divinities from as early as the Qin dynasty, the practice was relatively limited. Early Northern Song rulers followed the tradition and extended it to popular spirits in the eleventh century with edicts first in 1047 ordering popular temples (*miao*) to be repaired across the empire, and then, after a drought in 1050, requesting that the names of all spirits who brought rain be reported to the government. But prior to 1075, few titles were granted because it was difficult to gain information about miracles and the deities responsible for them from local authorities. Another edict was issued on December 16, 1074, after a serious drought in north China earlier in the year, requesting the names of deities in shrines and temples (*cimiao* 祠廟) known to respond efficaciously to requests for rain. By this time, the New Policies were fully in place, and the central government received a large number of names. In 1075 alone, thirty-seven deities were granted official titles.[62] Title-granting continued at this high level through the end of the eleventh century and into the twelfth, though the New Policies were first dismantled in 1086 and then revived in 1094 due to shift in power at court.[63]

Because the granting of titles to the Sage Mother and her shrine at Jinci parallels the implementation and revival of the New Policies, her promotion was likely due more to the local support facilitated by these policies than to imperial knowledge of her cult specifically. The Gentlewoman whose shrine was rebuilt to the west of the Jin Springs after 1032 was promoted to Sage Mother before 1063, perhaps as a result of the 1050 edict regarding efficacious rain spirits. She was given an additional noble title three years after the 1074 edict; then, after the New Policies were revived, the central government sponsored her hall's repair after the 1102 earthquake (at the request of a local official), issued official plaques to her temple, and added another two characters to her title. Because of local requests advanced to the central government through the reorganization under the New Policies, the Spirit of the Jin Springs was entered into the imperial sacrificial statutes (*sidian*), where her cult remained officially sanctioned for the rest of imperial Chinese history.[64]

Chapter Six

The Song-Dynasty Temple to the Sage Mother

Without a full-scale excavation, we may never know what the pre-Yuan-dynasty ritual compound at the Jin Springs looked like. Yet consideration of all textual and physical evidence indicates that the present Sage Mother Hall was always a hall for the worship of the Spirit of the Jin Springs. Beginning with her canonization in the late eleventh century, the textual record reveals that the Sage Mother, through her rain-giving miracles, was the primary object of veneration for local farmers and the expanding network of canal heads and hatch keepers who distributed the irrigation water emanating from the Jin Springs. For the first time, we can positively match extant structures with textual sources and examine the changing reaction of elite authors to the grandeur of the worship hall dedicated to a local water goddess. As Jinci was gradually rebuilt after the imperial interest in the cult of Shu Yu had waned at the end of the Northern Song dynasty, the modifications to the site increasingly focused it on the springs and the canals that extended from them. This later configuration placed the Sage Mother Hall at the center of the complex, making her the visually dominant divinity of Jinci and directly undermining the status of Shu Yu. In this chapter, I correlate epigraphical evidence with the earliest physical evidence of temple buildings extant at Jinci: the Sage Mother Hall, the Spirit or Flying Bridge, the Iron Man Terrace, the Offering Hall, and the statuary and wall paintings attributable to the eleventh and twelfth centuries. I first argue for a late eleventh-century date for the Sage Mother Hall's structure through a comparison with extant timber-frame buildings of the same period. Then I incorporate the sculptural and wall painting program to show that the building was always dedicated to the Spirit of the Jin Springs. While being an exceptionally dramatic and visually arresting example of Northern Song architecture, the Sage Mother Hall, with its elegant statuary and wall painting within the hall and the ritual structures added to the axis in front of it, is entirely consistent with other examples of popular goddess and rain spirit worship elsewhere in Shanxi province.

The Sage Mother Hall

Although the identity of the Sage Mother has been the subject of debate since the seventeenth century, the Sage Mother Hall and the buildings associated with her worship from the eleventh and twelfth centuries display her significance for the local population as a water spirit. The three major sources of evidence for understanding the appearance of the site and the Sage Mother Hall—before the Jin-Yuan wars in the 1230s destroyed much of the complex—are Zhao Changyan's stele inscription from 984 documenting the reconstruction of the site, the inscription from the thirteenth-century official Yi Gou dated to 1267, and the site itself. Although Zhao Changyan's inscription includes some discussion of the buildings and the environment in which they were placed, it follows poetic convention and describes a site that was largely destroyed by the middle of the thirteenth century. Consequently, his discussion of the complex does not provide enough information to identify the buildings positively. When this and Yi Gou's inscription from 1267 are examined in conjunction with an analysis of the interior and exterior of the extant Sage Mother Hall, we can see that the present structure dates to the late eleventh century and was always dedicated to the Spirit of the Jin Springs.

The undisputedly Song-dynasty Sage Mother Hall has been variously dated between 979 and 1102, according to differing and often ambiguous textual sources. In Liang Sicheng's (1901–72) and Lin Huiyin's (1904–55) first survey and subsequent article documenting the site, the date of the building was determined by correlating the date of the building given in a guidebook of the site—a *Jinci zhinan* 晉祠指南 by the archaeologist Wei Juxian 衛聚賢 (b. 1898)—and a comparison of the building's style to the Song-dynasty imperial construction manual *Yingzao fashi* (published in 1103; hereafter *YZFS*) by Li Jie (d. 1110). Wei Juxian stated that the Sage Mother Hall had been built in the Tiansheng reign period (1023–32).[1] Liang and Lin believed that the structure and outer appearance of the Sage Mother Hall pre-dated the *YZFS* and therefore accepted the 1023–32 date for the hall.[2] However, the hall is dated to 1102 in surveys of Shanxi architecture beginning from 1959.[3] The discrepancy in date is the result of differences among textual sources.

The first date is 979–84 and is based on the conclusion that the Sage Mother Hall was originally the main hall dedicated to Shu Yu of Tang from Zhao Kuangyi's rebuilding of the site. Although Peng Hai and Chai Zejun argue that the Sage Mother Hall was constructed during the rebuilding of the site completed in 984, the evidence from inscriptions and style of the building confirms that the hall was built between 1038 and 1087. The argument made by scholars such as Peng Hai, and more recently Chai Zejun, relies on the similarity between the present place of the Sage Mother Hall and the description of the main hall in Zhao Changyan's inscription (see Chapter 4):

Looking at the completed main hall, the galleries surrounding it, the interlocking rafters cover [us from] the sun, flying with [text lost] . . .

Hanging in the sky the great roof-ridges [text lost] (interlock?) in tangled undulation.

The hall and veranda extend and [text lost].

The myriad brackets gather like constellations; the chiliad pillars shimmer like *zao* aquatic plants.[4]

Bright walls, more brilliant and crystalline than the autumn moon; jade lintels, more colorful and dazzling than the morning clouds.

With magnificent [timbers] and beautiful [decoration] it is now completed on a grand scale.[5]

Furthermore, in front it faces onto an angular pool (*quzhao*); the spring is so deep one can fathom hundreds of feet. At the rear it embraces the steep hill, the mountains and hills, like a screen, reveal heights of ten thousand yards.

It is exactly [this kind of] marvelous site that encourages the residence of the spirits.

觀夫正殿中啓，長廊周布。連甍蓋日，□□而翬飛。巨棟橫空，蜿蜒而虬□。欄堂延而□□□□□□□，萬拱星攢，千楹藻耀，皓壁光凝於秋月，璇題色晃於朝霞。輪焉奐焉，於茲大備。況復前臨曲沼，泉源鑑澈於百尋。後擁危峰，山岫屏開於萬仞。實惟勝概，克助神居。

[Afterward, we] built this temple and courtyard. How could it not be for honoring that outstanding person?[6]

搆此祠庭，豈不以旌彼哲人。

The new main hall of the Shu Yu Shrine Complex discussed in Zhao Changyan's inscription was located between a steep mountain and an angular pool. Because the only palatial hall (*dian* 殿) presently located in a position matching that description is the Sage Mother Hall, Peng and Chai suspect that the Sage Mother Hall originally was the main hall, perhaps with both deities being worshiped within the one building.

In addition to the similarity in the placement of the buildings, new archaeological evidence found during the 1990s restoration contributed to the conclusion that the Sage Mother Hall was originally Shu Yu's main hall. Because eighty-seven coins from 959 CE or before were found beneath three columns during that restoration, Peng Hai believes the building was most likely the main hall, as described in the 984 stele inscription. A total of 368 coins were found inside the column bases of fourteen of the building's forty-four columns, including twenty-one different types of coins, ranging in date from the year 7 to 1796 CE.[7] Although many of the column bases contained coins from multiple time periods, three contained no coins dating later than 959.[8] Additionally, the restoration revealed multiple foundations beneath the contemporary foundation, leading Peng to believe that this was also the location of the Shu Yu shrine described by Li Daoyuan in his sixth-century *Shuijingzhu*.[9] Peng then speculates that the water spirit and the state founder were originally worshiped together in a single hall.

The remaining question of why Shu Yu would be moved out of his main worship hall and into another building is more difficult to answer. Zhou Zaijun postulated that the Sage Mother Hall was originally the main hall to Shu Yu of Tang in his 1686 documentation of the repair to Shu Yu's shrine.[10] Peng Hai follows this position and suggests that Shu Yu's statue would have simply been moved into a subsidiary hall with the rise in the Sage Mother's popularity during the latter half of the eleventh century.[11] As I will discuss below, Amy McNair has suggested that the Shu Yu Hall was replaced with the Sage Mother Hall by the Song empress and regent Liu 劉 (969–1033).[12]

Although these arguments are compelling, the only archaeology (reported) to have been done during this restoration was underneath the Sage Mother Hall, so the size and placement of other buildings in what was, according to that and later inscriptions, a large complex of ritual structures are unknown. Furthermore, the evidence from coins found during this excavation only proves that the building was erected at some point after the coins were minted (621, 955, and 959) and does not specify to whom the building would have originally been dedicated. The earlier foundation could have been dedicated just as easily to the Damsel worshiped by Cao Han as to Shu Yu of Tang. Following the description in the 984 stele inscription, Liu Yongde and Zhang Yipeng also speculated about the placement of the Shu Yu main hall and concluded that, prior to the Yuan dynasty, it would have been located south of the Sage Mother Hall and west of the Eternal Youth Spring in the location of the 1563 Dressing Tower.[13] Like the recent discovery of the Sage Mother Hall's earlier support structure, the Dressing Tower was also built atop an earlier foundation, but sixteenth-century builders did not know what that foundation had supported.[14] Prior to the eleventh-century water-management project, a large pond was directly east of the Everlasting Spring, perhaps something that could be described as an "angular pool," thereby fully matching Zhao Changyan's description.[15]

The second date associated with the Sage Mother Hall is the Tiansheng reign period, or 1023–32. This date derives from Yi Gou's inscription of 1267, which is the earliest textual source extant that mentions the actual building of the hall. As discussed in Chapter 5, even here the date of its first construction is ambiguous:

> From the sixth year of the [Later] Jin Tianfu reign period [941 CE] [Shu Yu of Tang] was enfeoffed as the King of Arising Peace. It was not until after the Song Tiansheng reign period that his title was changed to King of the East of the Fen River; furthermore, [they] rebuilt the Gentlewoman Shrine (Nülangci) west of the spring facing east. During the Xining reign period [1068–78] the title "Sage Mother of Manifest Aid" was first added; by this time her rank was already clear.[16]
>
> 自晉天福六年封興安王，迨宋天聖後改封汾東王，又復建女郎祠於水源之西東向。熙甯中始加昭濟聖母號，則其品秩既明矣。

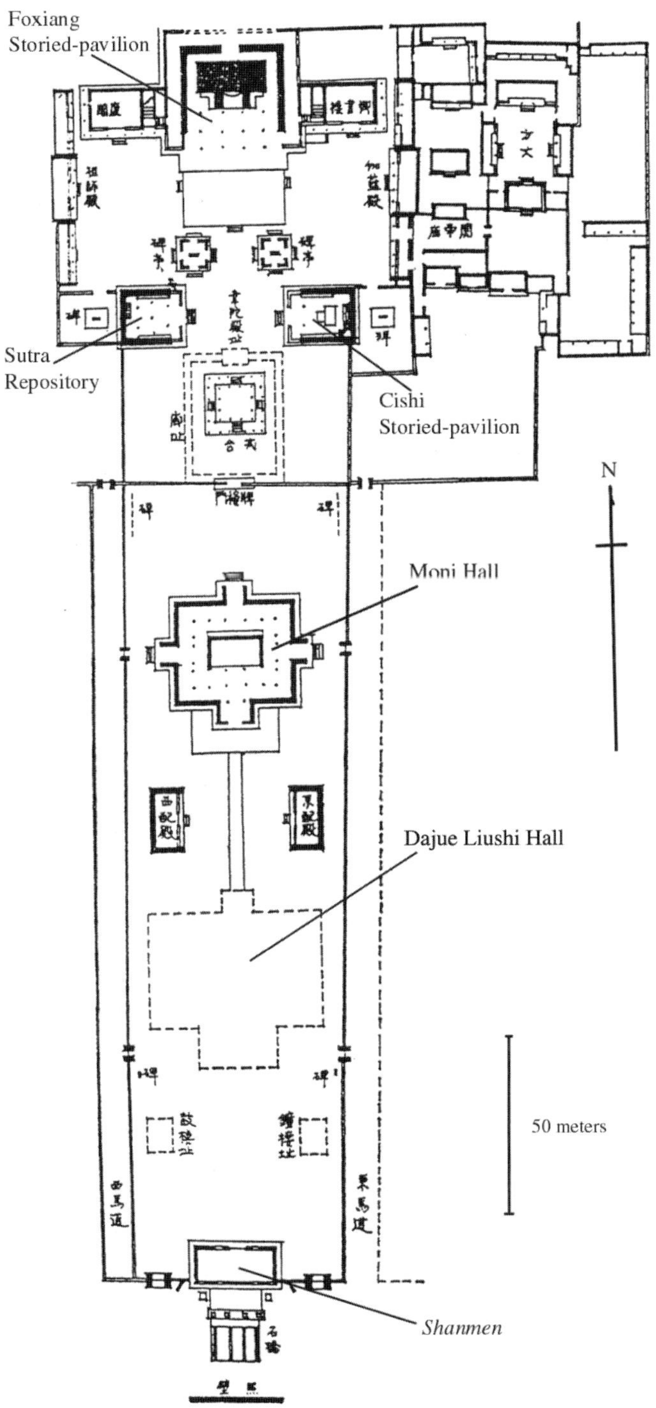

Fig. 6.2 Longxingsi plan (after Liang, *Wenji*, vol. 1, 174). This plan shows the relative size of the extant Moni Hall and the Dajue Liushi Hall, a significantly larger structure, which would have originally stood in front of it.

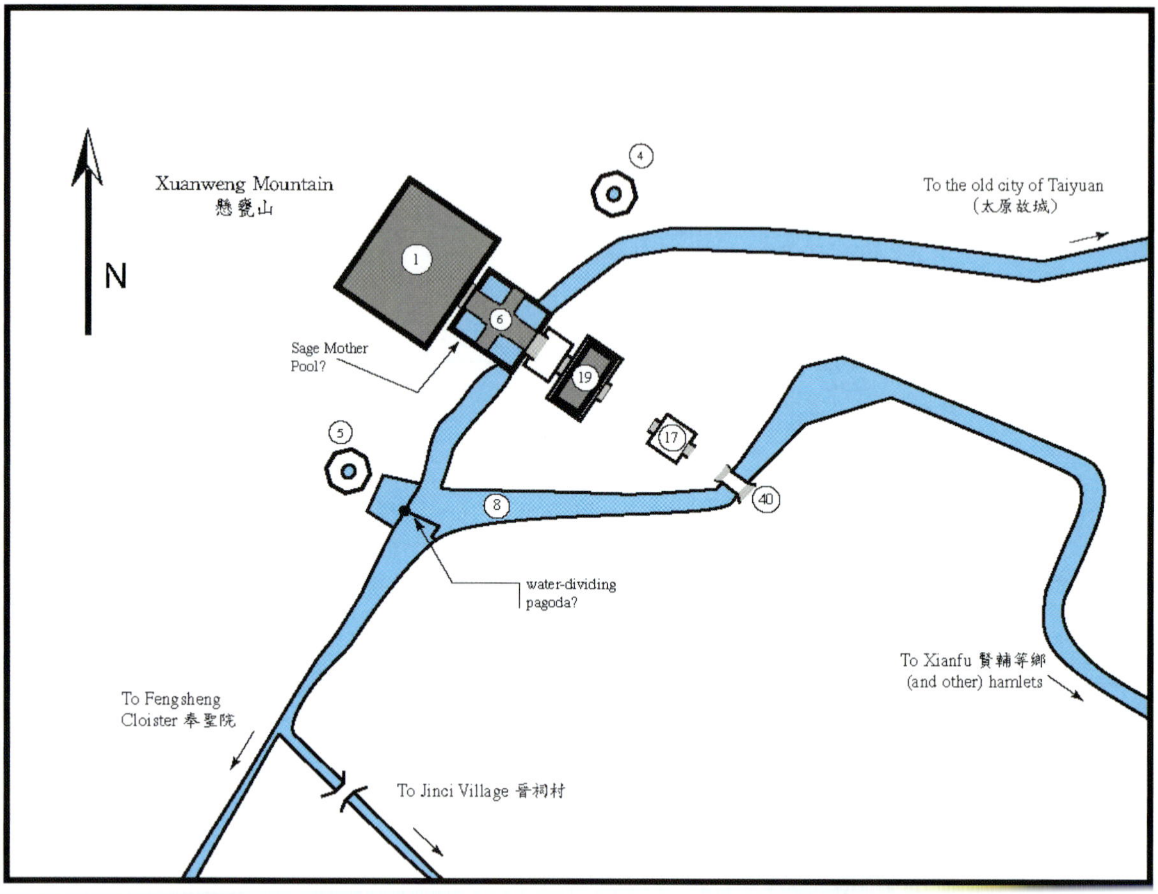

Fig. 6.3 Plan of Jinci showing the locations of extant structures from the twelfth century. Reconstruction of the waterways is based on the 1063 description of the canal expansion that took place in 1060. However, only Eternal Youth Spring and the Sage Mother Pool are mentioned; Perfect Benefit Spring and the Octagonal Pool are not discussed in the inscription. Because Yi Gou includes both the Eternal Youth and Perfect Benefit Springs in his inscription from 1267, one which is taken to mean that they had gazebos built over them in the Northern Qi Tianbao reign period (550–60), I have included both springs and gazebos in the drawing. The very few ritual structures seen on this plan reveals how little of the early complex is left to us today.

Key to Fig. 6.3

1. Sage Mother Hall 聖母殿, 1038–87
4. Perfect Benefit Spring *Ting*-gazebo 善利泉亭, 16th century
5. Eternal Youth Spring *Ting*-gazebo 難老泉亭, 16th century
6. Spirit Bridge 神橋 or Flying Bridge 飛梁, 11th century
8. Earl of Zhi Canal 智伯渠, Han dynasty, with later modifications
17. Iron Man Terrace 鐵人臺 or Lotus Terrace 蓮花臺, late 11th century
19. Offering Hall 獻殿, 1168
40. Meeting Transcendents Bridge 會仙橋

The Structure of the Sage Mother Hall

The structure of the present building suggests that it was originally designed to hold sacrificial offerings as well as to provide space for individual worship. One can see the hall's basic structure clearly by examining a section drawing (Fig. 6.4). The Sage Mother Hall is composed of a tall central section

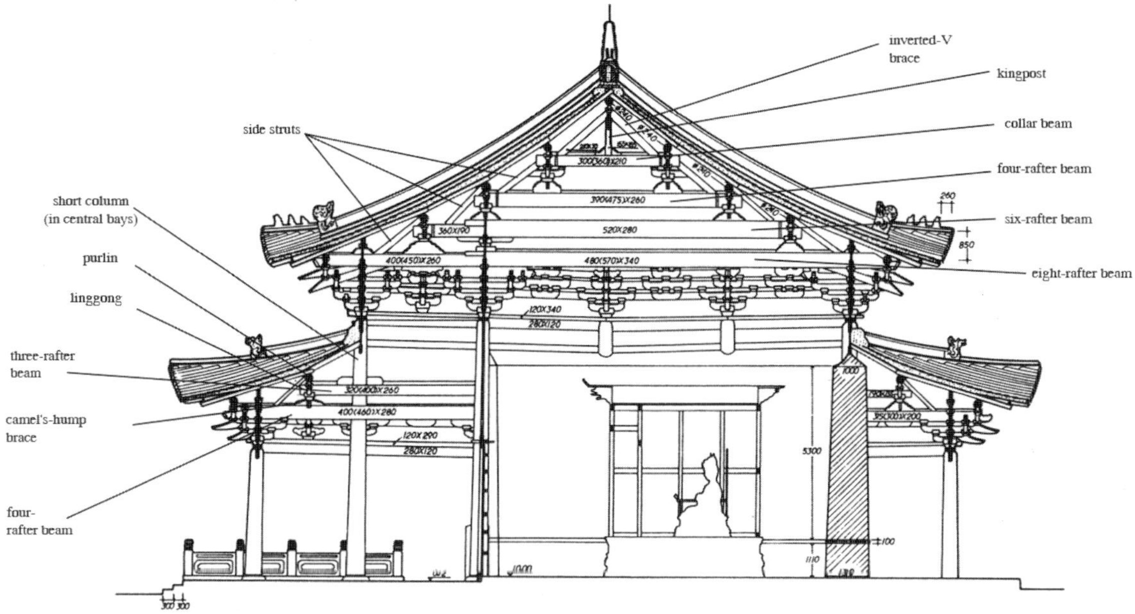

Fig. 6.4 Sage Mother Hall, side section (after Peng, *Jinci wenwu*, 176), note the similarity with the *Yingzao fashi* diagram of a *diantang*, shown in Fig. 6.5.

surrounded by a second set of eaves covering a veranda that is one bay deep along the side and back façades and two bays deep along the front façade. The upper eaves are supported by the eaves columns and bracketing of the main body of the building, and the lower eaves are supported by the eaves-columns and bracketing of the veranda. Bracket sets occur on top of all columns and intercolumnarly by joining through the column-top tie beam into the column-top or directly into the architrave itself. The roof frame begins above the bracketing level. This use of three distinct levels of column-network, bracketing, and roof frame is a distinguishing feature of the *diantang* 殿堂 (palatial hall) configuration, an example of which is shown in Li Jie's imperially commissioned *YZFS* (Fig. 6.5).[39] The use of an encircling

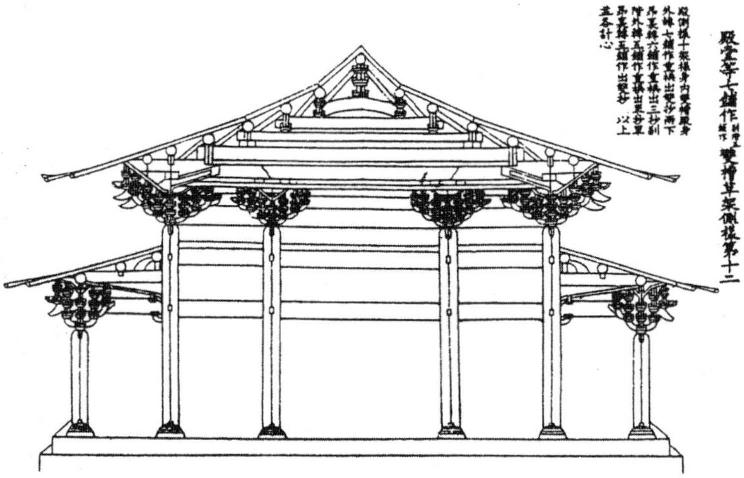

Fig. 6.5 Section drawing of a *diantang* (*Yingzao fashi*, 31/4) showing the different horizontal layers, foundation, column grid, bracketing, and roof typical of this system. The veranda columns are shorter and support a second layer of eaves that would make up a double-eaves roof system as seen in the Sage Mother Hall.

veranda with a second set of eaves must have been relatively common at the time, as three out of the four drawings of buildings labeled *diantang* remaining in the *YZFS* show the lower eaves attached.[40] However, few single-story double-eaves buildings remain in China from the tenth through eleventh centuries.[41] Consequently, what was probably a common building type at the time has come to be perceived as a majestic artifact of Northern Song architecture.

The plan of the Sage Mother Hall features extensive column elimination to create larger open spaces within the building, a characteristic of Song-Yuan-dynasty buildings that decreased in popularity in later times.[42] This is used to create the two-bay-deep veranda along the front façade, the most remarkable feature of the plan of the Sage Mother Hall. This unusual configuration extends the open area of the hall an extra bay into the main body of the building. The columns that would usually frame the wall of the body of the building are cut short and supported by tie-beams that span the two-bay space, resulting in a roughly 6.81-meter (subtracting 40 centimeters for the width of the columns) by 20.6-meter covered area free from obstruction in front of the cella proper (Fig. 6.6). The extent of the column elimination can be seen more clearly from the open floor space visible in a plan of the structure (Fig. 6.7). The veranda continues at one bay in width surrounding the rest of the building, thereby encircling a five-bay-wide cella that is three bays deep and accessed through double-panel doors (*shuangshan banmen* 雙扇版門) in the central three bays of the front façade. Prism-lattice windows (*pozi lingchuang* 破子櫺窗) allow light to enter into the outer bays. The side and back façades of the cella are enclosed by a 1.31-meter-thick wall, which presently has a single circular window in the upper portion of the back façade's central bay, a space that would have originally held an exit doorway (Fig. 6.8).[43] The covered space is increased and focused centrally through the elimination of the central four columns in the second, fourth, and fifth rows of columns (from front to back). Thus, there are no interior columns in the five bays of the open veranda directly in front of the door, nor within the interior walls of the cella proper. Because the Offering Hall was added to the complex in the Jin dynasty, the deep-front veranda would probably have been used to shelter offerings made to the Sage Mother.

The distribution of bays and the treatment of the eaves columns give the building a majestic and ancient appearance that is readily seen in the front façade. Tang- and Song-dynasty buildings are known for the way the central bay is emphasized by a greater size. Subsidiary bay size then decreases symmetrically outward, in this case with a difference of 90 centimeters between the widths of the central and secondary bays, a 34-centimeter difference in the widths of the secondary and tertiary bays, and a 60-centimeter difference in the width of the tertiary and outer bays. This results in a central bay on the front and back façades that is dramatically larger than the other bays, and outer bays that are dramatically smaller. By contrast, the width of the side-façade bays decreases by 60 centimeters only at the outer bay.

Fig. 6.6 Sage Mother Hall, front veranda. This view shows the two-bay depth of the front veranda created by the elimination (or cutting short) of the four central upper eaves columns along the front façade. This feature, which can be seen clearly in the plan (Fig. 6.7), increases the amount of open space in front of the cella for gathering or offerings and is common in buildings from the mid-eleventh–thirteenth centuries.

Three fundamental techniques used in rendering the columns of the Sage Mother Hall are consistent with descriptions found in the *YZFS*. The eight lower-eaves columns of the front façade gradually increase in height from the center outwards, with the two central-bay columns being 3.86 meters high, the secondary-bay columns being 3.92 meters high, the tertiary-bay columns being 3.98 meters high, and the corner columns being 4.04 meters high.[44] The 18-centimeter height difference between the center and corner columns gives a noticeable upwards curve to the column-top tie beam of the hall. This characteristic is called *shengqi* 生起, or "rise," and, according to the *YZFS*, the amount of rise in the column height is relative to the number of bays in the hall.[45] This effect is slightly more pronounced in the upper-

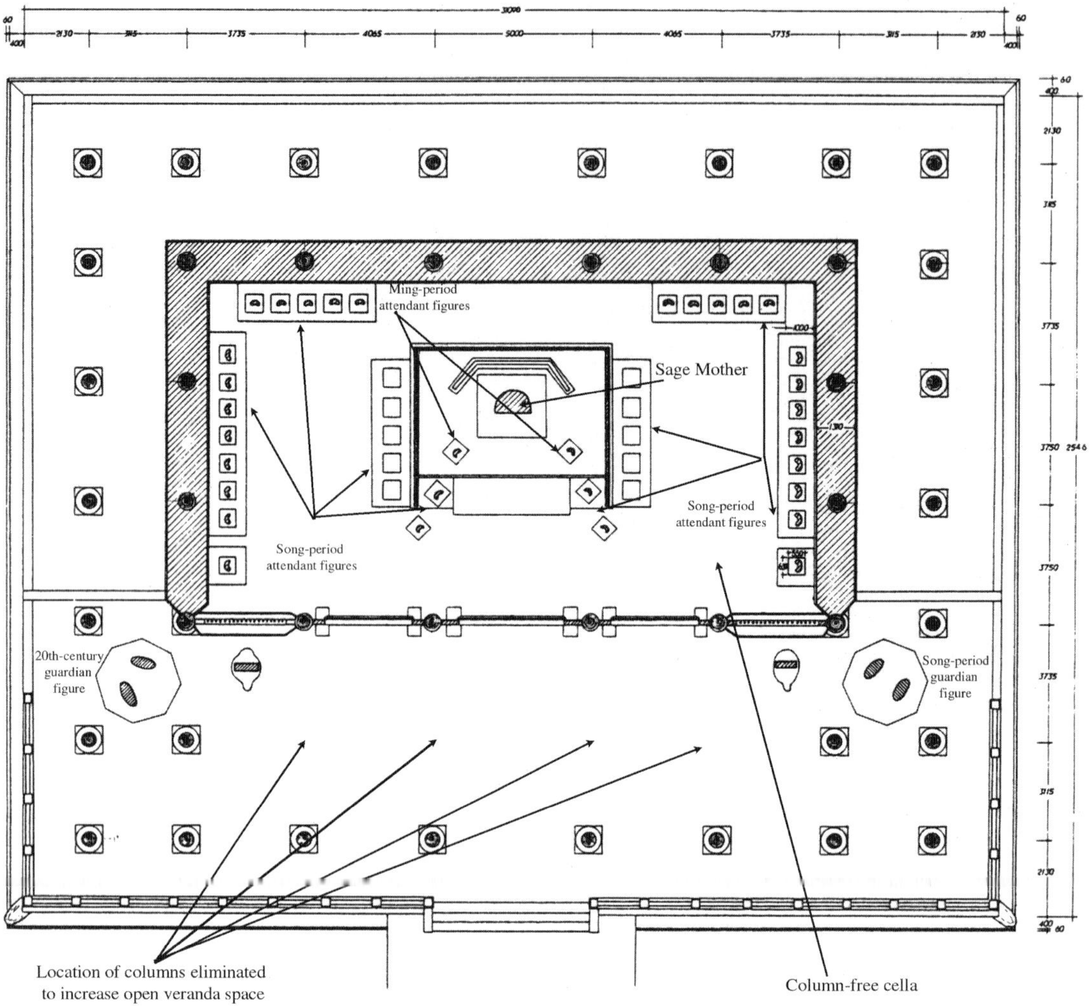

Fig. 6.7 Sage Mother Hall, plan (after Peng, *Jinci wenwu*, 177); note the space created through column elimination at the front of the structure.

eaves columns where the central bay columns are 7.79 meters high,[46] the secondary columns are 7.80 meters, and the corner columns are 7.92 meters—resulting in a rise of 26 centimeters.[47]

The second technique employed here that is named in the *YZFS*, where it is called *juansha* 卷殺 or "chamfering," is a reduction in the width of the column at the top, creating a "shuttle-shaped column" or *suozhu* 梭柱.[48] Beginning thirteen to fifteen centimeters from the topmost portion, the lower-eaves columns decrease in diameter from bottom to top by two to four centimeters. The chamfering on the upper-eaves columns begins fifteen centimeters from the top of the column, and the diameter of the column is reduced by six centimeters. A third technique of column manipulation that

Fig. 6.8 Sage Mother Hall, back façade showing a window at the approximate location of a door during the Song through Yuan dynasties. This window is not visible from the interior.

is in evidence in the construction of the Sage Mother Hall is called *cejiao* 側脚, or "batter."[49] In this case, the columns lean in toward the center of the building. Again, the degree to which this is in effect increases symmetrically outward from the central bay. On the lower eaves, the batter is 2.5 centimeters for the central bay columns, 4 for the secondary bay columns, 5.5 for the tertiary bay columns, and 7 for the corner columns. The batter is thus roughly 1.73 percent of the height of the columns at the corners. The batter of the upper-eaves columns is 5.5 centimeters at the corners, which is a significantly lower percentage of the total column height, only about 0.69 percent. The columns are joined at their tops first by a tall narrow timber (*lan'e* 闌額—what I am calling the "architrave"), which visually threads through the tops of the inner six eaves columns but does not extend through the corner columns. A column-top tie beam, or *pupaifang* 普拍枋,[50] is placed horizontally on top of the architrave. The individual sections of the column-top tie beam are joined at the center of the column tops. The eaves-bracketing is joined directly into the column-top tie beam, or through it to the columns below for column-top bracket sets.

Whereas the structure of the Sage Mother Hall is consistent with the *YZFS* and buildings of the Northern Song period, the bracketing style places it in the mid- to late-eleventh century when compared with other buildings from the area. The eaves bracketing of the Sage Mother Hall is similar to smaller buildings in Shanxi in both style and structure, while being different from buildings outside this area, indicating that local craftsmen were responsible for its design and construction. Thus, the bracketing style should be datable by comparison with the smaller dated halls in the vicinity.

The eaves bracketing of the Sage Mother Hall is unusual in its combination of early and late structural and stylistic aspects. Regional features such as beveled bracket-arms parallel to the building plane and the descending-cantilever-shaped *shuatou* 耍頭, the latter of which can be seen on the Sage Mother Hall in Figures 6. 9 and 6.10, became popular from the late tenth to

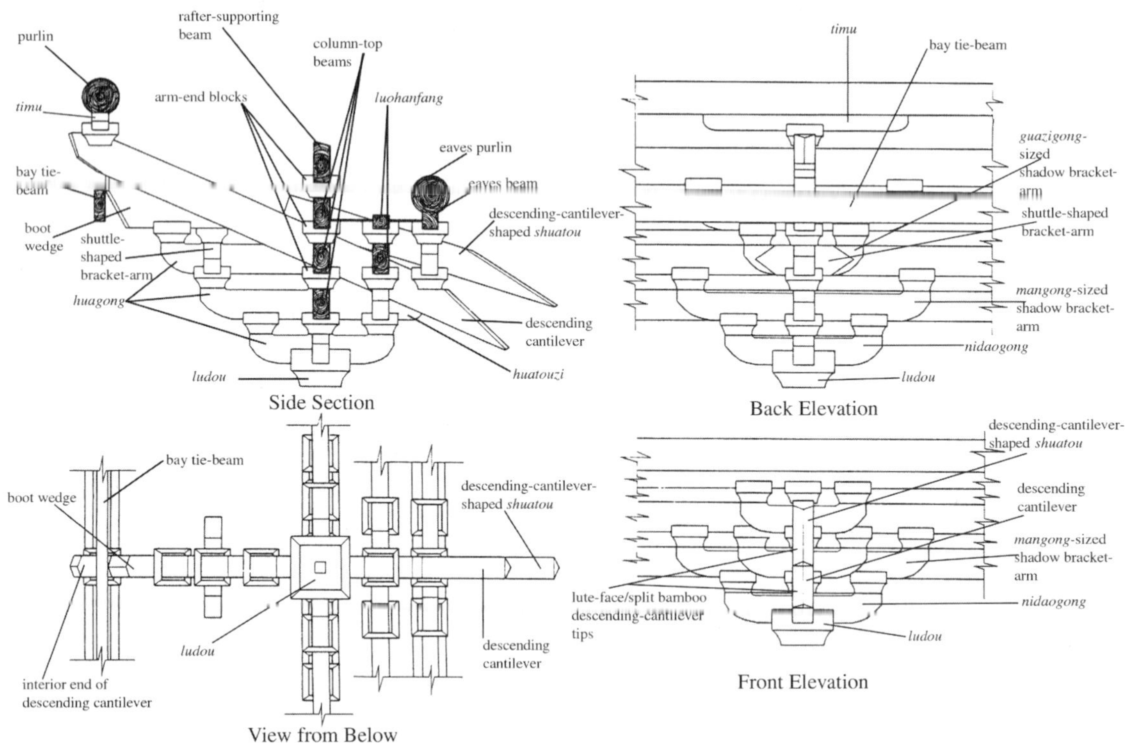

Fig. 6.9 Sage Mother Hall, lower-eaves intercolumnar bracket set (after Peng, *Jinci wenwu*, 179), note especially the descending-cantilever-shaped *shuatou* labeled here.

Fig. 6.10 Sage Mother Hall, lower-eaves intercolumnar bracket set showing the filled-heart *huagong* supporting the *huatouzi*, as well as descending cantilever and descending-cantilever-shaped *shuatou* with lute-faced and split-bamboo tips.

eleventh centuries in southern Shanxi. Additionally, the architrave was contained by the columns at the corners of most buildings in this area, including the Sage Mother Hall, until the middle of the eleventh century, when an architrave extending beyond the corners was the dominant style. Yet, the Sage Mother Hall also displays structural features of southern Shanxi buildings that were commonly used at the end of the eleventh century but are rarely seen in other buildings from the tenth century, including a cap block (*ludou* 櫨枓) and *nidaogong* 泥道栱 supporting intercolumnar, eaves-supporting bracket sets; a *huatouzi* 華頭子 underneath descending cantilevers; a column-top tie beam; and a filled-heart first step of *huagong* 華栱. All of these are present in the intercolumnar lower-eaves bracket sets of the Sage Mother Hall and point to a late eleventh-century date for the building as a whole (Figs. 6.9, 6.10).

The rendering of the cantilever tips in the Sage Mother Hall, something that could be considered more decorative than structural, also suggests a mid- to late-eleventh century date for the building. Cantilever tips from the eighth through early eleventh centuries were typically rendered in a simple, straight profile bevel at the end, termed "split-bamboo" (*pizhu* 批竹) in the *YZFS*.[51] This treatment was common in Shanxi province from the Tang

Fig. 6.11 East Great Hall of Foguangsi, Wutai County, Shanxi, 857, detail of eaves bracketing showing the straight beveled edge of the split-bamboo descending cantilever tip.

dynasty, as seen in buildings such as the East Great Hall of Foguangsi 佛光寺東大殿, 857, in modern Wutai county (Fig. 6.11; see Fig. 3.1 for location), through the first half of the eleventh century in the South Jixiangsi Middle Hall 南吉祥寺中殿, 1030, in modern Lingchuan county (Fig. 6.12; see Fig. 3.1 for location). By contrast, the cantilever tips of buildings of the tenth and eleventh centuries in the Yangzi delta, such as the Daxiongbao (Mahāvīra) Hall of Baoguosi 保國寺大雄寶殿, 1013, located in Yuyao 餘姚, Zhejiang, are curved in profile (Fig. 6.13). By the mid-eleventh century, we have examples of cantilever tips being finished with a pentagonal end in northern buildings, as can be seen in the Moni Hall of Longxingsi, 1052 (Fig. 6.14), part of a decorative treatment called "lute-faced" (*qinmian* 琴面) in the *YZFS*.[52] In the Sage Mother Hall, the bracketing appears transitional, with a combination of the styles popular in the period and region. The intercolumnar bracket sets of the lower eaves and the column-top bracket sets of the upper eaves display a variation of the split-bamboo cantilever end, where the profile is straight but the end has a shallow pentagonal tip. This unusual style was termed lute-faced/split-bamboo by Liang Sicheng and the *YZFS* research group[53] and appears in southern Shanxi buildings dating primarily from the late eleventh to early twelfth centuries.[54] By contrast, the intercolumnar bracket sets of the upper eaves

(*left*) Fig. 6.12 Middle Hall of South Jixiangsi, Lingchuan, Shanxi, 1030, a detail of an eaves bracket set showing split-bamboo treatment of the tips, similar to that seen in earlier buildings such as the East Great Hall of Foguangsi. (*right*) Fig. 6.13 Daxiongbao (Mahāvīra) Hall of Baoguosi, Yuyao, Zhejiang, 1013, detail of side façade eaves bracketing showing the curved profile of lute-faced descending cantilever tips. The eaves were enclosed by an exterior wall and a second set of eaves during the Kangxi reign period (1662–1723) and now appear on the interior. The consistency of intercolumnar and column top bracket sets typical of tenth–eleventh-century architecture of the coast is also clearly seen in this image.

and the column-top bracket sets of the lower eaves are carved in a slightly more slender but clearly curved lute-faced manner. Examples in southern Shanxi and northern Hebei indicate that by the beginning of the twelfth century, craftsmen appear to have moved away from either the split-bamboo or the lute-faced/split-bamboo cantilever tips visible in Figure 6.10. In the main hall of Erxianmiao 二仙廟 1107–1117 CE (Fig. 6.15)[55] and the Shijia (Śākyamuni) Hall 釋迦殿 of Chongshousi 崇壽寺, 1119/1157 CE (Fig. 6.16), both located in modern Jincheng 晉城 (see Fig. 3.1), the cantilever tips do not have a straight-edged profile. Rather, they have a pronounced curve that clearly distinguishes them from the buildings of only twenty years earlier in the same area (Fig. 6.15). This curved profile became the standard for later halls, and by the Yuan dynasty, the majority of buildings in southern Shanxi had this articulation of the descending-cantilever tip.[56] The combination of both types of bracket sets in the Sage Mother Hall strongly suggests a mid- to late-eleventh-century date for the building.

(*left*) Fig. 6.14 Moni Hall of Longxingsi, Zhengding, Hebei, 1052, detail of eaves bracketing showing the pentagonal cantilever tip. (*right*) Fig. 6.15 Main Hall of Erxianmiao, Jincheng, Shanxi, eaves bracketing, ca. 1107–17, showing the transition toward lute-faced descending cantilever tips by the beginning of the twelfth century.

For Liang Sicheng, one of the most unusual aspects of the Sage Mother Hall was the inconsistency between the column-top and intercolumnar bracket sets.[57] This characteristic is common in tenth- and eleventh-century buildings in Shanxi and Hebei provinces and separates them from the buildings of later times, as well as from those further south, even as near as the main hall of the Chuzu'an 初祖庵 in Dengfeng 登封, Henan province, dated to 1125 (Fig. 6.17).[58] Although the intercolumnar support is different from building to building—or is simply confined to the column plane—it is not the same for column-top and intercolumnar sets. Late tenth- to early eleventh-century examples of wooden halls and stone pagodas in Zhejiang (Lingyinsi 靈隱寺 Stone Pagodas in Hangzhou, 960 [Fig. 6.18], and the Daxiongbao Hall of Baoguosi [Fig. 6.13]), the Main Hall of Hualinsi 華林寺 in Fuzhou, Fujian, 964 (Fig. 6.19), and the 1015 Putian 莆田 Xuanmiaoguan 玄妙觀 Hall of the Three Pure Ones (Sanqingdian 三清殿, Fig. 6.20)[59] in southeastern coastal China all have intercolumnar and column-top bracket sets that are exactly the same. However, only one building in southern Shanxi prior to the Jin conquest of the area, the Great Buddha Hall of Dayunyuan 大雲院, 940, in Pingshun 平順 (Fig. 6.21; see Fig. 3.1 for location), displays such consistency in eaves bracketing.[60]

(*left*) Fig. 6.16 Shijia (Śākyamuni) Hall, Chongshousi, twelfth century (1119/1157; recently repainted). In this example, the curvature of the lute-faced descending cantilever tips (here not a structural feature) is clearly visible. (*right*) Fig. 6.17 Main Hall of Chuzu'an, eaves bracketing, 1125. In this detail, one can see consistency of bracketing across the façade as well as the use of lute-faced descending cantilever tips, characteristics of coastal architecture from as early as the tenth century.

The bracket sets of the Sage Mother Hall are clearly a product of a north China regional style but are unique in their combination of descending cantilever forms. The intercolumnar sets on the lower eaves and the column-top sets on the upper eaves both have two layers of lute-faced/split-bamboo descending-cantilever tips (or one cantilever, one descending-cantilever-shaped *shuatou*). The earliest building in southern Shanxi to have this combination was the Front Hall of Youxiansi 游仙寺, 990–95, in Gaoping 高平 (Fig. 6.22; see Fig. 3.1 for location), but it continued to be employed on buildings throughout the eleventh century and into the twelfth. The ends of the "double descending cantilevers" in the lower-eaves column-top sets and upper-eaves intercolumnar sets, however, are not consistent with tenth-century building practice. Descending cantilevers in these positions are curved with a pronounced pentagonal tip, that is, the lute-faced styling that appears to have come into common use in Shanxi only during the early twelfth century.

Other characteristics of the bracketing support this mid- to late-eleventh-century date. The lower-eaves bracket sets are entirely filled-heart

Fig. 6.18 East Pagoda, Lingyinsi, detail of one story, 960. Here we see a tenth-century example of the curved descending cantilever tip.

Fig. 6.19 Main Hall of Hualinsi, Fuzhou, Fujian, 964 (heavily restored in 1986), a view showing consistency of eaves bracketing across the façade.

(*left*) Fig. 6.20 Hall of the Three Pure Ones, Xuanmiaoguan, Putian Fujian, 1015, detail of original eaves bracketing showing consistency of intercolumnar and column-top bracket sets. (*right*) Fig. 6.21 Main Hall of Dayunyuan, Pingshun, Shanxi, 940, front façade showing consistency of eaves bracketing in the intercolumnar position, a rare feature of buildings in this time and place.

Fig. 6.22 Front Hall of Youxiansi, Gaoping, 990–95, detail of eaves bracketing showing cantilever-shaped *shuatou*.

Fig. 6.23 Sage Mother Hall, lower-eaves column-top bracket set. In this view from below, one can see two layers of nonstructural lute-faced descending cantilever supporting a *shuatou*. A *huatouzi* is carved into the bottom lower level of the cantilever.

while the upper eaves are stolen-heart on the first step, but filled with a wing-shaped short bracket-arm to alter its stolen-heart appearance. Of the firmly dated buildings I have examined in southern Shanxi, the popularity of filled-heart *huagong* begins at the end of the eleventh century. Additionally, a number of previously structural features of timber frame buildings here are used decoratively. For example, the bracket sets of the Sage Mother Hall all have *huatouzi*, or the column side of the descending cantilever arm is carved to appear as if there were *huatouzi* (Fig. 6.23). The lower-eaves column-top (shown in Fig. 6.23) and upper-eaves intercolumnar sets do not use structural descending cantilever but rather use *huagong* made to look like descending cantilever. The first firmly dated building in this group with nonstructural descending cantilever is the Shijia Hall of Chongshousi, 1119/1157 (Fig. 6.16).

Finally, two other structural features of the Sage Mother Hall eaves bracketing that appear only in the later buildings of this region are the use of *luohanfang* 羅漢枋 on the lower eaves and *shuatou* on the upper eaves. Both the Shijia Hall and the Sage Mother Hall use *luohanfang* above the *guazigong* 瓜子栱 on the first outward step (Fig. 6.9). This feature, as well as the second layer of *shuatou* joined though the eaves beam seen in the upper eaves of the Sage Mother Hall (Fig. 6.24), is also used in the Three Sages Hall (Sanshengdian 三聖殿) at Hongfusi 洪福寺 in Dingxiang 定襄 dating to 1096 (Fig. 6.25; see Fig. 3.1 for location).[61] Thus, the style of the bracketing on the building and the structural frame of the hall all point to a mid- to late-eleventh-century date for the Sage Mother Hall on the basis of structure alone.

Fig. 6.24 Sage Mother Hall, upper-eaves bracket sets showing nonstructural descending cantilever (right) and descending-cantilever-shaped *shuatou*, with a second layer of *shuatou* in the locust-head style (left).

Fig. 6.25 Three Sages Hall, Hongfusi, Dingxiang, Shanxi, 1096, this detail shows strong similarities to the Sage Mother Hall in the second layer of *shuatou*, the lute-faced / split-bamboo style descending-cantilever-shaped *shuatou*, filled-heart first step of *huagong*, and the use of eaves beam and eaves purlin.

The combination of bracketing styles shows an awareness of trends taking place elsewhere, specifically in the imperial capital at Bianjing (modern Kaifeng, Henan province) as documented in the *YZFS*. When this information on building style is correlated with other textual sources available about the hall and the site—the rebuilding of a Gentlewoman Shrine west of the spring after the Tiansheng reign period ending in 1032, a major earthquake in central Shanxi in January 1038, the presence of a "Sage Mother Pool" north of Eternal Youth Spring by 1063, the addition of six to eight dragons in 1087, and the fact that the hall was built in the vicinity of the prefectural capital (which would likely have a greater availability of resources and quality craftsmen familiar with the latest trends)—a conservative date for the hall would be 1038–87.

The Temple Program and Deity Identity

The palatial style of the Sage Mother Hall is consistent with goddess and water-spirit temples elsewhere in southern Shanxi province. As discussed in Chapter 2, most springs in Shanxi and elsewhere in the Chinese sphere had spring-spirit temples, but they were frequently too small or too common to be documented. Thus, the location of the Sage Mother Hall directly above a spring is one indication that it was a worship hall for a spring spirit. The remnants of the eleventh-century building program (including the Flying Bridge over the pool in front of the Sage Mother Hall and the addition of the Iron Man Terrace in the late eleventh century) further express the identity of the divinity as a water spirit. The sculptural and wall-painting program of the Sage Mother Hall supports this reading. Although the interior wall paintings and door placement have changed somewhat over the centuries, the iconography for representations of the divinities within the hall followed a conservative, and thus somewhat generic, interpretation of imperial court costume.[62] The interpretation of the Sage Mother as a Zhou-dynasty queen and mother of Shu Yu is therefore not in conflict with her appearance. Only when the entire architectural program is examined as a whole is the identity of the Jin Springs water spirit made clear.

Sculpture and Wall Paintings Within the Sage Mother Hall

The sculpture and wall-painting programs of the Sage Mother Hall are consistent with conceptions of the otherworldly realm in traditional Chinese religious thought, and the main ritual halls for nature spirits, as well as deities within the organized Chinese religions of Daoism and Confucianism, were decorated with imperial imagery. Because the same iconography is used for palatial and heavenly scenes, the interior of the Sage Mother Hall is what might generally be expected if the temple were dedicated to a Zhou-dynasty queen such as Yi Jiang, contributing to the multivalent interpretation of the deity's identity during late Ming and Qing dynasties. Overt references to water in the detail of the decoration, however, indicate that the deity's identity was originally a water spirit.

As one approaches the building, the eight dragons entwining each of the front façade columns are the first ambiguous aspect of the sculptural program (Fig. 5.1). The addition of these dragons may have been more than just decoration, and they were most likely thought to contribute to the rainmaking process as well as to denote the power the deity within the hall had over water. All these gilded wooden images should date from the late eleventh century. When the Sage Mother Hall was undergoing registration as a historic building in 1952, a donation record dated the equivalent of May 14, 1087, was found on the side of the plinth underneath the chair. It stated that six "column dragons" had been added to the front-eaves columns of the Sage Mother Hall in addition to a new chair for the Sage Mother.[63] Because the dragon was a symbol of the imperial house, Amy McNair postulates that the two dragons not mentioned in the inscription were original to the building, which, according to her article discussed above, would have been sponsored by Dowager Empress Liu.[64] But the dragon was primarily considered a sign of rain, and the display of images of them, through "sympathetic magic," was thought to cause rain.[65] Paintings of dragons, as Anning Jing argues, were used for this purpose in the Mingyingwang Hall 明應王殿, dedicated to the Spirit of Huo Spring, at the Guangshengsi Water God's Temple.[66] The addition of dragons to the front columns of the Sage Mother Hall would thus allow the building itself, rather than just the image within, to have rain-giving potency.

Because of the discrepancy between the present eight dragons and the six mentioned in the inscription, some debate has taken place over when the other two came into being. In his 1965 article on the inscriptions found in the Sage Mother Hall, Gao Shoutian wrote that because the two dragons winding around the columns framing the central bay appear to be more coarsely rendered, they may have been original to the building's construction. The six outer dragons would have been added in 1087.[67] Peng Hai was less confident about the difference in quality of the eight, proposing that the dragons on the corner columns were added later.[68] The report of the 1993–96 building restoration notes that another inscription was found on the north side of the seat, indicating that a local group had added to the project. The authors contend that this inscription, which is similar in style to the first that discussed the six dragons, was documenting the addition of two more dragons, so that all eight front-façade eaves columns were decorated with them. As the style and quality of the eight dragons presently coiled around the columns of the front veranda are virtually indistinguishable, they suggest that the final two were added a short time after the first inscription; if they had been added within the same year, that would explain the lack of a date on the second inscription.[69]

Fig. 6.26 Gu Kaizhi (345–404) attributed, *Spirit of the Luo River Rhapsody* (*Luoshenfu*), handscroll, ink and colors on silk, Palace Museum, Beijing, second quarter of the twelfth century, detail showing the river goddess in a chariot being pulled by six dragons. (Courtesy Palace Museum, Beijing.)

The addition of six dragons to the front columns may also have been a marker of the Sage Mother's identity as water goddess. One of the most well known of water goddesses, the Spirit of the Luo River, immortalized in Cao Zhi's 曹植 (192–232 CE) *Spirit of the Luo River Rhapsody* (*Luoshenfu* 洛神賦), was the subject of numerous pictorial narratives. An extant copy dating from the mid-twelfth century of a sixth-century design clearly displays the imagined form of this goddess so carefully described in the rhapsody.[70] Of particular significance here is the vehicle of the goddess: as she exits in the rhapsody and the scroll, she is pulled in a chariot by six dragons (Fig. 6.26).[71] The six dragons on the front columns of the Sage Mother Hall would have made the whole of the building the vehicle of the Sage Mother as Spirit of the Jin Springs. The final two dragons may have been added later to complete the look of the building by adorning all eight front-façade columns, despite the original iconographical antecedent.

Also similar to the Mingyingwang Hall, the Sage Mother Hall front veranda presently holds two extraordinary guardian statues, each in this case measuring over four meters high.[72] Symmetrically disposed to frame the center portion of the building, the figures are fully clad in armor and carry pole arms. The images are weighty, static, and imposing, with energy coming more from the wind-blown sleeves than any other aspect of the figure. The northern statue is said to be an original Song-dynasty work, and the craftsmanship on this piece is clearly superior to that on the southern piece

(*right*) Fig. 6.27 Door guardian on north side of the Sage Mother Hall veranda, painted clay, h. approx. 450 cm, Song dynasty. (*left*) Fig. 6.28 Door guardian on the south side of the Sage Mother Hall veranda, painted clay, h. approx. 450 cm, twentieth-century replacement.

(Fig. 6.27). He is light-skinned with head exposed but otherwise dressed in full armor. He holds what was originally a battle-ax or halberd (*fuyue* 斧鉞) with both hands, arms poised ready to attack.[73] His facial features are clearly articulated, with deeply furrowed brows, broad nose, and full chin and neck. The southern image is a 1950 replacement for an earlier damaged work (Fig. 6.28).[74] Dark-skinned, he is also in full body armor and carries a flanged mace (*jingua* 金瓜).[75] In contrast with his counterpart, the carving of facial features and overall posture of this piece lacks ferocity. The iconography and pairing of weapons (particularly as they have been identified by Liu Yongde) in these images are consistent with that of door gods (*menshen* 門神), common guardian figures seen in print form on residential doorways.[76]

Entering the hall, one immediately encounters the Sage Mother, grandly enthroned in the center of the interior framed by a screen and placed within a larger, elevated, statuary niche (Fig. 2.8). The royal presence of the statue leaves no doubt that this figure dominates the building and the water welling forth from underneath it. The Sage Mother sits on a phoenix chair, seemingly an appropriate symbol of an empress or queen, but details of her iconography depart from the period examples of empresses (Figs. 2.8 and

Fig. 6.29 Sage Mother (Jin Weinuo, *Taiyuan "Jinci,"* pl. 1), detail showing her phoenix chair, headdress, and elaborate robes. Although her robes are similar to those in other representations of goddesses from the Song-Yuan periods, her cross-legged position is iconographically closer to representations of the Buddha or deified Laozi than to other female deities from either the Daoist or popular pantheons. (Shanxi renmin chubanshe.)

6.29). Although the facial style, crown, and robes of the Sage Mother are consistent with other sculptural representations of the popular and Daoist deities from the Northern Song dynasty extant in Southern Shanxi, the 110-centimeter-tall image sits with her legs crossed in front of her in a manner entirely unfamiliar in representations of either popular female deities or images of empresses known from the period. Instead, her cross-legged position resembles Buddhist images but also, perhaps as a product of competition between the two religions, can be found in some representations of the Spirit Mother of the West, Laozi, and other canonized Daoist figures, as well as Buddhist lay women.

The facial style of the Sage Mother is poised and formal without appearing stiff or aloof. She has thin, high eyebrows and narrow, almost closed eyes. Her nose is refined but not petite and flares to the width of the slightly pursed lips below it. Full cheeks and neck make this work an image of a mature, respectable woman who is in control of the building she occupies. Her hair is pulled up, away from her face, and tucked into a now-damaged phoenix crown. Her pierced earlobes would have originally held earrings.

She wears a layered garment, with the first layer being a rounded collar, covered by a second, V-necked garment tucked under a high-waist skirt. Over this, she has an elaborate necklace that appears to be a combination of necklaces wore by Buddhist deities on top of a lotus-leaf base of the type frequently seen in other representations of female deities in the popular pantheon. Although her hands appear as if she were in mid-speech, they are completely covered by the long, sumptuous sleeves of her outer robe, which is draped loosely across her shoulders and around her folded legs. The low angle of the scalloped shoulder pieces, usually much more stiffly rendered, emphasize the relaxed manner in which she wears this garment. The drapery is finely carved and falls naturally around a two-tiered square plinth.

By 1087, the Sage Mother's new chair reiterated the rain-making potency of the building's exterior, as well as its use in identifying the Sage Mother as water spirit. In addition to the six to eight dragons being added to the front façade columns, the Golden Dragon Society also sponsored a new chair for the Sage Mother. The wooden chair is a combination of royal chair and Buddhist statuary plinth. The upper half is an over-sized chair with arms and back, each articulated at the corners with phoenix heads. The lower half, by contrast, takes the form of a Buddhist statuary plinth, whose square edges form an hourglass profile likely derived from the shape of Mt. Sumeru, the *axis mundi* of Buddhist tradition. However, this is not a fully Buddhist form, as the front panel has six dragons carved along the front edge, a direct reference to the dragons added at that time to the front columns of the building and perhaps also a reference to dragon vehicles for water goddesses. Behind her chair is a wooden three-panel screen adorned with phoenix heads of virtually the same make as those found on the chair. It is decorated with seven images: three on the upper portion and four on the lower portion. The upper portion has a dragon in the center, flanked on either side by images of waves. The lower portion contains images of moons in the outside panels and wave patterns on the interior two panels. Around the dragon and moon forms are images of clouds. The larger platform and niche containing the image of the Sage Mother was a Ming-dynasty addition[77] but employs a similar wave pattern, giving a strong sense of the significance of water to the patrons or creators of the object.[78]

Fig. 6.30 Attendant Figure, painted clay, h. 156 cm (Zhao Zhiguang, *Zhongguo Jinci Songsu*, pl. 27). Although repainted, this example of the forty Song-period attendant figures shows the highly sensitive expressions and lifelike quality of the Sage Mother Hall sculpture. (Courtesy of Shanxi renmin chubanshe.)

As famous as the building is itself, the attendant figures within the Sage Mother Hall are considered to be some of the best Northern Song-dynasty works extant (Fig. 6.30). The forty attendants dating to the Song period are all slightly smaller than life size with expressive, individuated facial features and body postures, and contrast sharply with the two smaller figures on either side of the Sage Mother that are Ming-dynasty additions.[79] The variety of images recreate a celestial court and include five eunuchs, four female officials who wear clothing otherwise reserved for men, and thirty-three ladies-in-waiting—all figures who would work in the inner quarters of a palace. The coiffure and clothing of the female attendant figures reflect a conservative style common in provincial areas and consistent with tenth-century representations of elite ladies. These images are renowned for their verisimilitude and liveliness, a characteristic some have linked to an interest in verisimilitude in Northern Song-dynasty art in general. Yet, the long drapery folds and jade rings of their clothing and their tall hairstyles are more like elite clothing of the tenth century rather than contemporary eleventh-century court costume. Shen Congwen speculates that they may be representative of a conservative regional tradition that was a holdover from the costumes popular during the Five Dynasties period.[80]

Evidence from the 1990s restoration of the building indicates that the wall surfaces of the Sage Mother Hall were fully painted from the Song dynasty and were repainted multiple times in the following period, obfuscating the Song-period iconography. Prior to the restoration, panels above the doorways still contained heavily damaged images of female figures, but no wall paintings remained on the interior. While dismantling the building, traces of paint were found on interior walls that were possibly part of the Song-period wall-painting program but not enough to positively identify the imagery. Chai Zejun believes this to be evidence of a fully painted Song period interior.[81] The rest of the remaining painting is thought to be from the sixteenth century, with repainting having taken place early in the eighteenth century.

Underneath the veranda, above the doors in the secondary bays and windows in the tertiary bays, is a wall-painting series measuring approximately 37-square meters in total painted surface that recreates the court scene of the sculptural program (Figs. 6.31–6.34). Traces of paint on the wall plane above the central bay indicate that it originally held images as well, but it is presently covered with a plaque bearing the official title of the goddess, Sage Mother of Clear Efficacy and Manifest Aid (Xianling zhaoji shengmu) from her elevation in 1111 (Fig. 6.35).[82] According to an inscription on the paintings, Canal-Head Zhang sponsored the repainting of these images in 1515.[83] Each of the paintings had traces of earlier Song- and Yuan-dynasty paintings beneath them, and the Ming-dynasty images overlaying these earlier works are thought to have been similar in content. The paintings have suffered enough damage that certain identification is difficult, and cartouches that may have helped to identify individual figures are obscured.

Fig. 6.31 Sage Mother Entourage, panel in southern tertiary bay, front façade of Cella, Sage Mother Hall, pigment on plaster, h. 265 cm, sixteenth century, showing guardian figures carrying pole arms and other courtly figures.

Fig. 6.32 Sage Mother Entourage, panel in southern secondary bay, front façade of Cella, Sage Mother Hall, pigment on plaster, h. 263 cm, sixteenth century, showing courtly female figures facing northward toward the central bay.

Fig. 6.33 Sage Mother Entourage, panel in northern tertiary bay, front façade of Cella, Sage Mother Hall, pigment on plaster, h. 265 cm, sixteenth century, showing guardian figures framing the north side of attendant figures.

Fig. 6.34 Sage Mother Entourage, panel in northern secondary bay, front façade of Cella, Sage Mother Hall, pigment on plaster, h. 263 cm, sixteenth century, showing courtly female figures facing southward toward the central bay.

Fig. 6.35 Plaque over door of Sage Mother Hall, pigment on wood, Song dynasty. Although this plaque is not dated, the title is from the 1111 elevation of the goddess to Sage Mother of Clear Efficacy and Manifest Aid, and the style of the plaque is similar to images passed down to us from the *Yingzao fashi*.

Although quite faint, one can still clearly discern a hierarchy of figures arranged in a formal, court-like configuration from the outer bays inward indicating that the missing central bay panel would likely have held an iconic image of the Sage Mother. The outermost figures in the tertiary bays wear armor and both hold pole arms, the one on the south side stands at attention at the back of the entourage, the one on the north faces away from the viewer toward the group of figures in the work, including what appears to be another armored guardian. Another bearded male figure appears in both of these outer paintings; on the north, he serves to frame seven female figures at least two of whom are attendants who hold fans behind the heads of their mistresses. On the south, he stands on the far side of five more females, only one of whom holds a fan for another who stands in a more prominent position. Other than the armored warriors, the figures are all in voluminous robes with expansive sleeves, and all are directed inward toward the central bay.

The figures above the doorways in both north and south secondary bays are all women, each panel containing those who either dominate or look outward toward the viewer (or both). Yet, the larger orientation of the group is still inward toward the central panel. In the south panel ten figures are discernible. Positioned in a somewhat semi-circular configuration behind three central women rendered in slightly larger scale, two figures hold feathered fans, one a flat fan, one a *ruyi* 如意 scepter, and one a ceremonial umbrella. Two of the three larger women hold *gui* 圭 tablets, and one has her hands folded within her sleeves in front of her. The northern panel contains eleven discernible images of women, at least two of whom are holding feathered fans. A hierarchy of scale is not as clear in this panel, and size seems to be used to indicate proximity to the viewer rather than importance. Although three of the women look directly outward, the body postures and positions of the figures as a group lead the eye toward the central bay of the building.

Because of the shared iconography between popular spirits and the imperial court, and the later interpretation of the Spirit of the Jin Springs as the mother of Shu Yu, the iconography of these paintings is not certain. In different publications, Chai Zejun and others have identified the theme as either a court tour of inspection, twelve brook transcendents (*shier xixian* 十二溪仙) attending the peaches of immortality, or twelve female officials (*shier nüguan* 十二女官).[84] Chai likens them stylistically and iconographically to representations of deities as palace ladies found in nature-spirit temples such as the Yuan-dynasty Mingyingwang Hall, at the Guangshengsi Water God's Temple and the main worship hall of the Ming-dynasty Earth Queen Sage Mother Temple in Fenyang 汾陽 (Houtu shengmumiao 后土聖母廟), seventy-five kilometers (just over forty-five miles) south of Jinci (Figs. 6.36, 6.37).[85] In Chai Zejun's analysis of the paintings, he states that the earlier paintings (found underneath the present wall surface) are similar in style to deities depicted on the walls of the Yuan-dynasty Daoist Monastery Yonglegong 永樂宮 now in Ruicheng 芮城, Shanxi (Fig. 6.38).[86]

The symmetrical configuration of the figures facing inward toward the central bay, the placement of guardians on the outermost edges, and the formal courtly dress and *gui* tablets resemble extant Yuan-period wall paintings showing deities holding court. Quite dissimilar to the paintings of women in the back palaces depicted in the Mingyingwang Hall, or the deity preparing to depart on a tour in the Fenyang Sage Mother Temple, the women here are in the formal postures of a court audience. A more comparable example is the audience with Mingyingwang, the Spirit of the Huo Spring, located on the west interior wall of the Mingyingwang Hall (Fig. 6.39). Here, male figures dominate the scene, yet we see the same placement of guardians framing the outside and standing courtiers in formal robes, sometimes holding *gui* tablets, fanned by attendants, all facing inward to an iconic image of Mingyingwang sitting on a throne. He is depicted frontally, and his throne is similar to the Sage Mother's chair, with a high-backed wooden upper portion and a solid pedestal base that narrows at the center. Although very

(*left*) Fig. 6.36 Ladies in the Back Palace, east side of north wall, Mingyingwang Hall, Water God's Temple, Guangshengsi, Wang Yanda et al., pigment on plaster, h. 350 cm, 1324 (Chai, *Shanxi siguan bihua*, 228). This detail shows courtly ladies making preparations of some kind in what appears to be the inner quarters of the Water God's palace. (Courtesy Wenwu chubanshe.) (*right*) Fig. 6.37 Earth Queen(?) and entourage exiting her palace, east wall, Shengmumiao, Fenyang, 16th century. Here we see a more narrative scene than that in the paintings in the Sage Mother Hall, with the central deity exiting through a doorway followed by ladies-in-waiting. Although not visible in this image, the narrative continues on this wall as the Earth Queen is taken on a tour in her dragon-drawn chariot.

faint, one can see that the style of the robes and facial features of the figures in Sage Mother Hall wall paintings bear more similarities to the Yuan-dynasty images than the Ming images of palace ladies (as seen in the Fenyang series), supporting Chai's theory that the sixteenth-century works were repaintings of Yuan images. Given the arrangement of the figures in the secondary and tertiary bays therefore, the original painting in the central bay was likely a frontal iconic image of the Sage Mother as Spirit of the Jin Springs, sitting on a throne. This scene was then repeated in sculptural form in the interior. When this central panel was covered with the plaque that is there today is uncertain, but it could have been quite early; the plaque itself may date from her promotion to Sage Mother of Clear Efficacy and Manifest Aid in 1111.[87]

Both the Song-dynasty sculpture inside the cella and the Ming-dynasty paintings on the exterior of the cella share the convention of imperial costume as a means of representing the status of the divinity. In his article on modularity in the religious painting of the Ten Kings of Hell, Lothar Ledderose identified a set of conventions for depicting high-status individuals,

Fig. 6.38 Earth Queen, east wall, Sanqing Hall, Yonglegong, Ma Junxiang et al., pigment on plaster, h. 398 cm, 1325 (Jin Weinuo, *Siguan bihua*, 102). This detail shows the Earth Queen in a formal court audience surrounded by standing attendant figures. (Courtesy Wenwu chubanshe.)

Fig. 6.39 Audience of Mingyingwang, west wall, Mingyingwang Hall, Water God's Temple, Guangshengsi, Zhao Guoxiang et al, pigment on plaster, h. 538 cm, dated 1324 (Chai, *Shanxi siguan bihua*, 225, courtesy Wenwu chubanshe).

Fig. 6.40 Empress of Song Renzong, hanging scroll, ink and colors on silk, 172.1 x 165.3 cm, Northern Song. This image is typical of portraits of empresses from the Northern Song dynasty in their costume, chair, and attendant figures. (Courtesy National Palace Museum, Taipei, Taiwan, Republic of China.)

be they representations of underworld deities, emperors or empresses, Chan Buddhist masters, or the more overtly secular images of famous literati—all employed elevated seats, high-backed armchairs, a raised dais backed by a screen, or an armchair backed by a screen as a frame for the sitter that emphasized his or her superior position vis-à-vis the viewer of the painting.[88] The images of the Ten Kings of Hell, deities of the Buddhist underworld, were all dressed in the official regalia of a Chinese magistrate, clad in voluminous robes, and placed in a high-backed armchair framed by a screen.[89]

Although these images of otherworldly beings were used in monasteries, the iconography is derived from the imperial bureaucracy. As Ledderose points out, Song-dynasty images of emperors and empresses display the same formulae of high-backed chairs and formal court robes (Fig. 6.40). The portrait of the Northern Song empress of Renzong (r. 1022–63), for example, shows her seated in a three-quarters pose on a high-backed chair that is punctuated at the corners of the back and armrests by dragons. A diminutive attendant figure stands on either side. The empress's head is covered with a dramatic crown that sits low on the forehead. She wears an intricately embroidered robe that crosses in front of her and is belted slightly above the waist. Below this, her hands are folded in front of her with one thumb revealed, in a manner consistent with other imperial portraits from this period. Her legs hang pendant in front of her and are placed on an elaborate footrest.

The Yonglegong image of the Earth Queen provides a high-quality standard by which to compare images of female divinities that had been incorporated into the Daoist pantheon with portraits of empresses extant from the Song imperial collection (Fig. 6.38). Like the empresses, the deities are shown in a three-quarter view, seated in high-backed chairs decorated with dragons. However, the details of their costume differ considerably. Although in the same formal posture, they sit on a throne surmounting an hourglass-shaped plinth commonly seen underneath Buddhist divinities and linked iconographically to the cosmic Mt. Sumeru. Their heads are framed by halos as well as by their chair backs. Their robes and crowns are also different with, in the case of the transcendent girl next to the Earth Queen, much more clearly defined phoenixes, as well as a type of formal chest and shoulder piece or *peijian* 帔肩, which may have derived from *pibo* 披膊 armor.[90] While not ubiquitous, this elaborate shoulder piece can be either stiff as if made of metal, as in this Yuan-dynasty image of a standing goddess from the National Palace Museum (Taipei), most likely the Spirit Mother of the West (Fig. 6.41), or more softly rendered in leather or fabric.[91] An entourage of attendant figures and subsidiary divinities dressed in flowing, layered robes stands on either side of the primary figures.

The sculptural image of the Sage Mother is therefore more similar to conventional representations of high-status deities on elaborate chairs framed by screens than to extant images of empresses. Subtle differences in seated position, costume, and chair separate these images of deities from Song-period ancestral portraits. In the above examples, dragon thrones were used rather than the phoenix-head decoration we see in the Sage Mother Hall—the chair of the Sage Mother reserves its six dragons for the lower panel. And, as subsidiary divinities in larger painting programs, a three-quarter view was used rather than an iconic, frontal image. But the clothing, robes, crown, and necklace of deities found in these paintings are consistent with the image of the Sage Mother. As a central icon, however, she bears more similarities to sculpture found in the temples of southern Shanxi. The costume and facial style of the Sage Mother can be compared to Northern Song images of popular and Daoist deities extant in the Erxianmiao and Yuhuangmiao 玉皇廟, both located near Jincheng in southeastern Shanxi province (Figs. 6.42 and 6.43).[92] Her seated position atop the square plinth recalls the tradition of Daoist sculpture in the Dragon Mountain

Fig. 6.41 "Blessings for Long Life," hanging scroll, 91 x 45.3 cm, ink and colors on silk, Yuan. This image shows a female deity in an elaborate costume similar to that of the Sage Mother, including what appears to be a metal shoulder-and-breast plate. The jade maiden standing beside her holding a plate of peaches suggests that the goddess is Xiwangmu, famous for the peaches of longevity that grow at her palace on Mt. Kunlun. (Courtesy National Palace Museum, Taipei, Taiwan, Republic of China.)

Grottos (*Longshan shiku* 龍山石窟), approximately three kilometers (less than two miles) north of Jinci (Fig. 6.44).[93] This simple cross-legged pose on an angular, hourglass-shaped pedestal was appropriated from Buddhism into religious Daoist imagery as early as the Tang dynasty,[94] and we have evidence for Buddhist elements such as the cross-legged position and lotus pedestal being used for indigenous Chinese religion in the Eastern

Fig. 6.42 Female Transcendent, Main Hall, Jincheng Ermiaomiao, painted and gilded clay, h. 245 cm (including seat), ca. 1107–1117 (Shi Yan, *Wudai, Song diaosu*, 90). The stiff-backed formal posture with legs hanging pendant is typical of central icons of both popular and Daoist pantheons as well as of imperial ancestral portraits, but the breast and shoulder plates distinguish her from contemporary images of empresses. (Courtesy of Wenwu chubanshe.)

Han (25–220 CE).[95] Even the hand positions, which at first glance are reminiscent of the Buddhist *mudrā*, are similar to those found in representations of Daoist and popular spirits from Shanxi province and elsewhere.[96]

Thus, the sculpture- and wall-painting programs of the Sage Mother Hall follow the traditional imperial metaphor used by popular and Daoist goddesses during the imperial, and even into the modern, period.[97] But, as a representation of the divine world, it differs from its contemporary counterpart in the real world. Dragons on the building and the Sage Mother's seat enhance the ability of the hall and the divinity within it to provide water to the community, as well as express the Sage Mother's identity as a water goddess. The sculptural program, with its guardian figures on the front

Fig. 6.43 Female Attendant, Yudi Hall, Jincheng Yuhuangmiao, painted clay, h. 173 cm, 1076 (Shi Yan, *Wudai, Song diaosu,* 89). Although this is an attendant figure, the shape of her face and high brow, diminutive eyes, and petite nose are strikingly similar to the somewhat older-looking Sage Mother. (Courtesy Wenwu chubanshe.)

veranda and entourage of attendants and officials, is repeated in pictorial form above the entrance into the cella in a design consistent with Yuan-period water-spirit temple programs elsewhere in Shanxi. The image of the Sage Mother is unusual in its use of the voluminous, layered costume and Buddhist cross-legged pose, which is unknown in imperial portraiture from the Song dynasty, but the costume and pose are common to the images of major Daoist and popular divinities in north China from as early as the Tang dynasty.

Fig. 6.44 Daoist Divinity, Dragon Mountain Grottos (Longshan shiku), stone, h. approx. 160 cm, Yuan dynasty, ca. 1236. In this image, located at grottos literally within walking distance of Jinci, the deity is sitting on an hourglass-shaped pedestal, similar to the lower portion of the Sage Mother's chair.

Song-Period Sculpture Outside the Sage Mother Hall

Jinci is also known for its iron sculpture of guardian generals and lions. Four guardian generals stand at the corners of the Iron Man Terrace, added on axis in front of the Sage Mother Hall in the Shaosheng-reign period (1094–98). The earliest inscription is on the southeast corner guardian, whose body was cast in 1089 but whose head was replaced in 1926. Two of the sculptures were cast in the Shaosheng period, the one on the southwest corner in 1097, which remains fully intact (Fig. 6.45). The torso of the northwest guardian was cast in 1098, but the head was replaced in 1423. According to the *Jincizhi*, a fourth sculpture was cast during the Ming Hongzhi period (1488–1506), but the one presently on the northeast corner is a 1913 replacement.[98] Thought to protect the temple against flood, they are similar to a set of four found at the Temple to the Central Peak (Zhongyuemiao) from 1064.[99] Unfortunately, they are movable, and thus it is difficult to be certain that they were originally placed in their current location. All of these sculptures display cast inscriptions that originally detailed the time of casting and the donors' names. Although much has been lost due to damage, the inscription on the 1097 figure on the southwest corner is still clear. As in the case of the column dragons on the Sage Mother Hall, the piece was donated by the members of the community—in this case, members of an elite family or families (including four *jinshi* 進士 and a new bride).[100]

Fig. 6.45 Iron Guardian, iron, h. 225 cm, dated 1097, this is one of four iron images at the four corners of the Iron Man or Lotus Blossom Terrace and the only such fully intact image from the eleventh century. Identified as a guardian figure because of its martial garb and stance, the inscription includes the names of donors as well as the date of casting.

Two pairs of guardian lions are also part of the Song-dynasty sculptural program at Jinci,[101] but again, we do not know where they were originally placed. Presently, one set frames the entrance to the Flying Bridge that leads to the Sage Mother Hall. The use of lions to guard entrances to temples was also an import from Buddhism but gained wide popularity through the late imperial period when they were used at the entries to palaces as well as to Buddhist and Daoist monasteries.

The Spirit Bridge (or Flying Bridge), Iron Man Terrace, and Offering Hall

Spirit Bridge or Flying Bridge (Shenqiao/Feiliang). The bridge in front of the Sage Mother Hall crosses a pool that was originally filled by the central of three springs at the site, allowing the visitor to physically traverse the spring water in order to reach the palatial realm of the goddess (Fig. 2.7). From an examination of the use of the term here and in textual sources, the significance of this bridge lies more in its placement between the Sage Mother Hall and the larger complex and in bridge symbolism in general rather than in any specific association with the name *feiliang*.

By the sixth century CE, *feiliang* were known in poetry to link terrestrial to celestial realms. The term is used as a link to temples in two rhapsodies in Xiao Tong's (501–31) *Wenxuan*, which became a canonical source of literature for China's educated elite.[102] In Yang Xiong's 揚雄 (53–18 CE) *Sweet Springs Palace Rhapsody*, the flying bridge is used to take the emperor into the heavens to meet Grand Unity, the supreme deity, when he went to the Sweet Springs Palace north of the capital to perform sacrifices.[103] A flying bridge is also mentioned in the *Eastern Metropolis Rhapsody* in the section describing the rite of Grand Exorcism, where it, too, is a link between this world and the heavenly realm with its Celestial Pond (Tianchi 天池).

Unfortunately, we do not know exactly when this name was applied to the bridge in front of the Sage Mother Hall. Although an analysis of its structure and the shape of its supporting columns places it in the Song dynasty,[104] we have no Song-dynasty reference to link this structure with the name, nor are other *feiliang* extant from other locations. The term seems instead to be a generic word for a cantilevered bridge or an elevated beam bridge of trabeated construction.[105] In his documentation of the restorations of Jinci in the 1560s, Gao Ruxing referred to the bridge as a spirit bridge (*shenqiao*), indicating that he did not consider it to be the one mentioned in the *Shuijingzhu* passage.[106]

The modern use of this name for the bridge appears to be a post-Ming reattribution of the name used in the *Shuijingzhu*, an attribution that would reassert the primacy of the worship of Shu Yu at the site of the Jin Springs by connecting the bridge in front of the Sage Mother Hall with bridges near the worship halls dedicated to Shu Yu. In the nineteenth century, Liu Dapeng believed that the use of this name for the bridge over the pool in front of the Sage Mother Hall derived from this source.[107] When Li Daoyuan used this term to describe the bridge (or bridges) over the waterways at Jinci during the sixth century, he portrayed the Jinci *feiliang* as a

Fig. 6.46 Offering Hall (1168), detail of eaves bracketing showing similarity with those of the Sage Mother Hall (shown in Figures 5.1, 6.10, 6.23, and 6.24).

popular meeting place. But because of the dramatic changes in the site documented in histories from the sixth to tenth centuries described above, Li was probably not describing a bridge in exactly that position. Given the location at a temple site, perhaps Li Daoyuan, too, was alluding to the bridges between earth and the heavens found in Yang Xiong's rhapsodies, thus referring to the same experience described in *ci* cantos—a location to meet a water goddess, the transcendent who presides over the springs.[108]

Iron Man Terrace. The Iron Man Terrace, also called Lotus Terrace (Lianhuatai), was added on axis in front of the Sage Mother Hall during the Shaosheng-reign period of Song Zhezong (1094–98; Fig. 2.4).[109] This small, square platform, called a *lutai* 路臺 at the Temple to the Central Peak, could either be an altar, worship platform, or theatrical stage (or conceivably all three, depending on the occasion).[110] Although we have no record of the activities that took place on this platform, information regarding invocations for rain in early China did include ritual dances.[111] As the Sage Mother became more important for providing rain, this terrace may have been added as a permanent structure for more regular ceremonies.

Offering Hall. In 1168, after the fall of the Northern Song and establishment of Jin-dynasty (1127–1234) control of north China as far south as the Huai River, the Offering Hall was added between the Spirit Bridge and the Iron Man Terrace. Despite changes in architectural style because of influences from Southeast China taking place across Shanxi, the bracketing of the three-by-three bay Offering Hall was made to match the idiosyncratic lower-eaves bracketing of the Sage Mother Hall (Figs. 2.6, 6.46). The addition of this structure during the twelfth century indicates the continued, and perhaps increasing, local support of the Sage Mother after the fall of the Northern Song. The building's continued maintenance into the present is a further testament to her significance to the local community.

The Pre-Yuan "Complex" of the Sage Mother as a Local Nature-Spirit Temple

The extant evidence of the pre-Yuan-period temple to the Sage Mother of Manifest Aid, though limited, emphasizes topography over cosmology and the creation of water above all else. From the earliest documentation of it, the site of the Jin Springs at the base of Xuanweng Mountain was known to be the location of nature spirits. Beginning from the Han dynasty, the Jin Springs began to be developed systematically to create a canal network that supplied the surrounding community with water for irrigation and hydraulic mills. During the second half of the eleventh century, the canal system was expanded to reach more than five times the amount of land it had previously irrigated.

Although the pre-Song textual record of the site emphasizes the worship of Shu Yu of Tang, the natural beauty of the Jin Springs and its economic significance is also a recurring theme in written sources. These sources display a conflict, or perhaps a competition, between the two divinities that gradually became more pronounced in the tenth century—emperors venerated Shu Yu, but poets were interested in the manifestation of spirits in kingfisher-blue. By the beginning of the Song, the distinction became more important, and the official Zhao Changyan sought to define the Jinci rebuilding as being exclusively for the benefit of Shu Yu, clarifying that neither transcendents nor the Earth Queen were being venerated with the construction project sponsored by the second Song-dynasty emperor.

But the expansion of the canal system in the eleventh century also expanded the patronage base of the spring spirit—along with its wealth. Her temple was rebuilt on a grand scale after the destructive 1038 earthquake, and her ability to provide rain allowed local officials to petition for her official entry into the sacrificial statutes and for the promotion to Sage Mother of Manifest Aid. Local patronage enhanced her worship hall with the addition of dragons and a throne that was consistent with the status expressed by her new title as well as her status as a powerful water goddess. Iconographic similarities among popular, Daoist, and imperial imagery in architecture and sculpture allowed the addition of a chair and framing screen to make the goddess look especially regal, just as these same elements made the images of royalty look especially divine. But the location of the building above the most central of the Jin Springs, and the temple rituals performed frequently enough to require a permanent location, clearly denoted her identity as a water goddess. The addition of the Offering Hall in 1168 is evidence of her continued local patronage after the fall of the Northern

Song, patronage that was clearly tied more to efficacy in providing water. Because of the destruction of the site during the Jin-Yuan wars, only the buildings associated with the Sage Mother of Clear Efficacy and Manifest Aid—the cult with the strongest indigenous patronage base—remained from the eleventh and twelfth centuries. Confusion about the date of the Sage Mother Hall and the identity of the Sage Mother stems from a late imperial interpretation of the site and is ultimately tied to the development of the complex from the Yuan through Ming dynasties. In the next chapter, I examine the re-orientation of the Jinci complex from ancestral shrine to nature-spirit temple as the site was rebuilt around the Sage Mother Hall, and the way in which the flexibility of the imperial metaphor in architecture and sculpture was manipulated to align the Sage Mother with the competing interests of the local farmers, nobility, and Confucian elite, all of whom were dependent on the economic force of the Jin Springs for their lives and livelihoods.

Chapter Seven
Manipulating the Spirits of Jin

In this chapter, I examine the effect of competing patronage groups on the development of the site of Jinci from the Yuan through the early Qing dynasties. Temples, including the main worship hall and other ritual structures that made up the larger Chinese temple complex, were considered direct expressions of the importance and spiritual presence of the deity enshrined within them. Because the Sage Mother Hall was the oldest, largest, and best-preserved hall in the post-Jin-dynasty complex of Jinci, visitors to the site understood the building to house the primary deity—even when they did not agree that the primary deity *should* be a female water spirit. Unable to displace the Sage Mother from this regal structure, scholars beginning from the early Qing dynasty addressed the issue of what they perceived to be ritual impropriety by questioning interpretation; they began to debate the true identity of the Sage Mother. Two factors contributed to this debate: the name of the site as Jinci (by that time implying an ancestral or lineage shrine) and the impressive size, grandeur, and antiquity of the building. From the Yuan through the early Ming dynasties, the deity resident within this hall was the Sage Mother of Clear Efficacy and Manifest Aid, who ensured regular agricultural production through irrigation water, rain, and hydraulic power for mills. Over this period, the Sage Mother Hall became the ritual focus for an irrigation community controlled by the canal heads and hatch keepers, who distributed the irrigation water to nobility, landlords, and private farmers in a strict rotation. By the sixteenth century, perhaps in an effort to break the power of this network, the literati elite sought to reclaim the site as an ancestral shrine. They did this architecturally as well as textually, and their efforts eventually changed the interpretation of the Sage Mother's primary identity in local gazetteers from that of a water spirit to the mother of Shu Yu, Yi Jiang.

The Development of the Jinci Ritual Complex from the Thirteenth to Fifteenth Centuries

As discussed in the previous two chapters, the detailed description of the buildings at Jinci recorded in Yi Gou's stele inscription of 1267 provides most of the information we have for the site from the eleventh to twelfth centuries. As mentioned in Chapter 4, this inscription informs us of the expansive size of the pre-Yuan site that was very likely oriented north-south and tells of a gatehouse being added on the east side of the complex, in addition to the main gatehouse, in order to facilitate access to the Sage Mother Hall.[1] This stele inscription also mentions a number of other structures associated with the spirits, which were repaired under official sanction during this period: the tombs of King Li of Jin 李晉王 and Duke Di of Liang 狄梁公; and the temples to Tai Tai, Hu Tu 狐突, and Du Mingdu 竇鳴犢. Most of these buildings were located within the larger Jinci compound, but not all.[2] There were also eight pavilions on the site: the River View *Ting*-gazebo (Wangchuanting 望川停) on Mt. Xuanweng, the *Ting*-gazebos covering the Everlasting and Perfect Benefit Springs, Even Fortune *Tang*-pavilion (Junfutang 均福堂), Benevolent Wisdom *Xuan*-pavilion (Renzhixuan 仁智軒), Emerging Snow *Ting*-gazebo (Yongxueting 湧雪停), Pure Flourishing *Tang*-pavilion (Qinghuatang 清華堂), and Encircled-by-Kingfisher-Blue *Ting*-gazebo (Huancuiting 環翠停).

In 1342, a larger project was completed to repair the multiple temple buildings within the compound. In that year, a serious drought plagued the region, and several officials went to Jinci to pray for rain. Noticing that the buildings were in poor repair, the officials made a deal with the deities: if rain fell within seven days of the prayer, they would renovate the temple complex. As the story is told, before they completed their journey back to the city, the rain had soaked through their clothing.[3] The leading official promised a portion of his salary toward the restoration, and members of the local population were expected to follow with private donations to the project. When donations were not forthcoming, water rights were threatened to ensure proper support for the restoration. Farmers were charged 200 cash (*wen* 文) per *mu* of land and a total of 1,000 ingots was collected. Combined with that offered by the officials, a total of 1,078 ingots were used to rebuild the complex, and the project was completed in just under six months.[4]

The description of the complex in the memorial inscription by Wang Sicheng written at the completion of the project in the tenth month of 1342 is the first stating that the Shu Yu Shrine Complex was oriented north-south and that the Sage Mother Hall sat above a spring between the Everlasting Spring and the Perfect Benefit Spring. There were three major halls extant before the restoration began: those dedicated to Shu Yu, those to the Sage Mother, and those to the True Lord of Manifest Benevolence and Spiritual Clarity (Zhaohui lingxian zhenjun 昭惠靈顯眞君). These three faced south, east, and north, respectively. Additionally, there were worship halls (*dian*) dedicated to the deities of Mt. Tai, Fujun 府君, and the Medicine King, as well as a Precious Ink *Tang*-pavilion (Baomotang 寶墨堂), all of which had been destroyed by the time the inscription was written.[5]

The record left by Gaochang Xieyu 高昌偰玉 (Yuan) provides a more detailed account of worship at Jinci, mentioning the traditional history as well as how the site was used:

the elite encouraged others to recognize and act on their social obligations.[23] The use of these ritual manuals by individuals not necessarily tied to the state bureaucracy allowed the literati elite to create networks of local organization based on perpetuating lineage and linking kin rather than producing monetary wealth—thereby asserting a moralizing trend in society.[24] Additionally, ritual manuals were both based in the Confucian classics and easy to follow, qualities that were, as Shang Wei has argued, particularly important to the development of ritualism among Neo-Confucian scholars of the seventeenth and eighteenth centuries.[25] By following the manuals closely, any literate person could perform proper rituals without having to engage a religious professional.

The philosophical contributions of Cheng Yi were also extremely important to the development of an alternative Confucian social order. Cheng Yi's innovation was to link descent groups defined by traditional mourning circles with the performance of ancestral rites; this gave commoners the right to worship the same number of generational ancestors as they had the right to mourn, reaching as far back as their great-great grandfather. Although not advocated until late in the thirteenth century, Cheng Yi also introduced the first ancestor (*shizu* 始祖)—a symbolic figure meaning the "first progenitor of humankind" (*juechu shengmin zhi zu* 厥初生民之族)—as an object of worship by officials. Zhu Xi opposed this idea because he believed that worshiping remote ancestors was too close to the "great descent line" system (*dazongfa* 大宗法) that was the exclusive right of the Zhou dynasty hereditary aristocracy.[26] But by opening the door to the worship of a distant ancestor, Cheng Yi made way for the veneration of the first migrant ancestor to a region, which, according to Chow, was the most common type of first ancestor for Ming and Qing Confucians.[27]

None of the officials responsible for rebuilding the shrine to Shu Yu from the Yuan through the Ming dynasties did so because it was a shrine to the ancestor of their lineage. Rather, because Shu Yu was the first member of the Zhou royal family to rule the Taiyuan basin, his name was in the sacrificial statutes, and his temple received imperial patronage, and officials were responsible for performing rites to him and, by extension, maintaining his shrine. But the Confucian elite of the sixteenth century believed that all the people of Jin should properly venerate the spirit of Shu Yu because he was both the ancestor of the Zhou royal house for the region and a moral exemplar. This is clearly articulated in Su You's dedicatory inscription discussed in Chapter 4:

> Presently the shrine is by the Jin River; its irrigation water benefits the people. They say [they just] go to [focus on] the other sacrificial affairs [the Spirit of the Jin Springs] in their prayers. Yet Shu Yu began his enfeoffment from the *wutong* leaf, his descendants survived throughout the Zhou Dynasty, and their merit and favor to this land can be researched [in the classics].[28]

今祠在晉水上，民之利其潤也，方曰詣他祠事報祈，乃叔虞自翦桐啓封，歷世與周久遠，則其功德於斯土可考也。

The "lineage orientation" of the literati that developed during the Southern Song, combined with the model of distant-ancestor worship established in the philosophical writings of Cheng Yi, allowed for Ming and Qing Confucians to worship first ancestors even though there was no classical precedent for it.[29] This may have also opened the door for Zhou-dynasty regional founders to be venerated as ancestors as well as deified historical figures. The focus on lineage building and the search for the earliest migrant ancestors emphasized the role that historical figures from the classics, including Zhou-dynasty state ancestral figures such as Shu Yu, could play in reintroducing moral obligation into society. The late Ming gentry re-established the rites to the founder of their region of Jin at Jinci in a manner similar to the construction and re-establishment of rituals to the Zhou moral exemplar Wu Taibo 吳泰伯, best known to us from the eighteenth-century novel *Rulin waishi* 儒林外史. The eldest son of Danfu 亶父, progenitor of the Zhou royal house, Taibo was exalted by Confucius because, seeing that his younger brother would be the superior ruler, he declined to take the throne. Instead, he traveled to Wu and Yue (the Yangzi delta region), where he remained even after the death of his father, thus enabling his brother to succeed to the throne. Taibo was worshiped in Nanjing primarily as a Confucian moral exemplar. But although Wu Taibo was known to have no male offspring, as the first member of the Zhou royal family to settle an area conceived historically to have been on the edges of civilization far from the Central Plains, he was seen as the ancestor of the region. According to Shang Wei, the rites performed to him in the novel, as well as in eighteenth-century reality, were permeated with the sense of ancestral worship.[30]

The late imperial Confucian ritual agenda also set increasingly rigid parameters for women in society, where the most exalted position was as a "chaste widow" and mother. Official granting of honorific insignia for women who did not remarry after the deaths of their husbands had existed since the early fourteenth century and had increased in popularity across the Ming. In the Qing dynasty, the requirements for the award were lessened. Whereas earlier a woman had to be over fifty and a widow since before the age of thirty, in 1723 new regulations included women who were as young as forty and had been widowed for only fifteen years. Additionally, the Qing government made a point of seeking out women from lower classes for the award, thereby promoting the value beyond the gentry. These activities resulted in a dramatic increase in the number of women eligible to receive the honor, which usually included the erection of a memorial gateway, and may have been an effort to assert an ideal of the proper role of woman as wife and mother in an age of increased literacy among gentry women.[31]

At Jinci, the gentry's solution to both of these problems—the perceived need for a more lineage-focused society and the desire to present women in a familial role that emphasized the position of mother—was to reinterpret the identity of the water goddess at Jinci as the historical mother of Shu Yu.

Because Jinci was the center of the irrigation community as well as being the oldest ancestral shrine in the vicinity, however, the site served as a symbolic battleground of symbols where different groups fought for authority. These groups asserted their association with the Spirit of the Jin Springs, and by extension the right to the spring water, by sponsoring temple buildings that reflected an interpretation of the water spirit's identity that would support their interests.

Water Management During the Late Ming

The private landowners in the villages surrounding Jinci held a different belief about the identity of the Spirit of the Jin Springs, which they believed gave them a fundamental right to the water. By the late Ming, an extensive irrigation community had developed around the Jin Springs with the ritual center at Jinci. Court cases involving water rites during this time indicate that the organization of canal heads and hatch keepers exerted a significant, and not always productive, force on local society. This irrigation community, similar to others across China from the late Ming through the nineteenth century, was based in a local hierarchy separate from government officials and gentry elite. Because the ritual system, which was centered around the water goddess, did not follow the same Confucian principles of local governance, it competed with the authority of the literati elite and the representatives of the imperial government.

During the sixteenth century, two cases were brought to court concerning the water management of the Jin River. The first comes down to us in a stele inscription requesting an imperial ruling on the abuses by the hatch keepers and canal heads along the northern branch of the Jin River canal system in 1543. By this time, the water from Eternal Youth Spring was still divided into ten shares as it had been during the Song, and the seven-three split seems to have originated from the area in front of Eternal Youth Spring, in a configuration similar to its present appearance (Figs. 3.3, 7.1).[32]

The conflict over irrigation water was focused on the northern seven shares of the canal, which irrigated lands more than ten kilometers (six miles) north of the source of the water at the Eternal Youth Spring.[33] Although the lands irrigated south of Eternal Youth Spring had no trouble gaining sufficient water for their crops (the stated reason was closer proximity to the spring itself), the lands along the northern canal were not always sufficiently supplied. By the fifteenth century, local people and garrison troops of the Jinwangfu 晉王府 and Ninghuawangfu 寧化王府 princely establishments using the water along the north canal had established a regular six-day rotation of water during the spring and summer, beginning on the first day of the third month.[34] The rotation, termed "three for the troops, three for the people" (*junsan minsan* 軍三民三), was evenly split with three twenty-four-hour periods for the garrison troops and three twenty-four-hour periods for the local people.

Fig. 7.1 Eternal Youth Spring, view showing the water-dividing pagoda and the 7/10–3/10 split in the spring water, thought to have been established in the eleventh century.

Beginning in the Hongzhi reign period (1488–1506), the canal head of the north canal, Zhang Hongxiu, "offered" (*xian* 獻) the night water rights of the local people to the Jinwangfu, resulting in a system in which the garrison lands received irrigation water for three days and six nights, and the people received water only during the day for the three days of their rotation. Consequently, the northernmost villages lacked sufficient water for their crops. The canal heads and hatch keepers, responding to the increased demand, began selling the water to the locals. During his investigation in the 1540s, Su Zhigao found this practice particularly disgusting because it resulted in years in which some farmers enjoyed a full harvest while their neighbors starved. For Su Zhigao, this was an egregious misuse of the spring spirit's gift of water.[35]

The 1543 proclamation, literally set in stone in the form of a stele inscription, returned the rotation to the traditional three twenty-four-hour-period rations for the garrison troops' and the people's lands. However, making a judgment and displaying it publicly on a stele was not sufficient to break the canal heads' control over such a lucrative source of revenue for long. Although Gao Ruxing noted in his 1551 county gazetteer that the ruling had transformed the evil of buying and selling water,[36] by the 1580s, canal heads had returned the nighttime water rights to the nobility. This inspired the local people, particularly those of the northernmost villages who were least likely to receive sufficient water, to seek their own solutions. The reversal in rotation may have been due to another large expansion of the canal system in the mid-sixteenth century.

A judgment made on May 14, 1589, details the conclusion of an *ad hoc* solution to the problem of water distribution along the northern canal.

There was at least one major drought in Taiyuan in 1582, and, although the Sage Mother provided a rainstorm that year, water shortages continued to be a problem for the northern reaches of the Jin River canal system. Liu Tongfeng 柳桐鳳, Zhou Mi 周密, and Yang Xilong 楊希隆 were concerned about the limitation of the irrigation water on the northern end of the rotation. Because the water was distributed from south to north, it was not continuously irrigating lands for the people during their three-day ration, and the flow of water was not sufficient to irrigate all of Jinshengcun 金勝村 and Dongrucun 董茹村. Liu Tongfeng, a resident of Jinshengcun, succeeded in convincing the garrison troops of the King of Jin's Residence to add a seventh day to the rotation, which would also be split between the troops' land and that of the commoners. This allowed the northernmost villages to receive irrigation water as well.[37]

Although this new rotation was eventually declared to be illegal—Liu Tongfeng was flogged and fined, and the King of Jin's garrison troops reappropriated the people's night water rights—the justification behind Liu's addition of the seventh day is quite interesting. Liu believed that the members of Jinshengcun deserved an extra day in the rotation because they needed the water for attendants and horses for when Ms. Liu, the girl who had transcended to become the Spirit of the Jin Springs, returned home. According to legend, the Spirit of the Jin Springs was originally a girl from Jinshengcun with the difficult task of drawing water for her family. One day she came upon an equestrian (gender undefined) in white requesting water for his/her horse. Because Ms. Liu was generous, she was given a whip in return for the water. The equestrian ordered her to put it into the bottom of her vat for drawing water (*weng* 甕), saying, "If you take out the whip, then water will naturally come forth." When the girl returned to her mother's home, her paternal aunt (*gu* 姑) mistakenly took out the whip, causing the water to begin flowing rapidly. Unable to stop the flow, the aunt called out for help. Liu came in and sat on top of the vat, and only then did the flow settle. The Sage Mother's position at the base of the mountain was thought to be the mouth of the vat. Although it is impossible to determine the origin of this legend, one could see how the name of the mountain where the Jin Springs is located, Xuanweng (Suspended-Vat or Well-Bucket) Mountain, could inspire such a story. The fact that Liu Tongfeng shared the girl's surname probably made the story more convincing to the garrison troops and canal heads who cooperated in the rotation change.[38]

The problems of corruption and disputes over water rights at Jinci during the sixteenth century are similar to those described by Prasenjit Duara in his study of local culture in north China during the nineteenth and early twentieth centuries. Similar to the irrigation communities studied by Duara, the network of canals filled by the Jin Springs sustained agricultural production in the villages surrounding the springs. As Henrietta Harrison has pointed out, during the Qing dynasty, the control of water distribution at the canal was tied closely with the belief system in place at the temple complex, and the Sage Mother Hall was the ritual focus of the irrigation network. Although it did not hold up in court, the belief that Ms. Liu, as the water goddess the Sage Mother of Manifest Aid, controlled the water from the Jin Springs was widespread enough that it was used to convince the canal heads to give the people of Jinshengcun irrigation water.[39] Observers of the site during the early twentieth century stated that the steles inscribed with judgments involving water rites were kept in the Offering Hall in front of the Sage Mother Hall.[40] The court cases of the sixteenth century reveal how corruption among the canal heads disrupted society at a fundamental level, causing harvest difficulties and even starvation. Because *ad hoc* arrangements were made with the operators of the canals and sluice gates, local society was as dependent on the leadership of the irrigation network as it was on the gentry or officials in managing the individual interests of community members.

Building Projects of the Late Ming and Divinity Identity

By the sixteenth century, extant documentation allows us to see how closely that period's building projects at Jinci were tied to patrons expressing their right to access the Spirit of the Jin Springs and the water under her control. As discussed in Chapter 4, the rebuilding of the Shu Yu Shrine Complex by the local gentry in 1548 was an effort to remind the people of the importance of the Zhou-dynasty historical figure to the Chinese settlement of the region and the creation of the Jin state. As in the situation at the end of the Song, this effort had to be made because money and attention were being lavished on the water-giving Sage Mother while Shu Yu was being ignored:

> Annually in the 25th day of the third month there is a local executive who supervises the sacrifice [at the Shu Yu shrine], which was recorded in the sacrificial statutes. From the Zhiyuan period to the present it has been more than 200 years, the beams are broken, and it cannot provide shelter from the wind and rain. Consequently, the gods have lost their residence and the sacrifices are no longer sincere.
>
> 歲以三月二十五日有司致祭，載在祀典。自至元迄今二百餘年，棟梁摧折，不蔽風雨，神失所棲，祀事弗虔。
>
> Beside [the King of Jin Shrine] is the so-called Sage Mother Shrine. Every day the candles and incense are offered in large quantities. But Shu Yu of Tang's shrine is alone by the water; people do not even know that he is the proper divinity. . . .
>
> 其旁有所謂聖母祠者，香火日極崇奉，而唐叔虞之祠，顧寂寞水濱，不知爲正神。。。。。。
>
> The [water's] benefit [can be used] to nourish the people and the wind's [influence] to enlarge the transformation. How could it be that only the people of Jin obtain good fortune and benefit [from the gods]? Those who are in charge of the government also rely on it.[41]
>
> 利以滋養，風以宏化。豈惟晉人獲樂利之休，司政紀者亦將可憑籍矣。

Even in this commemoration of the 1548 project, Su You understands the Sage Mother to be the Spirit of the Jin Springs. Her worship is not considered to be heterodox. This local official's only concern is that the historical figure, Shu Yu, not be ignored or considered secondary. Only through his influence can the people be "transformed." This is the first time that any official writing about Jinci mentions that people can be transformed through the worship of historical exemplars.

Gao Ruxing, in his 1551 *Taiyuan County Gazetteer*, also presents his understanding of the Spirit of the Jin Springs and her origin, displaying an open belief in the orthodox worship of female water spirits. For him, it was a simple, acceptable reality that water and mothers are both *yin*, and her efficacy over the centuries as a water spirit is sufficient to explain the presence of a temple, even one as grand as the Sage Mother Hall, at the site of the Jin Springs:

I would say that there is heaven and earth and there are mountains and waterways. Water is a *yin* object and mothers are *yin* spirits. [Local] residents established a shrine because of the water. At first it was named Gentlewoman Shrine, later because of her response to prayers for rain, titles and temple regulations [ceremonies] were gradually added.[42]

愚謂有天地即有山水。水陰物母陰神。居人因水立祠。始名女郎祠，後禱雨有應漸加封號廟制。

In 1561, the rest of the complex was repaired in a combined effort of scholars, nobility, and locals. This project introduced another set of players onto the field of patronage at the site: the Jinwangfu and the Ninghuawangfu with their farming garrison troops. As discussed above, they, too, had a vested interest in publicly supporting the Sage Mother, and for this project they donated more than 100 taels of gold (*jin* 金) to the restoration of the Sage Mother Hall, a project that was also partially funded by people who were identified in the inscription as villagers (*xiangmin* 鄉民) and Confucian officials (*dutong ruguan* 督同儒官).[43] Additionally, the Ninghuawangfu contributed specifically for restoration of the bridge in front of the Sage Mother Hall.

Yet the identity of the Sage Mother as a transformed village girl, rather than a nature spirit within the purview of the local administrative officials, also provided common farmers with an inherent right to their portion of the water. This resulted in the building of a separate structure for the use of the Spirit of the Jin Springs. As was shown above, the story of Ms. Liu and her magical vat was of great importance to local people, particularly residents of the northernmost reaches of the canal network at Jinshengcun and Dongrucun. The common people began their own fund for the addition of a Dressing Tower (Shuxilou 梳洗樓—literally, comb and wash tower) for the Sage Mother.[44] This project was led by the villager Wang Wentai in 1563. The building is a two-story tower located directly west of the Everlasting Spring, open to the water and independent of any central axis (Fig. 2.9).

Fig. 7.2 Ms. Liu as Village Girl, bronze with gilding, Dressing Tower first floor, 1563 (Ding et al., *Jinci*, pl. 74). This view shows the goddess in simple garb dressing her hair. She sits on a lotus blossom emerging from a black vat or well bucket, which is consistent with Ming-dynasty popular legend about the origin of the Spirit of the Jin Springs. (Courtesy Wenwu chubanshe.)

Within the hall, the local people asserted their own story of the historical origins of the Sage Mother. On the lower floor stands a bronze statue of a young girl sitting on a lotus seat that is emerging from a large vat (Fig. 7.2).[45] On the upper floor is an image of the Spirit of the Jin Springs transcended into the heavenly bureaucracy; she is dressed in the imperial garments common to goddesses in the popular pantheon (Fig. 7.3).

By the time this restoration project was completed, there were nine temples or temple complexes: the Shu Yu Shrine Complex, the Sage Mother Shrine, the Jade Emperor's Temple (Yuhuangmiao), the Temple to the Three Pure Ones (Sanqingmiao), the Mt. Tai Temple (Taishanmiao 泰山廟), the Descendants' Temple (Miaoyimiao 苗裔廟), the Tai Tai Temple, the Medicine King's Temple (Yaowangmiao), and the True Lord's Temple (Zhenjunmiao). There was also a total of twelve pavilions: Qinghuatang, Huancuiting, Junfutang, Renzhixuan, Yongxueting, the Flowing Cup *Ting*-gazebo (Liubeiting 流盃停), Baomotang, the pavilions over the Perfect

way, though not all did.[57] Careful examination of Zhou's essay, however, indicates that he was not fully convinced of his hypothesis:

In the Song the court elevated the spirit called King of Arising Peace to King of the East of the Fen River because of a spiritual response to prayers for rain; this was certainly crude and inappropriate. However, the text of the *jiao* festival during the Xuanhe reign period there was one called the Sage Mother of Clear Efficacy and Manifest Aid.[58] The intention was that she was Shu Yu's mother.

至宋以禱雨靈應，封其神曰興安王，爲汾東王；固已陋而不典。乃宣和醮文又有所謂顯靈昭濟聖母者，意以爲唐叔虞之母。

According to the commentary in the *Spring and Autumn Annals*, "When [the wife of] King Wu, Yi Jiang, was pregnant with the great Shu, she dreamt of the Thearch who said to her: 'I name your son Yu and will give him [the fief] of Tang, which is under the constellation Shen, and he will have many descendents.'" When he was born, he had a pattern on his hand that was "Yu," thus his mother so named him. When King Cheng destroyed Tang he enfeoffed Shu Yu therein. The Sage Mother, then, is probably Yi Jiang. Tang Shu was the first lord enfeoffed to Jin (*shifeng zhi jun*), [thus] it is certainly appropriate to have temple sacrifices [to him] at this place. However, Yi Jiang was King Wu's queen, the mother of all under heaven. How could it be appropriate for her to have descended to be sacrificed with her son? Furthermore, giving her a title as if she were an earth goddess, rather than giving her the orthodox name as the ancestral queen (*bi*) of the Jin, approaches defilement.

春秋傳言武王邑姜方震太叔，夢帝謂己「余命而子曰虞，將與之唐屬諸參，而蕃育其子孫。」既生有文在其手曰虞，遂以命之，成王滅唐而封太叔焉。是則聖母蓋邑姜也。唐叔爲晉始封之君，廟食於斯固宜。邑姜則武王之后，天下之母，豈宜降從其子以祀？又不正名爲晉之先妣，而冠以他號，若媼神之云，比於黷矣。

However, the vulgar and rude merely followed after the good omen of the pattern [character] on the palm, and the Sage Mother became a deity appropriate to worship for those who want children. Consequently, the devotees came from far and near and built a temple facing the sun; the incense and candles gather [in great amounts] like clouds. By contrast, the shrine for sacrifices to Tang Shu was placed to its side. Because of the numerous decaying rafters and weeds, it is impossible to worship. The esteemed imperially bestowed Zhenguan-period stele stands loftily alone; thus the shrine has not gone to the point of being destroyed. Scholars investigating antiquity can still examine it. Alas! The fallacy and reversal of the sacrificial statutes are quite ancient. The positions of historian and master of ancestral sacrifices were abolished, and the teachings of religious Daoists and Buddhists became popular. Embellished temples are all over the empire, not twenty to thirty percent of which are in accord with the rites. Suppose people like Duke Di of Liang came around and expunged the incompliant temples? What would it be like then?

然流俗昌昧，徒以手文瑞，故相傳聖母爲宜子孫之神，遠近尊奉，作殿當陽，香火雲集。而唐虞之祠反退居其旁，朽椽數楹，草茀不可以拜，尚賴貞觀之碑，巋然獨存，故祠不遂泯滅。稽古之士，猶有考焉。嗟呼！祀典之譌翻久矣。太史祝宗之職廢，而方士浮圖之教盛行，琳宮貝闕遍天下，應禮者十不得二三。使有狄梁公其人者出焉，其所釐剔，當何如也？

> This sacrifice to Tang Shu in Jinci and the Taibo temple in Wu are just the same, and it is certainly appropriate that it should not fall into ruin generation after generation. Although the Sage Mother's temple does not comply with the classics on rites, if later people worship the one who gave birth to Shu Yu, this is better than the other [option of worshiping a deity who is] strange and groundless (unhistorical). Because people's attitudes have been thriving [in this perception] for a long time, it is difficult to suddenly abolish them. *If we could sacrifice to Shu Yu in the main hall and establish the Sage Mother in another [side] hall, that would be close to appropriate.* (Emphasis mine)[59]
>
> 惟是晉祠之祀唐叔與太伯之廟於吳正同，固宜世世無毀。其聖母廟雖不應禮經，特以唐叔故，追崇其所生，猶愈其他，怪迂無稽者。又以民心肸蠁之久，勢難驟廢。若奉唐叔於正祠，而以別殿居聖母，庶幾近之。

Although Zhou Lingshu was interested in finding a classical, historical explanation for the identity of the Sage Mother, he acknowledged that interpreting her as Yi Jiang was contrary to Zhou tradition. As discussed in Chapter 4, official ancestral temples should be located in the capital of the appropriate state or nation. Worship of Yi Jiang should therefore be located in the Western Zhou capital in Shanxi's Wei River Valley. But by the seventeenth century, mother figures were becoming increasingly common in pictorial iconography, at least for deified humans. Julia Murray has described how the miraculous birth of sages such as Confucius, as well as other apotheosized mortals, ultimately developed from Buddhism and its tradition of giving evidence for the divine status of the historical Buddha, Gautama Siddhartha, through his own miraculous birth from Queen Maya's side. Departing from the earlier tradition of rendering historical sages singly as adults in dignified official garb, by the end of the fifteenth century pictorial hagiographies of Confucius (as well as other popular divinities) employed the conventions of illustrating lives of divinities such as the Buddha in which miraculous conception and birth figured prominently.[60] As in the cult of women's chastity, which developed during the same period, in this purified conception of womanhood, the husband/male sexual partner is completely absent, leaving only the woman as mother to a glorious son.[61]

Zhou may also have been influenced by other examples of female spring spirits who were later identified as the mothers of male rain deities. As discussed in Chapters 2 and 5, female water spirits were plentiful in premodern China, though they rarely received much attention by compilers of local histories.[62] When they did, they were often "masculinized," rendered as kings or dukes, or having their powers transferred to their sons. In Zhou's interpretation of the Prayer in Thanks for Rain, he appears to have no knowledge of the gradual increase in titles given to the Gentlewoman and later Sage Mother during the eleventh century in reward for rain; rather, he indicates that Shu Yu was the rain spirit, even though he had no history of that power. Kenneth Pomeranz's work on late imperial spring/rain deities in north China suggests that though goddess cults did not fare well across imperial Chinese history, the situation for water goddesses became even worse during the Qing dynasty. In his study of the Handan Rain Shrine 563 kilometers (350 miles) south of Beijing, Pomeranz shows how a Dragon Mother became a Dragon King as women were progressively excluded from rain-spirit worship across the Qing dynasty and into the twentieth century.[63] By the time Zhou Lingshu arrived at Jinci, the stage had already been set for a reinterpretation of the local water goddess as a Confucian moral exemplar, a historical queen of the Zhou dynasty whose son was portended by the Thearch. His inscription clearly expresses his desire, and yet practical inability, to enact any change in the ritual landscape.

However, a much more active scholar in the vicinity, Yan Ruoqu, agreed with Zhou and became a strong advocate of his argument. Yan's ancestral home was Taiyuan, even though his family had lived in Shanyang 山陽 (modern Huai'an, Jiangsu province) for generations.[64] Because of restrictions on the number of exam graduates allowed from the Jiangnan area, members of the Yan family returned to Taiyuan to take the exams. Following this tradition, Yan traveled to Taiyuan for the provincial civil service exams in 1663.[65] There he met with his father's friend, the famous calligrapher Fu Shan. It was through Fu Shan that Yan met the Ming loyalist and early evidential scholar Gu Yanwu in 1672, the same year that Zhou Lingshu wrote his inscription.[66] Yan actively debated the authenticity of ancient documents and historical geography. Perhaps because of his contentious nature, he disagreed with Gu Yanwu about the original location of the Tang fief and the identity of the Sage Mother. Gu followed the line of thinking, later supported in the twentieth century by archaeology, that Tang was located in the southern portion of Shanxi in the vicinity of modern Quwo and Yicheng. In his discussion of Li Shimin's "Jinci ming bingxu," Gu considered it unfortunate that Shu Yu had been forgotten as the regional founder, but he had no question about the identity of the Sage Mother—she was a water spirit.[67]

Yan Ruoqu, on the other hand, was a staunch defender of Taiyuan as the location of the original Tang fief.[68] In his afterword to Zhou Lingshu's essay commemorating the restoration of the pavilion that contained Tang Taizong's stele, Yan stated that, after rereading Zhou's inscription, he went to the county gazetteer and examined the Prayer in Thanks for Rain. He was elated to find that Zhou Lingshu's assertion that the Sage Mother should be venerated as the mother of Shu Yu had a textual, historical precedent.[69] In a separate essay, *Sishu shidi xu* (An explanation of geography in the *Four Books*, continued), Yan devotes a section specifically to Yi Jiang, telling of her temple at the Jin Springs, only eighteen *li* from his ancestral home. He explains that the addition of the Sage Mother Hall on the right side of the Shu Yu Shrine Complex represented the son submitting to the domination of his mother.[70]

Yan's interest in historical geography and reinterpreting the identity of the Sage Mother may have been the result of his own place in the Neo-Confucian "conquest generation." Like Wu Taibo, Shu Yu was the first representative of Zhou culture to rule an otherwise barbarian land. If Tang was located further south, then Taiyuan may not have been part of the Confucian Zhou dynasty, and Yan Ruoqu's understanding of the Yan ancestral home would have been either inaccurate or forced to change to admit it as part of the northern steppe. Additionally, interpreting the Sage Mother as Yi Jiang may have involved more than just transforming an unattached water goddess into a proper Confucian mother and queen. The Yan surname is one of seven with an ancestry that can be traced directly back to Shu Yu of Tang.[71] By making the Sage Mother the mother of Shu Yu, Yan Ruoqu transformed her into the direct ancestress of his clan. This was not intended as a "superscription" of identities, but rather a rectification of the whole of Jinci to include all of the ancestors of Jin found in the *Zuozhuan*:

> I was pleased to obtain evidence [by finding the stele containing the Prayer in Thanks for Rain], and I told the local official that they should send this up to the court in order to rectify [the identity of the Sage Mother of Clear Efficacy and Manifest Aid], since this is a historical incident/fact of this place. Someone said, "Since it has been rectified, then we should establish a separate shrine to the Spirit of the Jin Springs." I replied, "This is correct, but how can we merely limit this to the Jin Springs? There is also a temple to Tai Tai that should be augmented with one to Shi Chen in order to sacrifice to the god of the [constellation] Shen.[72] Otherwise [this place] will only have a knowledge of topography but no knowledge of cosmology." Someone ridiculed me as a busybody only wanting to show off my knowledge of constellations.[73]
>
> 喜得一典證，屬有司當上聞於朝以釐正之，此鄉邦故蹟。或曰「既釐正矣，則當別建晉源神祠。」余曰「然，豈惟晉源？此間有臺駘廟當補入實沈以祀參神。不然，是只有地理而無天文。」或笑余爲多事強知星宿。

Yan's interpretation was not immediately adopted,[74] and evidence exists to show that the commoners never understood the Sage Mother in this way.[75] The elite of the eighteenth century found it useful to follow Yan's interpretation, however, since it would not only Confucianize the water spirit but also would tie Shu Yu more closely to local patronage.

From 1768 to 1771, the shrine to Shu Yu of Tang was enlarged to its present size, a project that was meant to give Shu Yu an architectural setting appropriate to his importance in history, and by extension, at Jinci. Textual, pictorial, and architectural evidence from this period reveals the extent to which this was accomplished. In his inscription of 1772 documenting the rebuilding of Shu Yu's shrine, Zhu Gui 朱珪 (d. 1806) specifically mentions that, although some say the Sage Mother is a water spirit, Yan Ruoqu has shown that she is really the historical mother of Shu Yu, Yi Jiang. For the elite writing about the site, this interpretation made complete sense and showed the link between Taiyuan and the Zhou heartland.[76] An inscription written by Hu Qijing 胡其敬 to commemorate the rebuilding of the Jade Emperor's shrine complex of 1795 stated that the earlier rebuilding of the Shu Yu complex was an effort to present Shu Yu as the primary deity of the Jin Springs (以唐叔爲晉源主神).[77]

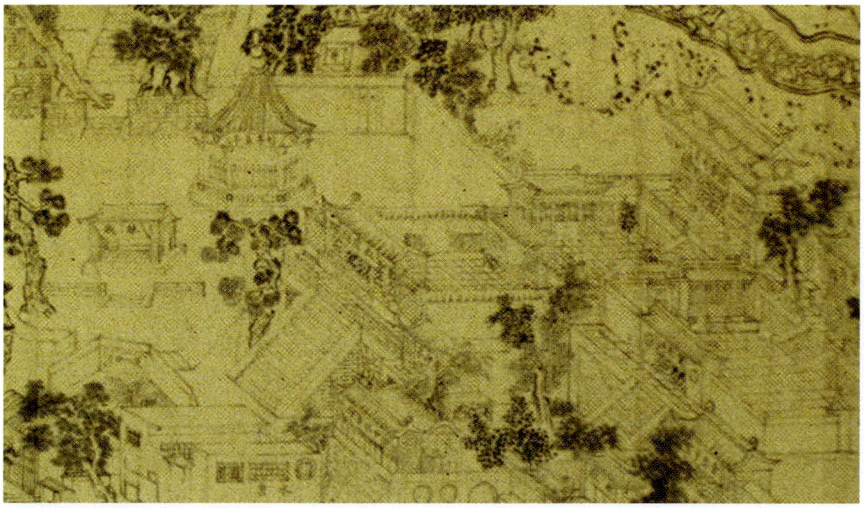

Fig. 7.7 Painting of Jinci, ink and color on paper, late eighteenth century, detail of Shu Yu of Tang Shrine. The painting of the Shu Yu complex shows how effective the front façade veranda was at presenting the main worship hall as a double-eaves building—the painted version of the building has the second set of eaves extending around to the side façades as well. (Courtesy Peng Hai and the Jinci Museum.)

Zhu Gui's inscription also describes the new complex. The foundation was expanded and a new front gatehouse added at the top of a high stair. A new, enlarged main hall was added behind the foundation of the earlier main hall, which itself had fallen into disrepair. A three-bay offering hall was then constructed on the old main hall foundation. Side halls were added to the back courtyard and the whole enclosed with surrounding galleries. Zhu Gui's description emphasizes the commanding presence the new complex had over the northern side of the site, with its dramatic height, its orientation to the cardinal directions, and its location with its back nestled into the hillside.[78] This image is what we see in the eighteenth-century painting of the site (Fig. 7.7). The complex is a formal, two-courtyard compound with steep stairs leading to a gatehouse high above the Octagonal Pool and the rest of the site. A diminutive offering hall leads to the back courtyard framed on the west and east with side halls. At the north end of the compound we find a dramatic main hall, further elevated on its own high platform and crowned with a double-eaves, hip-and-gable roof. Given the intention of the patrons (as described by Hu Qijing), the building style must have been selected in direct reference to the Sage Mother Hall.[79]

Contrary to what we see in the painting, however, the smaller Shu Yu of Tang Shrine fails to achieve the countenance of the Sage Mother Hall. The steps to the gatehouse are indeed steep, and lead to a regular front courtyard framed by galleries on left and right, and a small offering hall at the back. After walking through the offering hall east and west side halls frame a formal back courtyard, but the main worship hall on the north end of the courtyard is not as elevated as it appears in the painting, and the eaves are somewhat compacted (Fig. 7.8). The uncomfortable quality of the lower set

Fig. 7.8 Shu Yu of Tang Shrine Complex, Main Hall, front façade, 1770–71. The main worship hall of the Shu Yu Shrine appears to have two sets of eaves from the front façade.

of eaves was likely the result of economizing on the construction of the largest building in the complex—they only occur on the front façade of the main hall. The building has one set of eaves on the back and side façades, but this is visible only outside the courtyard enclosure and would go unseen during normal worship (Fig. 7.9). Evidently, constructing a standard courtyard complex, with an overall two-courtyard structure elevated above the larger Jinci compound was thought to more effectively communicate Shu Yu's status than a single hall that fully duplicated, or was built larger, than the Sage Mother Hall.

Yan also wrote that he wanted his new interpretation of the Sage Mother's identity to be used in future county gazetteers, and this eventually came to pass.[80] In his 1826 *Taiyuan County Gazetteer*, Yuan Peilan stated that the Spirit of the Jin Springs was, in fact, the spirit of the mother of Shu Yu, Yi Jiang.[81] This was also the interpretation adopted by Liu Dapeng in his *Jinci Gazetteer*, published posthumously in 1986.

The site continued to develop after the 1768–71 rebuilding of the Shu Yu Shrine, but additional structures were still subordinated to the flow of the spring water through the complex. Additional buildings included two major temple complexes dedicated to the nationally venerated deities

Fig. 7.9 Shu Yu of Tang Shrine Complex, Main Hall, side façade, 1770–71. The side façade shows that the double eaves occur only on the front façade of the building.

Fig. 7.10 Wenchang Temple Palace, Entry Gatehouse, front façade, 1773. This view shows the bridge crossing the Earl of Zhi canal running directly in front of the complex.

Wenchang (Fig. 7.10), Guandi, the Three Pure Ones, and the Jade Emperor (Fig. 7.11). These complexes were similar to that of Shu Yu's in their standard courtyard style and enclosing walls.[82] They also shared the general north-south orientation of the Shu Yu Shrine Complex. Yet, none of the three complexes is oriented exactly north-south, and their central axes are not parallel to each other. Their only common feature is a (visually)

Fig. 7.11 Haotianshen Shrine Complex, Entry Gatehouse, front façade, 1795. This combined shrine contains worship halls dedicated to Guandi, the Three Pure Ones, and the Jade Emperor.

perpendicular relationship to the body of water located in front of them. Regardless of the attempts to reinterpret the Sage Mother's identity, the development of the complex in late imperial times was a reflection of the significance of the production of water to the internal hierarchy of the complex and the larger community surrounding it (Fig. 7.12).

Spirits of Jin Transformed?

Conceptions of the water spirit and Shu Yu were made manifest in the distribution of buildings within the temple complex at the Jin Springs. The building projects of the sixteenth century display how temple architecture reflected ideas of divine identity and status, and how patronage allowed competing groups to lay claim to the irrigation water by asserting an identity for the spring spirit that was in line with their individual interests. Three elements came into play during the development and reinterpretation of the site in the sixteenth and seventeenth centuries—social hierarchy, efficacy, and cultural identity.

The cult of the Spirit of the Jin Springs was central to the regular distribution of irrigation water in the immediate vicinity of the shrine complex. In this context, the physical site of the complex became a map of competing

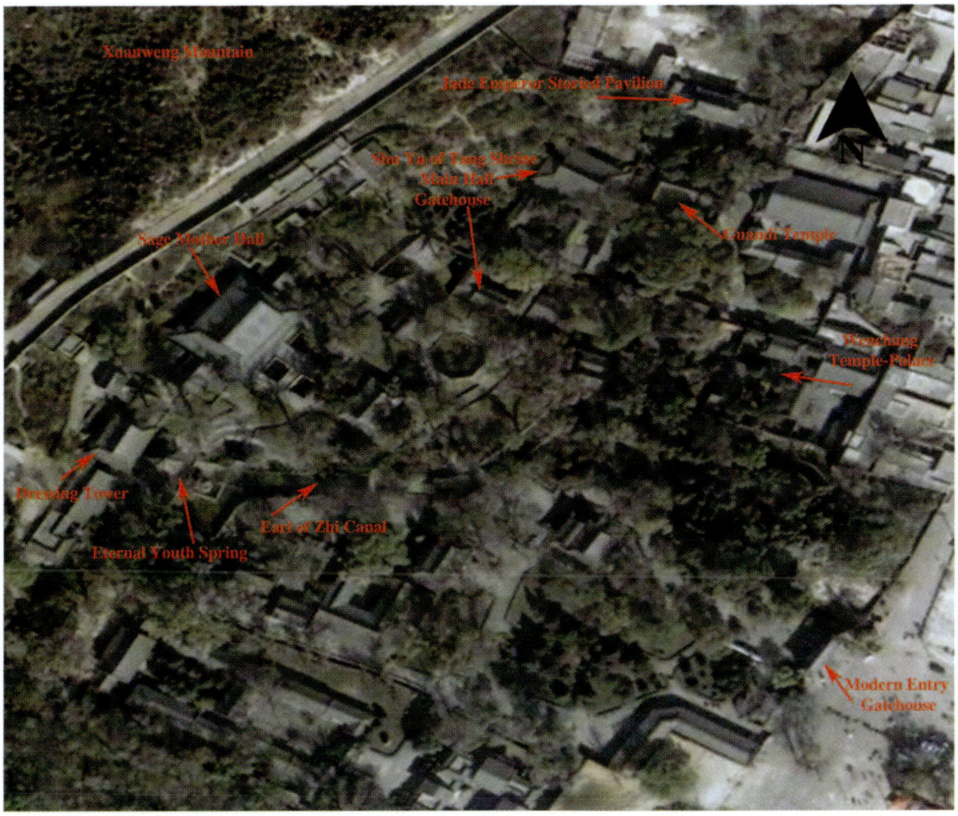

Fig. 7.12 Satellite photograph of the Jinci Shrine Complex taken on November 3, 2003. Here the orientation of the buildings primarily to the bodies of water on the site is clearly visible. (Courtesy Digital Globe.)

interest groups.[83] Canal heads and the local nobility asserted their control over the water goddess by supporting her as supreme goddess of the springs with a main worship hall to match. Private farmers and other members of the surrounding communities cast an image in bronze of the water goddess as a local village girl, preventing this interpretation from being erased by members of the elite who were becoming less sympathetic to their needs. Neo-Confucian literati of the sixteenth century may not have been able to change the beliefs or ritual practice of the locals, but they were able to enhance the shrine in a manner that might eventually convince some of the patrons that the water spirit was the mother of Jin in a historical, and not just metaphorical, way. It seems, however, that the people they were most effective in convincing were the later literati.

The enacting of social roles that took place within the complex of Jinci on a regular, cyclical basis broke down during periods of drought when the efficacy of the deity took precedence.[84] At this point, nothing mattered but obtaining rain, and even those who may have hoped to communicate a different message about the hierarchy of deities at the shrine had to acknowledge that the Sage Mother was the most effective for rain production. The parallel worlds of the celestial and terrestrial bureaucracies were aligned, and officials were held to their duties as human representatives to the other world.

Finally, we see that in the sixteenth and seventeenth centuries, Chinese cultural identity was asserted through increased Confucian ritualism and a desire to reclaim rights to the heritage of the Zhou dynasty. The Neo-Confucian reading of the classics emphasized lineage and encouraged an interpretation of women as moral exemplars within the lineage. As the chaste widow/mother became increasingly important, memorial gateways were established to acknowledge publicly women who were known to have fulfilled this role. In the wake of the Manchu conquest, historical figures from the Zhou dynasty became important icons of civilization in a China ruled again by a foreign power. This environment allowed for the creation and propagation of a new identity for a very old water goddess, at least in textual sources. But the social fabric of traditional China was harder to transform, and the orientation of the buildings and complexes of Jinci reiterate that topography and the power of the water flowing through the landscape define the territory of Jin.

Chapter Eight

Conclusion: The Temple and Shrine as an Expression of Divine Presence

Through a close reading of the existing physical and textual evidence regarding the development of the Jinci site from the sixth through the eighteenth centuries, I have detailed in the preceding chapters the complex and changing relationship between the water goddess of the Jin Springs and the founder of the Jin state, the two primary divinities of Jin for the people of Jinyang. In this study, I have made use of multiple methodological perspectives for what each can tell us about the motivations of the patrons who contributed to the construction of this remarkable place. By asking questions about the archaeology, anthropology, art and architectural history, and political, social, and religious history of the site, we can understand at least a portion of what different individuals saw when they went to pray at Jinci.

Modern archaeology has shown that, in all likelihood, neither Shu Yu of Tang nor any member of the Zhou royal clan ever occupied the lands of the Taiyuan basin. Although archaeology is a relatively young discipline in China, excavations in the Central Plains and Yellow River Valley have allowed us to connect many of China's historical city and place-names with actual locations. New data from excavations made in the second half of the twentieth century support the hypothesis that the fief of Tang given to Shu Yu by his older brother was located in the Quwo/Yicheng area rather than in the Taiyuan basin.

If this is the case, then the name of the Jin state would have become associated with the Jin River at a much later date. Thus, locating a shrine to the state founder at this site, rather than the ritually orthodox placement of a Zhou-dynasty feudal ancestral temple within the capital city walls, asserts a topographical claim to Zhou-dynasty legitimacy by emphasizing the Jin River as the eponym of the Jin state. By the sixth century, the connection was accepted, at least by the elite residents of north China, and was important enough to aspiring emperors of the periods of disunion to have provided a continued patronage base through the Northern Song dynasty. Although we do not know where the main worship hall to Shu Yu was placed prior to the thirteenth century, at that time his shrine complex was located on the north side of the springs and canals, situating Shu Yu perpetually in "Jinyang," whether or not his temple ever actually existed within the city walls.

Current limitations on resources for excavation, as well as the interests of historic preservation, prevent fuller archaeological exploration of living sites such as Jinci. Without this data, we must rely exclusively on textual sources to reconstruct the pre-Song dynasty site. The majority of the authors of early imperial texts focused on Jinci's connection to the historical Shu Yu of Tang and his significance to the political control of the region. Not surprisingly, Shu Yu was particularly important to rulers such as Gao Huan, Li Shimin, and Shi Jingtang, whose military power was located in the Shanxi area and/or who then named their empires Tang or Jin. After Zhao Kuangyi conquered Taiyuan in 979 and moved the capital of Taiyuan from Jinyang to Yangqu, Shu Yu's cult was eventually eclipsed by that of the water goddess. However, the historicity of Shu Yu again became important to legitimizing worship at the site after the fall of the Ming dynasty.

Other textual sources provide some clues to another version of early Chinese local society. The *Shanhaijing*, a pre-imperial textual source of a much less official genre than the dynastic histories, provides an alternative perspective on the area of the Xuanweng Mountains. Rather than being only a possible portion of the Tang fief, in this text the Xuanweng range and the Jin River emitting from its base were the location of numerous spirits to whom there should be sacrifices. Documentation of multiple expansions of the canal system beginning from the Han dynasty reveals that the Jin River was central to local agriculture and the livelihoods of Taiyuan area residents. The importance of the springs figures prominently in the first extended text designed for local consumption—the Jinciming inscription, written by Tang Taizong, Li Shimin.

Beginning in the Song dynasty, the evidence of the site reveals the centrality of the spring to the spiritual experience of the place. The limited archaeology that has been done, especially underneath the foundation of the Sage Mother Hall, has proven that the site, and the very location of the Sage Mother Hall behind the central of the three springs for the Jin River, had been built and rebuilt over the centuries. Documentation of a foundation below the Dressing Tower behind Eternal Youth Spring suggests that even the early building complex was constructed around the springs. But that is the limit of our knowledge; the orientation of the buildings and full extent of the Song-dynasty complex are hidden underneath the later constructions.

The earliest building at Jinci for which we have both physical and substantiating textual evidence is the Northern Song–dynasty Sage Mother

Hall. Although we still do not know the exact date of construction for the present Sage Mother Hall, it is stylistically consistent with other halls in southern Shanxi from the late eleventh through early twelfth centuries. The most reliable method of dating a timber structure is a combination of style and internal inscriptions on the beams of the building. At the Sage Mother Hall, the interior inscriptions provide a date of 1087 for the addition of the phoenix chair and column dragons, a date of 1102 documenting the imperially sanctioned restoration after an earthquake in January of that year, and a date of 1120 on the side of an earlier doorway in the back facade.[1] The earliest textual source we have documenting the full rebuilding of a "Gentlewoman Shrine" west of the spring places the reconstruction after the Tiansheng reign period and before the Xining reign period, when the deity was promoted to Sage Mother of Manifest Aid. A severe earthquake took place in January 1038, shortly after the end of the Tiansheng period in 1032, providing a probable *terminus post quem* of 1038 for the building. Documentation of six of the eight dragons presently wrapping around the front columns of the Sage Mother Hall provides a *terminus ante quem* of 1087. Although numismatic evidence found during restoration of the building in 1993–96 opened the possibility that the building itself was from the 979–84 rebuilding of the Jinci site, the style of the hall combined with epigraphical evidence indicates that the building dates from the mid- to late-eleventh century.

This building and the present configuration of the sculpture of female divinities within it portray the Sage Mother as a supreme goddess reigning over a celestial court. The building is fully in the official imperial style to the extent that it has a timber frame, double-eaves hip-and-gable roof, and dramatic five-*puzuo* eaves bracketing with intercolumnar bracket sets on the front eaves. Beyond the wide veranda, appropriate to shelter a large number of offerings, the Sage Mother sits cross-legged on a phoenix chair, her importance emphasized by the wooden screen used to set her off from the expansive internal space of the hall. We do not know the configuration of the Song interior or the original placement of the forty Song-dynasty statues of palace women, female officials, and eunuchs that fill the hall. However, traces of figural wall paintings indicate that the building would have originally been fully painted on the interior. Inscriptions on the side of a doorframe in the back bay show that the back bay held a central door through the thirteenth century to allow devotees to exit and walk back around the surrounding veranda to reach the rest of the site.

The iconography of the sculptural and painting program is largely consistent with a fully formed imperial metaphor for deities of the Chinese popular pantheon, yet the statue of the Sage Mother is incongruous with Song-period imperial iconography and borrows instead from a tradition of images designed to compete with Buddhism for spiritual legitimacy and patronage. Her cross-legged posture matches no extant Song-period ancestral portrait, nor does it follow the paradigm for representations of popular and Daoist female divinities, such as the Earth Queen and Spirit Mother of the West, from the Song-Yuan periods. However, Daoists in Shanxi from as early as the Tang dynasty did make use of this Buddhist meditative posture in their own sculpture, some of which is extant in the Yuan-dynasty Daoist grottos of Longshan, within walking distance from Jinci. The six low-relief dragons carved on the front of the phoenix chair supporting the Sage Mother paralleled the rest of the 1087 enhancement project, which also supported the addition of six dragons to the front columns of the hall. As with the presence of dragons in the Water God's Temple at Guangsheng Monastery, as well as other dragon-spirit temples located near springs across north China, these sculpted dragons, sponsored ten years after the Sage Mother's imperial promotion for relieving the people of the area from drought, may have helped to make the hall a magically charged talisman for invoking rain.[2] Other eleventh-century remains perhaps used in rain ceremonies include the rectilinear pool in front of the hall (perhaps for ceremonial frogs) and a small platform that could have held ritual dances.

The later history of Jinci can also be viewed through different methodological lenses, through which we can see the religious experience being mediated by and manipulated due to the economic importance of the water from the Jin Springs. The people who encountered the springs at the site of Jinci reacted to the spiritual presence of deity there; we see this in the poetry and stele inscriptions throughout history. Although one expects inscriptions and prayers documenting miracles to discuss the power of the divinities being venerated, even statesmen took note of the spiritual quality of the place, as did Fan Zhongyan in his poem, written outside the official ritual context:

How spiritual is the Shu Yu Temple!
How marvelous the land [from which] emerges the auspicious springs.[3]
神哉叔虞廟！地勝出嘉泉。

The visceral response to the beauty of nature was interpreted as proof of divine presence. It also formed the foundation for cantos describing the female nature spirits known to dwell near rivers and springs, a tradition beginning as early as the third century BCE. Travelers to Jinci wrote of the water and the water spirit even before they discussed the details of a temple built for rites to communicate with her. However, these deities were frequently left out—or purposely written out—of standard historical sources, as has been noted by scholars such as Rolf Stein, Suzanne Cahill, Edward Schafer, and (following Schafer) David Johnson, who have examined early goddess worship in China and Southeast Asia. Prior to her official elevation to Sage Mother of Manifest Aid in 1077, the water goddess of Jinci was acknowledged in writings about the spiritual power of Jinci, but because she had neither been entered into the sacrificial statutes nor had been a historical figure for whom a larger context could be given, she seems to have been simply taken for granted as part of the fabric of the Jin Springs ritual site.

Her entry into the official record, most likely facilitated by the widespread institutional changes brought on through the New Policies of Wang Anshi, made her impossible to ignore, since her worship became part of the responsibilities of the local magistrate.

Although the development of the site after the wars of the thirteenth century reveals the importance of the water through the buildings' orientation toward the springs and canals, textual sources document another side to the centrality of the springs. By the middle of the Ming dynasty—if not before—Jinci was also an important site of patronage for groups vying for their rights over the irrigation water emerging from the springs. Over the twenty-eight years following the restoration of the Shu Yu Shrine Complex by Taiyuan's local literati in 1548, a battle of building patronage was fought in the temple precinct around the Jin Springs. The patrons varied from independent farmers to nobility and noble estates, to the literati. All of these groups agreed on one thing: the Sage Mother was the most powerful divinity on the site. But during this time, the conflict over the interpretation of her identity became an overt part of the Jinci complex. Both Duara and Watson have shown how a single divinity can be given multiple identities or powers according to the interests of its patrons.[4] The various powers or legends that came to be associated with divinities such as Tianhou (Mazu) or Guandi reflected the needs of an individual or a group of devotees. Duara notes that the varying identities follow a semantic link—that is, each individual aspect does not stray too far from any other.[5] The evidence from the Jinci site reveals how the temple complex could be physically changed to assign a particular divinity a different identity, one that was representative of the interests of the patron. The reinterpretation of the Sage Mother from the goddess of the spring to the mother of Shu Yu, and by extension the Jin state, was further played out through the manipulation of the architecture of the temple complex. While retaining the deity's female identity (Duara's semantic link), the building projects were used to assert different interpretations of her origin. The nobility and noble estates supported her as a nature spirit, the officially recognized Spirit of the Jin Springs, first by patronizing the restoration of the Sage Mother Hall and the bridge in front of it. The local farmers preferred to support the legend of the Sage Mother as local peasant and did so by sponsoring the construction of a Dressing Tower containing an image of the Sage Mother as a village girl from along the Jinci Northern Canal. Finally, the local officials and literati supported Yan Ruoqu's belief that the Sage Mother was the deified mother of Shu Yu found in the *Zuozhuan* by adding the Duiyue Memorial Gateway along the axis of the Sage Mother Hall. In 1606, the strong central axis marked by the Duiyue Gateway was emphasized and symbolically reoriented to the south by the addition of bell and drum towers, which would usually have been placed to the east and west, respectively. These additions gave the undeniably dominant Sage Mother Hall an appearance of legitimacy that, for Qing and modern literati, would have been appropriate only for an ancestral figure such as Shu Yu, or his mother. Yet, this was the perspective of an increasingly conservative, educated elite, who needed textual sources—preferably canonical histories or stele inscriptions—to legitimize their deities. The competition between Shu Yu and the Sage Mother continued into the seventeenth and eighteenth centuries as patrons of Shu Yu sought to interpret the Sage Mother as the historical Yi Jiang, and even rebuilt his shrine so that it could compete with hers in scale and grandeur.

Literati interest in promoting the worship of historical human spirits over nature spirits can be traced to the early centuries of the imperial period with firm documentation from the Song dynasty.[6] However, the shift in focus from the late Ming through the early Qing to Confucian ritualism, described by Kai-Wing Chow, gave new importance to the veneration of historical figures.[7] Shang Wei's research on Confucian ritual in the *Rulin Waishi* shows that Zhou-dynasty regional founders such as Wu Taibo were thought to be bearers of Yellow River Valley civilization to barbarian areas. Like Wu Taibo, Shu Yu of Tang was also a deity with a historical pedigree deserving of veneration, as Zhou Lingshu noted in his 1672 stele inscription.[8] As I have shown, textual analyses of Jinci led to the conclusion that the shrine had a pedigree extending back to the Northern Wei. Because Shu Yu of Tang and his mother Yi Jiang are mentioned by name in canonical sources such as the *Shangshu*, the *Zuozhuan*, and the *Lüshi chunqiu*, as well as in Zhu Xi's commentaries on *The Four Books*,[9] early Qing scholars influenced by "evidential scholarship" (such as that of Zhou Lingshu and Yan Ruoqu) could conclude that the most efficacious deity at the site, the Sage Mother, was the historical Yi Jiang. Even though Zhou Lingshu himself doubted the orthodoxy of worshiping a Zhou-dynasty queen at Jinci, for Yan Ruoqu, whose family could trace its surname back to its original ancestor, Shu Yu of Tang, the oblique reference in Jiang Zhongqian's "Text Giving Thanks for Rain" provided sufficient textual basis to prove that the water spirit was actually the historical mother of Shu Yu and thus his family's ancestral mother.

This interpretation had no classical precedent, but it was well within the increased veneration of the divine mother in late imperial China. The late seventeenth century was a time when an emphasis on the mothers (as well as on any magical aspect of conception and birth) of deified historical figures such as Hou Ji or Confucius had become an important part of proving the deity's divine status. This period also saw the rise of the cult of the chaste widow, who, according to Susan Mann, was frequently memorialized through the efforts of a devoted son.[10] And although the "masculinization" of female deities had begun in the early centuries of the imperial period, Kenneth Pomeranz's research on other goddess cults in north China suggests that people in the early Qing made an even more pronounced effort to transform any female deity that fell outside traditional familial roles into one who fulfilled the most important of those roles—the success of her son.[11] Yet the evidence of the Jinci site indicates that this interpretation was only representative of the agenda of a small group of the elite whose abilities to enact change in ritual sites did not extend far beyond the histories they were writing.

Over the past fifteen years, historians examining local temple culture have identified limitations to anthropological approaches to religion and society (such as that of James Watson) that tend to exclude belief from their theoretical formulations. Incorporating a perspective seen more frequently in the writings of historians of religion influenced by Mircea Eliade, historical studies in the 1990s of local cults have taken into consideration not only the interaction of patrons vying for power in the very public sphere of the local temple, but also the response of patrons to the perception of spiritual presence—the awe of the divine forces on which the livelihood of the surrounding community was thought to depend. As Kenneth Pomeranz has pointed out, the desperation of patrons requesting miracle rain creates a different kind of social interaction than the interest of other patrons in establishing their position in the local social hierarchy through the performance of regular ritual activities, where "orthopraxy" could be of pre-eminent importance.[12] The perceived efficacy of the Sage Mother in delivering rain played a fundamental role in sustaining her patronage base. Shu Yu of Tang's patronage was, on the other hand, first based in the support of a ruler's sovereignty over the Taiyuan basin, and later as a link between this region and the Zhou-dynasty heartland. Across the late imperial period, although different patrons held different ideas about who *should* be the primary deity of Jinci, all writings regarding the site express *belief* in the power of the divinities worshiped there, particularly of the Sage Mother. If we understand the creation of religious art to be, as Walter Otto has suggested, a part of this belief, then everything constructed at a temple site—every poem, work of sculpture, and building—can be seen as the physical manifestation of the reaction to the spiritual encounter.[13] Given the genuine faith of the whole variety of patrons at Jinci, the construction and manipulation of the site becomes more than just bartering with the gods; it is evidence of their presence.[14] We see this perspective in the text of the inscription documenting the rebuilding in 1548:

> From the Zhiyuan period to the present it has been more than 200 years; the beams are broken, and [the Shu Yu Shrine] cannot provide shelter from the wind and rain. Consequently, the god has lost his residence, and the sacrifices are no longer sincere.[15]
>
> 自至元迄今二百餘年，棟梁摧折，不蔽風雨，神失所棲，祀事弗虔。

Su You indicates with this inscription that the presence of the divine and the sincerity of the devotee were lost when the building in which the ritual took place was not maintained. Facing the loss of his residence and, as a consequence, the impossibility of patrons' performing a sincere ritual for invoking the spirit, Shu Yu would no longer descend and would be unable to help "transform" the local people. When the late-imperial Neo-Confucians entered the site, they saw that the most important deity was the Sage Mother of Manifest Aid (the name plaque was prominently displayed on the hall), a title that, by this time, was not acceptable for a historical figure.[16] Although enclosed in a southern-oriented courtyard compound expressive of the high status and elite patronage of the deity worshiped within it, the main worship hall of Shu Yu was dilapidated and smaller than the Sage Mother's; therefore, his spirit was clearly less powerful than the female deity's, and perhaps no longer present at all.[17] The late-Ming Neo-Confucians, who believed in the power of these exemplars to transform the local people, were motivated to rebuild Shu Yu's temple and so inspire his presence. This effort was continued in the eighteenth century when Shu Yu of Tang's shrine was elevated and enlarged to contain a main worship hall with double eaves in an attempt to express that Shu Yu was architecturally, as well as historically, the main deity of Jinci.

But even today, the Sage Mother Hall, built on top of the central of the three Jin Springs, still commands the entirety of the Jinci site. Her identity as a spring spirit is expressed architecturally by her location and by the location of her Dressing Tower atop the springs. Furthermore, as subsequent temple complexes were added to Jinci, their physical orientation was not defined by the cardinal directions; rather, their orientation was subordinated to the emerging Jin River. Despite attempts to create an ancestor and historical mother of the Spirit of the Jin Springs, the literati were unable to alter the shrine fully to conform to the southern-oriented courtyard complex that would have allowed the deity to be understood in this way. The local patronage of a powerful irrigation community, which had sustained the spring-spirit shrine since its reconstruction in the mid-eleventh century, added buildings in accordance with the pathway of the spring water, and thereby asserted the identity of the Sage Mother as the life-giving force for the community and Spirit of the Jin Springs.

Appendixes

Appendix A
Dates of Extant Structures in the Jinci Complex

The numeration follows that used in Fig. 1.2, p. 4.

1 Sage Mother Hall 聖母殿
Mid-eleventh century

I have dated this hall by style and building inscriptions to 1038–87. A major repair is also documented in 1342.[1] See Chapter 6 for more detail.

2 Shu Yu of Tang Shrine Complex 唐叔虞祠
1770–71

Expansion of the complex was initiated in 1768 by a plan to build an offering hall on the foundation of the old main hall and a new main hall behind it. The mountainside rises more than a *zhang* 丈 (approximately ten feet) behind the main hall. Small doors to the right and left of the main hall link it to the east with the Haotianshenci 昊天神祠 and to the west with the Jingyiyuan 靜怡園.[2] According to the inscription for the repair, actual construction was begun in August/September of 1770 and completed in October/November of 1771.[3]

3 Dressing Tower 梳妝樓/梳洗樓
(present Water Mother Tower 水母樓)
1563

First built in the 42nd year of the Ming Jiajing reign period (1563); repaired in the 24th year of the Qing Daoguang reign period (1844). The building is two stories with three arcuated chambers or caverns (洞) in the first story and a three-bay second story. The central cavern contains a gilt bronze image of the water goddess as a village girl. Stairways are located in the second two caverns. The upper story is an open worship hall with narrative wall paintings on the north and south walls, and the water goddess in more regal garb consistent with representations of high-ranking goddesses elsewhere. She is housed within a wooden statuary niche located along the west wall.

As discussed in Chapter 7, this building was originally a Dressing Tower for the Sage Mother, who was officially the Spirit of the Jin Springs. The building was still understood as a Dressing Tower as late as 1826.[4] In 1874, Provincial Governor Bao memorialized the throne to add a title to the "Water Mother" 水母 in the hall to the right of the Sage Mother Hall, which would be the tower. At that time, two plaques were bestowed by the emperor, one with the characters 惠普桐封 to be placed on the Sage Mother Hall, the other with the characters 功資樂利 in the hall to its right, that is, the Dressing Tower. It is thus possible that the building came to be called the Water Mother Tower at about that time. In 1878, Provincial Governor Zeng requested that the Water Mother be given her own title; consequently, two characters were added, making her "Water Mother Who Expounds and Transforms" 敷化水母.[5]

4 Perfect Benefit Spring *Ting*-gazebo 善利泉亭
16th century

The gazebos over both Perfect Benefit and Eternal Youth Springs were first built with imperial funds donated by the Northern Qi emperor Gao Yang during the Tianbao reign period (550–60 CE) when he visited the site. The Perfect Benefit Spring gazebo was destroyed at the beginning of the Ming Zhengde period (1506–22) and rebuilt in the Jiajing period (1522–67).[6]

The name Shanli comes from the *Daodejing*, chapter 8: "The highest good (*shangshan* 上善) is like water; water is good at benefiting (*shanli* 善利) the ten thousand things, and yet it does not compete with them."[7] It is uncertain when the spring was given this name. The first reference I have found is from Yi Gou's stele inscription of 1267.[8]

5 Eternal Youth Spring *Ting-gazebo* 難老泉亭
16th century

First built during the Northern Qi Tianbao period, Eternal Youth Spring Gazebo was rebuilt in the Ming Jiajing reign period.[9]

The name Eternal Youth comes from a phrase in "Panshui," found in the *Shijing*: "He will forever enjoy eternal youth" 永錫難老.[10]

6 Flying Bridge 飛梁 or Spirit Bridge 神橋
11th century?

Unknown when the name was first attributed to this bridge; the name comes from the *Shuijingzhu* description of the site. According to Lin Huiyin and Liang Sicheng, the present structure is consistent with the construction techniques of the Song dynasty, and should date to the same period as the Sage Mother Hall and Offering Hall.[11] Liu Yongde states that restoration of the bridge and pool underneath it in 1953 revealed the cavity for the spring directly underneath the Sage Mother Hall. The structure was such to warrant the conclusion that they were built at the same time.[12] See Chapter 6 for a more detailed discussion.

7 Octagonal Pool 八角池
terminus ante quem 1551

This pool has three names: Octagonal Pool, Pool for Liberating Captive Animals 放生池, and Lotus Pool 蓮花池. Located in front of the Shu Yu shrine, it is filled by water from the Perfect Benefit Spring and water from the pool in front of the Sage Mother Hall (Yu zhao shui 魚沼水).[13] No date of earliest construction given. The Octagonal Pool is not mentioned in Yi Gou's description of the site from 1267, nor in the description found in Wang Sicheng's record of the 1342 repair. It does appear in the 1551 *Jinci zhitu*, published in Gao Ruxing, *Taiyuan xianzhi*.

8 Earl of Zhi Canal 智伯渠
Han dynasty, with later modifications

Also called Haiqing beihe 海清北河, the Earl of Zhi Canal winds from the Eternal Youth Spring eastward, then turns northward to flow underneath the Meeting Transcendents Bridge, turning eastward again where it would have originally been further filled with the water from both the spring underneath the Sage Mother Hall and Perfect Benefit Spring, to then travel underneath the bridges leading to the Mt. Tai and Wenchang ritual complexes. Finally, after passing the Wenchang Temple Palace, it turns southward and again eastward flowing out of the complex and into the irrigation canals in the northern portion of the community around Jinci Town. Portions of this canal may date to the Han dynasty expansion of the irrigation network stemming from the Jin Springs in 116 CE, which may, ultimately, have its origin in the canals used by the Earl of Zhi to flood Jinyang in the mid-5th century BCE. See Chapters 3 and 5 for more detail.

9 Haotianshen Shrine Complex 昊天神祠
1795

This temple complex is dedicated to the Jade Emperor, the Three Pure Ones, and Guandi. The whole is called the Haotianshen Shrine, after the title given to the Jade Emperor during the Northern Song dynasty.[14] This combined shrine was constructed after the 1770–71 rebuilding of the Shu Yu of Tang Shrine. According to the stele inscription documenting the construction of the combined complex by Hu Qijing of 1801, originally individual temple buildings dedicated to the Jade Emperor and the Three Pure Ones were on the right (west side) of the shrine to Shu Yu, and a temple to Guandi was located to the left (east) of the Shu Yu Shrine. These buildings appear on the 1551 map of Jinci in Gao Ruxing's *Taiyuan xianzhi*, and I have numbered them 42 (Jade Emperor's Temple 玉皇廟) and 43 (Temple to the Three Pure Ones 三清廟) on my plan of Jinci from 1606 (Fig. 7.4), which is largely based on Gao Ruxing's map. The 1801 inscription states that after the Shu Yu Shrine was rebuilt in the 1770s, the contrast between the new shrine and the old buildings inspired people to rebuild the surrounding temples as well. Twenty-two years later, the new complex was built on top of the old foundation to the Guandi Temple.

The complex has an entry gate with two courtyards, each with a worship hall at its rear to the north, and side halls to the east and west. Guandi is worshiped in a three-bay-wide central hall located on the north end of the first courtyard. In this inscription, the back hall is said to have been built like the Wenchang palace-temple next to it, with an arcuated lower story (described as cave-like 洞) and a timber upper story (called a *ge* 閣). The Three Pure Ones are worshiped in the lower story, the Cavern of the Three Pure Ones (Sanqingdong 三清洞), with the central cavern dedicated to Yuanshi tianzun 元始天尊, the left cavern dedicated to Lingbao tianzun 靈寶天尊, and the right cavern dedicated to Yuqing tianzun (Laozi) 玉清天尊. The upper story is, by itself, the Jade Emperor's Storied Pavilion (Yuhuangge 玉皇閣).[15]

10 Temple/Shrine to the Eastern Peak 東嶽祠
16th–18th centuries?

The earliest documentation of a temple to the Eastern Peak is in Wang Sicheng's stele inscription of 1342, where it was called a Taishanmiao 泰山廟. Gao Ruxing also shows a Taishanmiao on his map of Jinci published in 1551,[16] and it was still called this in a 1567 repair inscription.[17] However, Liu Dapeng was uncertain of the age of the temple. By his time, the name of the temple had also been changed from Taishanmiao to Dongyueci. Documentation exists for repairs in 1825 and 1877.[18]

11 Wenchang Temple Palace 文昌宮 and Jin River Seven Worthies Shrine 晉水七賢祠
1773

The present structure was built in the 38th year of Qianlong period (1773). According to the stele inscription by Yang Eryou 楊二酉 (1705–80) documenting that construction, the shrine was originally a one-bay-wide building on the south bank of the Earl of Zhi Canal. During the Yongzheng period (1723–36), it was moved to a location on the north side of the canal. In 1763, with the completion of the pagoda in Fengshengyuan 奉聖院, a new site was divined, and the building was built on previously endowed temple lands (香火地) located north of the canal.[19] Originally the Jin River Worthies Shrine was dedicated to five worthies and was located in the Jinxi Academy. In the 38th year of the Qianlong reign, the shrine was moved to the central cavern below the Wenchang *ge*-pavilion and was changed to include seven worthies. They are, from the Zhou dynasty: Yu Rang 豫讓 (mid-5th century BCE); from the Tang dynasty: Li Bai 李白 (701–62) and Bai Juyi 白居易 (772–846); from the Song dynasty: Fan Zhongyan 范仲淹 (989–1052) and Ouyang Xiu 歐陽修 (1007–72); from the Ming dynasty: Yu Qian 于謙 (1398–1457) and Wang Qiong 王瓊 (1459–1532).[20]

12 Juntianyue Terrace 鈞天樂臺
1795

Built during the Qianlong period, this stage faces the Haotianshen Shrine.[21] Liu Yongde states that it was constructed at the same time as the shrine expansion.[22] Juntian is the central of the nine heavens and the palace of Shangdi 上帝. The music produced in Juntian is called Juntian guangyue 鈞天廣樂.[23] Song Naizhong suggests that the name is thus another way of describing the music of transcendent beings (*xianyue zhi daicheng* 仙樂之代稱).[24] Additionally, *Juntianyue* is the name of a *chuanqi* 傳奇 drama written by You Tong 尤侗 (1618–1704).[25] Given that the structure was built in the late 18th century, it is possible that the name may also allude to this work.

13 Three Sages Shrine Complex 三聖祠
1737?

Originally two temples dedicated to Yaowang 藥王 (Medicine King) and Zhenjun 眞君 (True Lord). In the 2nd year of the Qianlong period (1737), they were combined into one temple and, with the addition of a Dragon King 龍王 (Longwang), it was called the Shrine of the Three Kings 三王祠, which was later changed to the Three Sages: Medicine King in the center; Cangwang 倉王, which is the True Lord, at left; and a Black Dragon King at right. A short wall surrounds the building, and there is an entrance through a *fang* 坊 gateway that serves as the front gate to the complex.[26]

14 Water Mirror Terrace 水鏡臺
16th century?

Original date of building unknown, it was repaired in the 24th year of the Daoguang reign period (1844).[27] The structure faces west and is oriented between the Sage Mother Hall and the Dressing Tower. The front portion of the building looks like a worship hall, and the back is a stage. Gao Ruxing, *Taiyuan xianzhi*, shows a *yuelou* 樂樓 stage in that location; so a stage was located here as early as 1551. The structure is considered to be Ming dynasty, with Qing-dynasty restoration to the stage portion.[28] Tiles on the roof ridge of the Water Mirror Terrace are dated to the first year of the Wanli reign period (1573).[29]

15 Tower of the Beautiful Ying Island 勝瀛樓
17th–18th century

The name likens Jinci to the famous Isle of Transcendents, Yingzhou 瀛洲. First construction unknown, located between the Jinqingmen and the Eternal Youth Spring. Thought to be built at the beginning of the Qing.[30] Liu Yongde states that the style of the building is consistent with late Ming or early Qing structures, and that it was likely named in response to the poem by Yu Qian, which states that because of Jinci's beauty, local people say that it is a little Yingzhou.[31] The Qianlong-period painting of the site shows this building, but it does not appear in Gao Ruxing's *Taiyuan xianzhi*.

16 Unified Rejoicing *Ting* Complex 同樂亭; Fu Shan Memorial 傅山紀年館
Expanded to current configuration in 1963

Originally a small sanctuary (*jingshe* 精舍), it later became a residence for Daoists and was called a Daoist Cloister. Modified in the 2nd year of the Qianlong period (1737) to include a five-bay hall on the south side, two three-bay halls on the east and west, and *pingmen* 屏門 gate at the front. Also called Yijianju 一鑒居.[32] The name Tongle is a reference to Mengzi's discussion about rulers sharing his pleasures with the people in order to gain their favor.[33] High ministers would stay here when they were visiting and "rejoice together" with the people of the Jinci area. And because ministers stayed here, it was also called a Shangguan ting 上官亭.[34] It was expanded to current configuration in 1963 and made into a memorial hall to the scholar and calligrapher Fu Shan.[35]

17 Iron Man Terrace 鐵人臺 or Lotus Terrace 蓮花臺
Late 11th century

Originally built during the Shaosheng reign period of Song Zhezong (1094–98). Four cast-iron statues located in the four corners of the terrace are considered to be water-guarding spirits. They are nicknamed the Four Iron Han; each is more than five feet tall. Two were cast in the Shaosheng period, one in the Huizong's Zhenghe period (1111–18) and one in the Ming Hongzhi period (1488–1506).[36] The original purpose of this terrace, as well as later repairs to the statues, is discussed more fully in Chapter 6.

18 Duiyue Memorial Gateway 對越坊
1576–1606

According to Liu Dapeng, this structure was built in 1606, but this may have been a rebuilding because in the case of the Bell and Drum Towers, also built in that year (the 34th year of the Wanli reign period), he uses "initially built." At the time of his writing, the central space on the east side (facing toward the pathway of approach) was inscribed with Wangu liufang 萬古流芳, and the Duiyue plaque, which is dated 1576, was on the west side between the gateway and the Offering Hall. Peng Hai follows Liu Dapeng in asserting that this structure was built at the same time as the Bell and Drum Towers. Liu Yongde disagrees and places initial construction of the gateway in 1576 with the Duiyue plaque.[37]

The Duiyue plaque was on the east side, visible to a devotee approaching the Sage Mother Hall, from at least the 18th century, as it appears in this position on the Qianlong-period painting of the site. An inscribed map of the site dated 1877 shows Wangu liufang 萬古流芳 on the east façade of the gateway.

Liu Yongde states that in 1956, four images were added to replace the Western-style buildings painted on the interior of the gateway in the early 20th century. The additions were: east façade/left side: Yi Jiang gives Shu Yu his assigned name; east façade/right side: Shu Yu enfeoffed by his older brother King Cheng; west façade/left side: Earl Yao of Zhi floods Jinyang; and West façade/right side: Yu Rang 豫讓 attempts to stab Zhao Xiangzi 趙襄子 on the stone bridge.

19 Offering Hall 獻殿
1168

First built in the eighth year of the Jin Dading reign period (1168), this was repaired in the 22nd year of the Wanli reign period (1594) and again (re-roofed?) in the 24th year of the Daoguang reign period (1844).[38] It was restored (*fanxiu* 翻修) using original materials in 1955.[39]

20 Drum Tower 鼓樓
1606

Located to the right (south) of the Offering Hall. First built in 1606, repaired in 1844.[40]

21 Bell Tower 鐘樓
1606

First built in 1606, repaired in 1844. Located on the left (north) side of the Offering Hall.[41]

22 Tang Taizong Stele *Ting*-gazebo 貞觀寶翰亭
1770

Located on the southeast corner of the Shu Yu of Tang Shrine. According to Liu Dapeng, this pavilion was originally only one bay facing west, first built in the 21st year of the Tang Zhenguan reign period (647) and repaired over the dynasties. Liu Dapeng and Liu Yongde both state that in the 35th year of the Qianlong reign (1770), it was expanded to three bays, and the foundation was moved to be reoriented southward.[42] Gao Ruxing's 1551 *Jinci zhitu* shows a small stele gazebo to the east of the Shu Yu of Tang Shrine clearly oriented southward.

There is some reason to doubt that the original pavilion at Jinci was built during the 7th century. The *Yuanhe junxian tuzhi* of 813 documents the stele location on Qianyangmen jie 乾陽門街 in Taiyuan prefecture.[43] However, a pavilion for the stele is not discussed in either of the two Yuan-dynasty records describing the site.

The two stelae within the pavilion are the Taizong original and a recarving of the Taizong stele completed in the 37th year of the Qianlong period (1772) following the original.

23 Gong Shuzi Shrine Complex 公輸子祠
17th–18th century?

Gong Shuzi is the name of Lu Ban, the ancient craftsman, and a statue of him is worshiped in the main hall. The complex consists of a main hall of three bays, a surrounding wall, and an entry gateway. The original date of establishment is unknown and does not appear on Gao Ruxing's *Jinci zhitu*. The statuary niche was repaired in the 8th year of the Yongzheng period (1730); the complex was repaired again in the 35th year of the Qianlong period (1770).[44]

24 Tai Tai Temple 臺駘廟
1533, with later repairs

A Tai Tai temple has existed at Jinci since at least the Yuan period, as Yi Gou's inscription of 1267 mentions a temple dedicated to him, but it is unclear where this temple was located.[45] However, the temple building was originally built in its present location by Gao Ruxing in 1533 as a reward to thank Tai Tai for saving Gao Ruxing during a river crossing. The temple was repaired/maintained by the Gao Family, with repairs documented in 1730, 1772, and 1847.[46] Liu Yongde states that the temple continued to be maintained by the Gao family until 1956.[47]

For the significance of Tai Tai as a deity of the Fen River and his importance to the state of Jin, see Chapter 3. Other deities worshiped within the shrine are the God of the Five Paths (Wudaoshen 五道神) and the local Earth God (Tudishen 土地神).[48]

25 Descendants' *Tang*-hall 苗裔堂 (also called Descendants' Temple 苗裔廟) 1511?

Date of first construction unknown; Liu Dapeng states that Descendants' *Tang*-hall was rebuilt in 1st year of the Song Zhenghe reign period (1111) and repaired in the 6th year of the Ming Zhengde reign period (1511).[49] Liu Yongde maintains that the hall was rebuilt in the 1st year of the Yuan Zhihe reign period (1328) and repaired in 1511. It contains images of female deities, which are thought to be Ming-dynasty works.[50]

26 Fangzhang Cavern 方丈洞 (also called Laojun Shrine 老君祠) pre-17th century?

Located to the south of Chaoyang Cavern. Three caves, originally the residences of Daoist priests who placed images of Laozi and guardian warriors in the shrine.[51] Then the Daoist priests were replaced with Buddhist monks, and Fangzhang Cavern was consequently named "abbot's quarters."[52] None of the caverns along this portion of the mountain (numbers 26–32) is shown on Gao Ruxing's *Jinci zhitu*.

27 Chaoyang Cavern 朝陽洞 and Lingguan Hall 靈官殿 17th century?

No date of excavation or first establishment. One of two caves located north of the Fangzhang Cavern. A timber-frame façade is attached to the front, which is called the Lingguan Hall 靈官殿. Within this structure is an image of Lingguanshen 靈官神.[53]

The cavern is named because it is located on the east side of Mt. Xuanweng, and the east sides of mountains are called *chaoyang* (west sides of mountains are called *xiyang* 夕陽).[54] The Chaoyang Cavern, along with the Ancestor Lü *Ge*-pavilion (see 32 below) is mentioned in an inscription dated to Qianlong 28 (1763).[55] Peng Hai lists the Chaoyang Cavern *Ting-pavilion* (Chaoyangdong ting 朝陽洞亭) as being built in 1785.[56] The whole complex is depicted on the Qianlong-period painting of the site.

28 Tea Smoke Cavern 茶煙洞 17th century?

Also called Yuntaodong 雲陶洞. Located north of Chaoyang Cavern, it was originally called Chaoyang bieyi dong 朝陽别一洞 (the other Chaoyang cavern) but is deeper than Chaoyang Cavern. Within it is another small cave, a tea stove, and a stone bed.[57] According to Liu Yongde, this place was thought to have been excavated for the use of troops in the area and was where Fu Shan (1607–84) was said to have been imprisoned. It came to be called Tea Smoke Cavern after this time, when Daoist priests brewed tea to entertain troops.

29a God of Wealth Shrine 財神祠 (also called Open Spring Cavern 開源洞) 17th century?

There is an image of the God of Wealth within the cave. The date of initial construction is unknown.[58]

29b Awaiting the Phoenix *Xuan-pavilion* 待鳳軒 1718[59]

On the north of the Chaoyang Cavern are three bays. In the 30th year of the Guangxu reign (1904), an interior room of one bay was added; the door opens from the back wall of the pavilion.[60]

30 Triple-Terrace *Ge-pavilion* 三臺閣 17th–18th century?

Eastward facing, north of the Lü (Dongbin) Temple-pavilion, connected to the Reading Terrace, also located to its south. Constructed at the beginning of the Guangxu reign period (1875–1909) by the abbot monk Xutan 續曇, who raised the money to have it built.

According to the *Jincizhi*, those who try to explain the name say that the emperor has three terraces: a spiritual terrace (*lingtai* 靈臺) for looking at the stars, a seasonal terrace (*shitai* 時臺) for looking at the four seasons, and a park terrace (*youtai* 囿臺) for looking at birds and beasts.

Another possibility for the meaning is from the *Tianwenzhi* 天文志:

> There are three terraces composed of six stars:
> Upper terrace on the west: the two stars of Wenchang in charge of destiny
> Middle terrace: next two stars, in charge of official rank (nobility)
> Lower terrace: two eastern stars, in charge of salary.[61]

31 Reading Terrace 讀書臺 (also called Bantongting 伴桐亭) 1785

The first Reading Terrace is said to have been built further up Xuanweng Mountain on Huanxi Peak 歡喜岭 at the place where Yang Yin 楊愔 of the Northern Qi (550–77) read.[62] According to Liu Dapeng, the Reading Terrace was originally built in the 27th year of the Ming Jiajing period (1548). Located between the Ancestor Lü *Ge-pavilion* on its south and the Triple Terrace *Ge-pavilion* on its north.[63]

32 Ancestor Lü *Ge-pavilion* 呂祖閣
17th–18th century

Located on the Chaoyang Cavern peak, halfway up the mountain. On the left (north) it is connected to the Reading Terrace and the Triple Terrace *Ge-pavilion* and on the right to the temple wall. Unknown exactly when built, this shrine was not mentioned in Gao Ruxing's writings on Jinci. According to Liu Yongde, an Ancestor Lü *Ge-pavilion* was already built in the 38th year of Kangxi's reign (1689).[64] In an inscription dated to Qianlong 28 (1763), both Chaoyang Cavern and a Duke Lü *Ge-pavilion* are mentioned.[65]

33 Pine River *Ting-gazebo* 松水亭

Built with the timbers from the River View *Ting*-gazebo (Wangchuanting 望川亭) when it was dismantled due to the frequent suicides that took place there after dark at the end of the Qianlong period (1736–95). Located between the Descendants' Hall, Octagonal Pool, Perfect Benefit Spring, and Longevity Pine, and so it is called Pine River Gazebo. Used by locals as an offering hall during festival times.[66]

34 Qinghua *Tang-pavilion* 清華堂

First built in the Tianbao period of the Northern Qi (550–60), it is unknown when it was destroyed or where it was originally located. A five-bay hall was rebuilt north of the Lotus Terrace (Iron Man Terrace) in the Daoguang period (1821–51) and given the same name.[67] No longer extant.

35 White Crane *Ting-gazebo* 白鶴亭
16th–19th centuries

A south-facing gazebo over the water across from Tongleting. First built in the Jiajing reign period (1522–67), repaired and expanded in Qianlong 43 (1778) and Daoguang 2 (1822). Also called River Pavilion (Shuiting 水亭) or the Little Orchid Pavilion 小蘭亭.[68]

36 Genuinely Wonderful *Ting-gazebo* 眞趣亭
1916–17

Construction began in autumn of 1916 and finished in autumn of 1917. Built by the KMT Brigade Commander Huang Guoliang 黄國梁 after a discussion about the site of Jinci with Liu Dapeng. It was named according to Huang Guoliang's thought that Jinci was genuinely wonderful (眞趣) and that the most genuine and wonderful place in the complex was the stairway to the stone tank leading from the Eternal Youth Spring.[69]

37 Sluice-Gate *Ting*-gazebo 水閘亭
1953

Is not discussed as a separate structure in the *JCZ* or found on the Qianlong- or Guangxu-period maps. According to Song Naizhong, this pavilion was built in 1953 and is presently the residence of the Jinci water managers stationed at the site by the Taiyuan City Water Conservancy Bureau (Taiyuanshi shuiliju 太原市水利局).[70]

38 Lock Rainbow Bridge 鎖虹橋
(also called Wenchang Stone Bridge 文昌石橋)
1773

Built after construction of the new, relocated Wenchang Temple Palace. According to Yang Eryou's stele inscription of the construction, stone was used to prevent the need for replacement due to rot common in wooden bridges.[71]

39 Mt. Tai Bridge 泰山橋
(also called Emerald Wave Bridge 碧瀾橋)[72]

Original date of construction unknown. A bridge appears in this location on Gao Ruxing's *Jinci zhitu* and may have been built at the same time as the Taishan Temple, prior to 1342. It is labeled Taishan Bridge on the Qianlong painting of the site.

40 Meeting Transcendents Bridge 會仙橋

Original date of construction unknown. A bridge appears in this location on Gao Ruxing's *Jinci zhitu*. According to Liu Dapeng, legend has it that in the past, on the 14th day of the 4th month, transcendents meet on this bridge.

41 Suspended Snow Bridge 掛雪橋
(also called Double Bridge 雙橋)
Pre-19th century

Original date of construction unknown. Shown on Qianlong painting and on Yuan Peilan's 1826 map of Jinci.

44 Five(-Colored) Clouds *Ting* Complex 五雲亭
1773

Built at the same time as the Wenchang Temple Palace and accessible to it from a doorway in the southwest corner. Originally the east wall abutted the Jinci Town wall. According to Liu Dapeng, the local literati would gather here annually on the third day of the second month when Wenchang was worshiped. Because colored clouds were a symbol of a flourishing period, those who gathered in this place would gain even greater abilities.[73]

Q

qifugong 騎栿栱 beam-top bracket-arm—bracket-arm of various lengths that is joined into the top of a tie-beam

qindian 寢殿 vestry

qinmian 琴面 lute-face—descending cantilever tip that is concave and pentagonal in section

qinmian/pizhu 琴面/批竹 lute-face/split-bamboo—term coined by Liang Sicheng and the authors of the *Yingzao fashi zhushi* to describe the not quite lute-faced/not quite split-bamboo articulation of the Sage Mother Hall's descending cantilever tip. The form was widely used in the Song architecture of southern Shanxi.

qipuzuo 七鋪作 seven *puzuo*—"seven-layer bracket set": a bracket cluster of bearing block + four perpendicular extensions + *shuatou* + intermediate timber/eaves purlin or eaves beam

qixindou 齊心枓 central block—small block located in the center of a bracket-arm

R

rufu 乳栿 *rufu* tie-beam—"breast tie-beam": tie-beam two rafters in length that spans between eaves bracketing and interior columns. According to Liang et al., this timber usually spans from eaves bracket sets to the body of the column, but there are cases of it spanning from eaves bracket sets to interior column-top bracket sets; contrast *dingfu* tie-beam.

ruyi dougong 如意枓栱 scepter bracket sets—bracket sets with 45°-angle bracket-arms located on the building façades rather than on corners

S

sandou 散枓 separate block—small block placed between beams, frequently at the ends of shadow bracket-arms

shangpingtuan 上平槫 upper interior purlin

shengqi 生起 rise—increase in column height from the central bay to corner columns

shuangshan banmen 雙扇版門 double-panel doors

shuatou 耍頭 *shuatou*—"trifling-tip": bracket-set timber that extends perpendicular to the wall plane and is joined through the *linggong*; frequently rendered in the locust-head shape

shunfuchuan 順栿串 beam-following tie—low interior beam that joins columns below regular rafter-length tie-beams along the bay line

shuzhu 蜀柱 queen-post—short column supporting either end of a collar beam; this term is also widely used for any column in the roof frame of similar height

sichuanfu duirufu yongsanzhu 四椽栿對乳栿用三柱 four-rafter beam facing a *rufu* tie-beam with three columns in cross-section

sipuzuo 四鋪作 four *puzuo*—"four-layer bracket set": a bracket cluster of bearing block + one perpendicular extension + *shuatou* + intermediate timber / eaves purlin or eaves beam

suantingfang 算桯枋 *suantingfang*—"planning-table beam": plain tie-beam connecting *linggong* on the interior portion of the eaves bracket sets; similar to the ceiling tie-beam, except that it does not necessarily support a ceiling; used in the Ten-Thousand Buddhas Hall of Zhenguosi

sufang 素枋 *sufang*—plain beam

suoxinggong 梭形栱 shuttle-shaped bracket-arm—*see* short bracket-arm

T

taoban tuofeng 掐瓣駝峰 hollow-chamfered camel's-hump brace

timu 替木 intermediate timber—timber, rectangular in section, which is located between the *linggong* and the purlin; on the Sage Mother Hall, this timber runs the length of the eaves purlin, a variation called *tongti* 通替 by Peng Hai

tingtang 廳堂 great hall—hall where interior columns are taller than eaves columns; the ceiling is, consequently, usually open frame; smaller timbers are used in this system than in that of a palatial hall

touxin 偷心 stolen-heart—bracketing construction by which perpendicular bracket-arms (*huagong*) hold only the next level of perpendicular extension (either another *huagong* or a descending cantilever)

tuanfeng 槫縫 purlin line—axis of structure running parallel to the purlins

tuojiao 托腳 side strut—strut that extends from tie-beam to purlin; these are often called inverted-V braces when they support the roof pole

W

wupuzuo 五鋪作 five *puzuo*—"five-layer bracket set": a bracket cluster of cap block + two perpendicular extensions + *shuatou* + intermediate timber or eaves purlin or eaves beam

X

xiapingtuan 下平槫 lower interior purlin

xia'ang 下昂 descending cantilever

xia'angxing shuatou 下昂形耍頭 descending-cantilever-shaped *shuatou*

xin 心 heart—a bracket set's center line running perpendicular to the building plane, i.e., the perpendicular extension of the *huagong*; if the separate block joined on to the end of the *huagong* contains a bracket-arm parallel to the building plane (such as a *guazigong* or *mangong*), the combination is referred to as a "filled-heart construction" (*jixin* or *jixinzao* 計心造); if a second step of *huagong* is joined into this position, it is referred to as a "stolen-heart construction" (*touxin* or *touxinzao* 偷心造)

xuexie 靴楔 boot wedge—wedge-shaped timber that is placed between an interior *huagong* and the tail of a true descending cantilever

Y

yacaofang 厭槽枋 rafter-supporting beam—column-top beam that directly abuts the rafters

yanchuan 檐椽 eaves rafter

yatiao 壓跳 *yatiao*—"wedge-step": intermediary timber placed horizontally between the upper interior *huagong* and the axial tie-beam

yidou sansheng 一斗三升 triple-rise bracket set—bracket set in which *ludou* supports bracket-arm with both central and arm-end blocks. This is presently the most commonly used term for this timber; however, it is a Qing term. The earlier version is *batou jiaoxiang zuo*.

yinggong 影栱 shadow bracket-arm—bracket-arm that is used along the wall plane; also called wall-supporting bracket-arm (*fubigong* 扶壁栱)

yixinggong 翼形栱 wing-shaped bracket-arm

you'ang 由昂 corner cantilever—"facilitating cantilever": uppermost cantilever on a corner column-top bracket set

yuanyang jiaoshougong 鴛鴦交首栱 mandarin-ducks bracket-arm—elongated timber, usually in the *linggong* position supporting the eaves purlin, which extends from the façade *huagong* across the 45°-angle line and is articulated to appear like two bracket-arms that cross over and share a single arm-end block where they meet

yueliang 月梁 moon-beam—axial tie-beam rendered in a curved "crescent moon" fashion, common from the Tang to the Song. The full-round moon-beam lost popularity in the north from the middle of the tenth century but continued to be used in southern areas at least through the Yuan (with some reduction in the length of the angled neck [*xiexiang* 斜項]).

yuntoushi-tuofeng 雲頭式駝峰 cloud-style camel's-hump brace

yunxinggong 雲形栱 cloud-shaped bracket-arm

Z

zhechuanban 遮椽版 rafter-screening panels—panels supported by side ceiling rafters (or column-top beams/*luohanfang*) used to hide the inner portion of the eaves rafters

zhidou 直枓 vertical strut—post or strut, crowned by a small bearing block, usually found in intercolumnar position of Tang (or Liao) architecture supporting an eaves bracket set; also present in the Ten-Thousand Buddhas Hall of Zhenguosi

zhilingchuan 直欞窗 straight-lattice window—window with straight-slat lattice work

zhuruzhu 朱儒柱 king-post

English-Chinese

A

architrave *lan'e* 闌額—tall tie-beam that is joined through the tops of columns

attached hall *jiawu* 夾屋—small hall attached to the hip or gable end of a main hall and oriented in the same direction; similar to an ear hall except that it shares a wall with the main hall

B

back hall *houdian* 後殿—axial hall at the back of the complex

batter *cejiao* 側腳—incline toward the center of a building from the bottom to the top of a column

bay line *jianfeng* 間縫—axis of structure running parallel to the gable ends of a building.

bay tie-beam *panjianfang* 襻間枋—tie-beam located underneath and parallel to the purlin

beam-following tie *shunfuchuan* 順栿串—low interior beam that joins columns below regular rafter-length tie-beams along the bay-line

beam-top bracket-arm *qifugong* 騎栿栱—bracket-arm of various lengths that is joined into the top of a tie-beam

bearing block *ludou* 櫨枓—largest bearing block, usually found crowning columns and as the support for the bracket cluster at the column-top and intercolumnarly

beveled *moxie* 抹斜

beveled bracket-arm *moxiegong* 抹斜栱

beveled *linggong* *moxie linggong* 抹斜令栱

boot wedge *xuexie* 靴楔—wedge-shaped timber that is placed between an interior *huagong* and the tail of a true descending cantilever

bracket set *puzuo* 鋪作—"layered bracket set": Song term for a combination of bracket-arms supporting the roof system; *dougong* (枓栱) in Qing parlance

bracket-arm *gong* 栱

C

ceiling rafters *ping'anchuan* 平闇椽

ceiling tie-beam *pingqifang* 平棊枋—plain beam supported by *linggong* on the building interior and supporting a paneled ceiling (different from the *suanchengfang* in that it is only used in buildings with ceilings)

central block *qixindou* 齊心枓—small block located in the center of a bracket-arm

chamfering *juansha* 卷殺—technique of rendering a curved appearance to a timber by planing off the corner with multiple straight edges; used for column tops as well as the ends of moon-beams

chenfangtou *chenfangtou* 襯枋頭—uppermost perpendicular timber in a bracket set; does not extend beyond the exterior parallel timber (either *linggong* or eaves beam)

chin-wiping bracket-arms *dinghua mokegong* 丁華抹頦栱

cicada-back *chanbei* 蟬背—chevron pattern: here found on the bottom of a descending cantilever where it enters into the bracket set

cloud-shaped bracket-arm *yunxinggong* 雲形栱

cloud-style camel's-hump brace *yuntoushi-tuofeng* 雲頭式駝峰

collar beam *pingliang* 平樑

column-top tie-beam *pupaifang* 普拍枋 (also *pubofang* 普柏枋)—tie-beam joined between the column tops and the cap block

corner cantilever *you'ang* 由昂—"facilitating cantilever" uppermost cantilever on a corner column-top bracket set

cross block *jiaohudou* 交互枓—block that supports timbers in two directions resulting in a "+" opening in plan

cross-shaped *linggong* internal, column-top bracket-arm extending both parallel and perpendicular to the building façade (my term)

D

descending cantilever *xia'ang* 下昂

descending-cantilever-shaped *shuatou* *xia'angxing shuatou* 下昂形耍頭

***dingfu* tie-beam** *dingfu* 丁栿—a short tie-beam that extends from the column-top bracket sets of the gable-end eaves columns to the top of the side-bay axial tie-beam making a T-shape

double-panel doors *shuangshanbanmen* 雙扇版門

E

ear hall *duodian* 朵殿—subsidiary halls placed on the left and right of a main hall, oriented in the same direction and separated from the main hall

eaves beam *liaoyanfang* 撩檐枋—"eaves-raising beam": rectangular timber located between outermost exterior *linggong* (above *shuatou*) and eaves rafters

eaves purlin *liaofengtuan* 撩風槫 (also *liaoyantuan* 撩檐槫)—"eaves-raising purlin": lowermost purlin located between *timu* and eaves rafters

eaves rafter *yanchuan* 檐椽

eaves-beam/eaves-purlin—combination of *liaoyanfang* and *liaoyantuan* used on the Sage Mother Hall. The *liaoyanfang* in this case has also been called a *tongtimu*, or "continuous intermediate timber." This kind of combination is frequently seen on Ming and Qing buildings, where it is called *taoyanfang* and *taoyanhang* 桃檐枋/桃檐桁.

eight-rafter beam *bachuanfu* 八椽栿—an axial tie-beam the length of eight rafters

eight-rafter-deep hall with *rufu* tie-beam and six-rafter beam supported by three columns in section *bajiachuanwu rufu duiliuchuanfu yongsanzhu* 八架椽屋乳栿對六椽栿用三柱

F

filled-heart construction *jixinzao* 計心造—bracketing construction by which perpendicular bracket-arms (*huagong*) hold both a parallel bracket-arm (usually *guazigong* or *linggong*) and the next level of perpendicular extension (either another *huagong* or a descending cantilever)

five *puzuo* *wupuzuo* 五鋪作—"five-layer bracket set": a bracket cluster of cap block + two perpendicular extensions + *shuatou* + intermediate timber or eaves purlin or eaves beam

flying eaves *feiyan* 飛檐—a second set of eaves rafters that extend out at a slight upward angle from the eaves rafters; the tips of these rafters (the amount that extends beyond the eaves rafters) are called *feizi* 飛子

four *puzuo* *sipuzuo* 四鋪作—"four-layer bracket set": a bracket cluster of cap block + one perpendicular extension + *shuatou* + intermediate timber/eaves purlin or eaves beam

four-rafter beam facing a *rufu* tie-beam with three columns in cross-section *sichuanfu duirufu yongsanzhu* 四椽栿對乳栿用三柱

G

great hall *tingtang* 廳堂—hall where interior columns are taller than eaves columns; ceiling is, consequently, usually open frame; smaller timbers are used in this system than in that of a palatial hall

guazigong *guazigong* 瓜子栱—short bracket-arm used away from the wall plane and underneath a *mangong* or, in the case of Sage Mother Hall, a *luohanfang*

H

heart *xin* 心—a bracket set's center line running perpendicular to the building plane, i.e., the perpendicular extension of the *huagong*; if the separate block joined on to the end of the *huagong* contains a bracket-arm parallel to the building plane (such as a *guazigong* or *mangong*) then the combination is referred to as a "filled-heart construction" (*jixin* or *jixinzao* 計心造); if a second step of *huagong* is joined into this position it is referred to as a "stolen-heart construction" (*touxin* or *touxinzao* 偷心造)

hip-rafter *jiaoliang* 角梁

hollow-chamfered camel's-hump brace *taoban tuofeng* 掐瓣駝峰

huagong *huagong* 華栱—"petal bracket-arm": bracket-arm that is placed perpendicular to the building plane

huatouzi *huatouzi* 華頭子—"bud" timber that supports a structural descending cantilever at the point of intersection with the bracket set. In the Sage Mother Hall this is the back end of the first step of interior *huagong*.

I

intermediate timber *timu* 替木—timber, rectangular in section, which is located between the *linggong* and the purlin; on the Sage Mother Hall this timber runs the length of the eaves purlin, a variation called *tongti* 通替 by Peng Hai

inverted-V brace *chashou* 叉手—two-pronged strut that supports either side of the roof pole or *linggong* supporting the roof pole

K

king-post *zhuruzhu* 朱儒柱

L

linggong *linggong* 令栱—"lead bracket-arm": regular bracket-arm, usually supports the intermediate timber and purlin on eaves and in interiors

locust-head arm *mazhagong* 螞蚱栱—short timber finished in the locust-head style

locust-head style *mazhaxing* 螞蚱形—style of finish for the end of a timber commonly used for *shuatou*

lower interior purlin *xiapingtuan* 下平槫

luohanfang *luohanfang* 羅漢枋—"arhat beam": beam running parallel to the building frame that is supported by the *guazigong* and (usually) *mangong* either inside the building or under the eaves

lute-face *qinmian* 琴面—descending cantilever tip that is concave and pentagonal in section

lute-face/split-bamboo *qinmian/pizhu* 琴面/批竹—term coined by Liang Sicheng and the authors of the *Yingzao fashi zhushi* to describe the not quite lute-faced/not quite split-bamboo articulation of the Sage Mother Hall's descending cantilever tip. The form was widely used in the Song architecture of southern Shanxi.

M

mandarin-ducks bracket-arm *yuanyang jiaoshougong* 鴛鴦交首栱—elongated timber, usually in the *linggong* position supporting the eaves purlin, which extends from the façade *huagong* across the 45°-angle line and is articulated to appear like two bracket-arms that cross over and share a single arm-end block where they meet

mangong *mangong* 慢栱—"extended bracket-arm": the longest bracket-arm, supported by the *nidaogong* on the wall plane (*nidao mangong*) or the *guazigong* away from the wall plane (*guazi mangong*)

moon-beam *yueliang* 月梁—axial tie-beam that is rendered in a curved "crescent moon" fashion, common from the Tang to the Song. The full-round moon-beam loses popularity in the north from the middle of the tenth century but continues to be used in southern areas at least through the Yuan (with some reduction in the length of the angled neck [*xiexiang* 斜項]).

N

nidao mangong *nidao mangong* 泥道慢栱—"plaster-channel extended bracket-arm": extended bracket-arm along the wall plane that, typically, is supported by the *nidaogong* and supports the column-top beams

nidaogong *nidaogong* 泥道栱—"plaster channel bracket-arm": bracket-arm joined into the capital block parallel to the wall plane

P

palatial hall *diantang* 殿堂—hall where interior columns are the same height as eaves columns resulting in a tripartite structure of columns, bracketing, and roof-frame

prism-lattice window *pozi lingchuang* 破子櫺窗—straight lattice whose slats are triangular in cross-section

purlin line *tuanfeng* 槫縫—axis of structure running parallel to the purlins

Q

queen-post *shuzhu* 蜀柱

R

rafter-screening panels *zhechuanban* 遮椽版—panels supported by side ceiling rafters (or column-top beams/*luohanfang*) used to hide the inner portion of the eaves rafters

rafter-supporting beam *yacaofang* 厭槽枋—column-top beam that directly abuts the rafters

residential quarters *liaoshe* 寮舍

rise *shengqi* 生起—increase in column height from the central bay to corner columns

roof pole *jituan* 脊槫

rounding *see* chamfering

rufu **tie-beam** (breast tie-beam) *rufu* 乳栿—tie-beam two rafters in length that spans between eaves bracketing and interior columns. According to Liang et al., this timber usually spans from eaves bracket sets to the body of the column, but there are cases of it spanning from eaves bracket sets to interior column-top bracket sets; contrast *dingfu* tie-beam

S

scepter bracket sets *ruyi dougong* 如意枓栱—bracket sets with 45°-angle bracket-arms located on the building façades, rather than corners

section *fen* 分—the basic proportional unit of measure. By using this unit to measure individual components, buildings can remain proportional even when the structural necessities of larger buildings require larger timbers (traditionally divided into eight sizes according to number of bays). Within this division, a single unit (*dancai*) is 10 × 15 sections and a full unit (*zucai*) is 21 × 10 sections.

separate block *sandou* 散枓—small block placed between beams, frequently at the ends of shadow bracket-arms

seven *puzuo* *qipuzuo* 七鋪作—"seven-layer bracket set": a bracket cluster of cap block + four perpendicular extensions + *shuatou* + intermediate timber / eaves purlin or eaves beam

shadow bracket-arm *yinggong* 影栱—bracket-arm that is used along the wall plane; also called wall-supporting bracket-arm (*fubigong* 扶壁栱)

short bracket-arm small bracket-arm that usually holds one single block in its center and usually rendered in wing, cloud, or shuttle shapes (*suoxinggong* 梭形栱). Commonly found on the wall plane in the intercolumnar position of tenth–twelfth-century buildings in southern Shanxi.

shrine *ci* 祠

shuatou *shuatou* 耍頭—"trifling-tip": bracket set timber that extends perpendicular to the wall plane and is joined through the *linggong*; frequently rendered in the locust-head shape

shuttle-shaped bracket-arm *suoxinggong* 梭形栱—*see* short bracket-arm

side brace *heta* 合踏—strut placed on top of a *rufu* tie-beam or a collar beam that usually supports a king-post or queen-post

side ceiling rafters *junjiaochuan* 峻脚椽—short rafters extending from the vertical architrave to the ceiling beams or *luohanfang* supporting rafter-screening panels (*zhechuanban* 遮椽板)

side strut *tuojiao* 托脚—strut that extends from tie-beam to purlin; these are called inverted-V braces when they support the roof pole

single unit *dancai* 單材—basic unit of timber with a proportion of 2 × 3, which is then divided into 10 × 15 sections (*fen* 分)

six *puzuo* *liupuzuo* 六鋪作—"six-layer bracket set": a bracket cluster of bearing block + three perpendicular extensions + *shuatou* + intermediate timber / eaves purlin or eaves beam

six-rafter beam *liuchuanfu* 六椽栿—axial tie-beam that extends six rafters

split-bamboo *pizhu* 批竹—descending cantilever tip finish in the shape of a simple beveled edge with a squared tip, common on Tang, Liao, and Song buildings but gradually going out of fashion beginning in the eleventh century

split-bamboo style *shuatou* *pizhuxing shuatou* 批竹形耍頭—*shuatou* finished in the split-bamboo style

stolen-heart *touxin* 偷心—bracketing construction by which perpendicular bracket-arms (*huagong*) hold only the next level of perpendicular extension (either another *huagong* or a descending cantilever)

straight-lattice window *zhilingchuan* 直欞窗—window with straight-slat lattice work

suantingfang *suantingfang* 算桯枋—"planning-table beam": plain tie-beam connecting *linggong* on the interior portion of the eaves bracket sets; similar to the ceiling tie-beam, except that it does not necessarily support a ceiling; used in the Ten-Thousand Buddhas Hall of Zhenguosi

sufang *sufang* 素枋—plain beam

T

temple *miao* 廟

triple-rise bracket set *yidou sansheng* 一斗三升 or *batou jiaoxiang zuo* (把頭絞項作)—bracket set in which *ludou* supports bracket-arm with both central and arm-end blocks. The most commonly used version is *yidou sansheng*; however, this is a Qing term. The earlier version is *batou jiaoxiang zuo*.

trough *cao* 槽—circuit of space between the eaves columns and the interior columns

U

unit *cai* 材

upper interior purlin *shangpingtuan* 上平槫

upturned basin *fupen* 覆盆—pre-Yuan-dynasty decorative treatment, mostly used for column bases, for a rounded form similar to the look of an upturned shallow basin. Can be carved (雕花覆盆) or plain (素覆盆); term also applied to column tops (or other architectural elements) when they have this shape.

V

vertical strut *zhidou* 直枓—post or strut, crowned by a small capital block, usually found in intercolumnar position of Tang (or Liao) architecture supporting an eaves bracket set. Also present in the Ten-Thousand Buddhas Hall of Zhenguosi.

vestry *qindian* 寢殿

W

wall-supporting bracket-arm *fubigong* 扶壁栱—bracket-arm that is used along the wall plane; also called "shadow bracket-arm" (*yinggong* 影栱)

wing-shaped bracket-arm *yixinggong* 翼形栱

Y

yatiao *yatiao* 壓跳—"wedge-step": intermediary timber placed horizontally between the upper interior *huagong* and the axial tie-beam

Reference Matter

Notes

For complete author names, titles, and publication data for the items cited here in short form, see the Select Bibliography, pp. 243–56. The following abbreviations are used in the Notes.

JCZ	Liu Dapeng 劉大鵬 (1857–1942). *Jincizhi* (Jinci gazetteer) 晉祠志.
SHY	Xu Song 徐宋 (1781–1848), comp. *Song huiyao jigao* (Draft recovered edition of the *Song huiyao*) 宋會要輯稿.
SJZ	Li Daoyuan 酈道元 (d. 527 CE). *Shuijingzhu* (Commentary on the Book of Waterways) 水經注. *Sibu beiyao* edition.
SXTZ	Wang Xuan 王軒 (1832–87) et al. *Shanxi tongzhi* (Shanxi gazetteer) 山西通志. Guangxu reign period, published 1892.
TPHYJ	Yue Shi 樂史 (930–1007). *Taiping huanyu ji* (Gazetteer of the world during the Taipingxingguo reign period) 太平寰宇記.
TYXZ	Yuan Peilan 員佩蘭 (Qing) and Yang Guotai 陽國泰 (Qing) et al., eds. *Taiyuan xianzhi* (Taiyuan county gazetteer) 太原縣志. Originally published 1826. Taipei: Chengwen, 1976.
XCB	Li Tao 李燾 (1114–83). *Xu Zizhi tongjian changbian* (Long draft of the continuation of the *Zizhi tongjian*) 續資治通鑑長編.
YHJXTZ	Li Jifu 李吉甫 (758–814). *Yuanhe junxian tuzhi* (An illustrated gazetteer of counties and commandaries of the Yuanhe reign period) 元和郡縣圖志.
YTZ	Muzhang'a 穆彰阿 (Qing) et al., comps. *Jiaqing chongxiu da Qing yitongzhi* (Comprehensive gazetteer of the Qing, Jiaqing-period recompilation) 嘉慶重修大清一統志.
YZFS	Li Jie 李誡 (?–1110) *Yingzao fashi* (Construction methods) 營造法式. Originally published 1103.

Chapter 1

1. *SHY*, 1233/3b.

2. My thanks to Peng Hai for helping me gain access to this painting.

3. For this idea with respect to Chinese city planning, see Wheatley, "The Ancient Chinese City," 147–58. The extension of this as a general characteristic of Chinese architecture can be seen in Ledderose, *Ten-Thousand Things*, 113–17.

4. This type of orientation can also be seen in temples to the Empress of Heaven (Tianhou 天后, also known as Mazu 媽祖) in southeastern coastal China and Taiwan. Because she was a water goddess and patron saint of fishermen, Mazu temples are frequently oriented to the ocean, nominally so that the goddess can watch over the sea and save fishermen in distress; see Bosco and Ho, *Empress of Heaven*, 18–20.

5. Qishan 岐山, the location of this palace (or temple) complex was the ancestral home of the Zhou kings; see Shaughnessy, "Western Zhou History," 301.

6. *Zhouli*, "Kaogongji," 41/642. For an extensive study of this text, see Wen, Kaogongji *daodu tuyi*. For information on the late date of the *Kaogongji* and the recompilation of the *Zhouli* during the Western Han, see Boltz, "*Chou li*," 25–27.

7. Zhang Gong, *Han-Tang fosi*, vol. 1, 166. I would like to thank Liu Shufen for directing me to this source.

8. Faure, *Chan: Insights and Oversights*, 155–56.

9. Lin Huiyin and Liang Sicheng, "Jin-Fen gujianzhu," 58; Duan, *Zhongguo simiao*, 154–94. For more on the relationship between gardens and sacred sites, see Ledderose, "The Earthly Paradise"; and Miller, "Synthetic Nature."

10. Wheatley, "The Ancient Chinese City," 150–52; Peng et al., *Jinci wenwu*, 99–101; Duan, *Zhongguo simiao*, 154–68; and Miller, "An Experiment."

11. Taiyuan shi Nanjiao qu difangzhi bianzuan weiyuanhui, *Taiyuan shi Nanjiao qu zhi*, 105.

12. McNair, "On the Date of the Shengmudian Sculptures," 243. Based on her understanding that the Sage Mother Hall was constructed during the Tiansheng reign period (1023–32), McNair speculates further that such a regal hall must have been sponsored by the regent of the period, Dowager Empress Liu. I discuss my dating for the hall and reasons why this was unlikely further in Chapter 6.

13. Otto, *Dionysus*, 26. I am indebted to Kalliopi Nikolopoulou for directing me to this text.

14. Watson, "Standardizing the Gods," 300.

15. Ibid., 293.

16. Michael Szonyi, a social historian whose work includes an examination of a local Fujian cult to the Five Emperors, has criticized Watson's research because of the problems created by the bias of the local gazetteers, as opposed to what can be found in stele inscriptions at temple sites; see Szonyi, "The Illusion." Additionally, Robert Hymes, in his recent work comparing Daoist and lay worship of local gods in Fujian province, questions the ability of the state to impose an identity onto a local divinity; see Hymes, *Way and Byway*.

17. For an account of the origin and transformation of the Wenchang cult, see Kleeman, "The Expansion" and *A God's Own Tale*.

18. Watson, "Standardizing the Gods," 294.

19. Duara, "Superscribing Symbols," 791.

20. Brook, *Praying for Power*, 178.

21. Pomeranz, "Water to Iron, Widows to Warlords," 63.

22. Pomeranz, "Cult of the Goddess of Taishan," 204.

23. Jordan and Overmyer, *The Flying Phoenix*, 11.

24. Jing Anning, *The Water God's Temple*, especially 70–143.

Chapter 2

1. The earliest of these may be the courtyard complex at Fengchu, Shaanxi province, dated to roughly 1050 BCE.

2. This configuration was detailed early in the study of Chinese architecture, however, the concept was blocked out into sectarian categories. For an early outline of the courtyard complex in shrine architecture, see Liang, *Liang Sicheng wenji*, vol. 2, 76–111. For a later study discussing the use of enclosing galleries in Song-dynasty Buddhist architectural complexes, see Xu Pingfang, "Beisong Kaifeng," 362.

3. Wang Shiren, "Ji Houtu," 273–77. An example of such reuse is Chongfusi, which during the Jin dynasty was used by the Pure Land Buddhist sect and then reused as a Chan monastery without substantial changes to the buildings. Even the wall paintings of the main Amitābha Hall (Mituodian) were kept intact; see Chai Zejun et al., *Shuozhou Chongfusi Mituodian*, 3. Further examples of temple complexes being reused by different sects in the Ming and Qing dynasties can be found in Naquin, *Peking: Temples and City Life*, 33–35. I am following Michael Loewe in translating *Houtu* as Earth Queen; see Loewe, "The Religious and Intellectual Background," 663.

4. See Wang Shiren, "Ji Houtu," 276–77.

5. For a discussion of the capital-I-shaped (also called "sideways-H-shaped" or *gong* 工) plan, see Nancy S. Steinhardt et al., *Chinese Traditional Architecture*, 154–55; and Ruitenbeek, *Carpentry and Building*, 51–54 (residential architecture) and 196–97 (ancestral temples). I have translated *qindian* in this work as "vestry" because, from at least the Han dynasty, the smaller hall behind the main worship hall in an ancestral temple (*zongmiao* 宗廟) was used for the storage of ritual clothing. This was considered parallel to secular architecture where the front halls were for audience and back for sleeping or resting; see Fan Ye, *Hou Hanshu*, 9/3199.

6. The semi-circular enclosure at the north part of the Temple to the Goddess of Earth is the most notable exception. Wang Shiren points out the similarity of this configuration to the pre-Jiajing emperor Temple of Heaven in Beijing and speculates that it is round because north is *yin*; see Wang Shiren, "Ji Houtu," 276. Rolf Stein notes that as early as the fifth century BCE, cities had been

constructed round on one side and square on the other three as a microcosmic representation of the heavens; see Stein, *The World in Miniature*, 221 and 294*n*128. My thanks to Jenny Liu for directing me to this source.

7. One of the best examples of the *gong* plan in a Buddhist monastery is the 1482 image of Chongshansi in Taiyuan. This should be representative of the complex from its 1381 construction. Liu Dunzhen, *Gudai jianzhu*, 363–64, notes the similarity of this complex with the Fenyin Temple to the Earth Queen and the Temple to the Central Peak. Additionally, the Amitābha Hall (*Mituodian*) dating to 1143 in Shuozhou's *Chongfusi* is followed by a smaller building that, at least stylistically, is from the same period, creating a *qindian* configuration (though reconstruction drawings do not link these buildings with a covered corridor); see Chai Zejun et al., *Shuozhou Chongfusi Mituodian*, 3. For ancestral temples designed in this manner in the *Lu Ban jing*, see Ruitenbeek, *Carpentry and Building*, 196–97.

8. The measurements in building orientation were taken by myself using a Chinese military-issue compass, October 10, 1997.

9. *Zhouli*, 41/642.

10. This new gatehouse was built in 1964 in the location of an entryway that opened in 1955. It effectively orients the visitor to the "central axis" of the Sage Mother Hall. This axis is considered to consist of the Water Mirror Terrace, Meeting Transcendents Bridge, Lotus Terrace, Duiyue Gateway and bell and drum towers, Offering Hall, Flying Bridge, and Sage Mother Hall; see Qi, "Jinci Shengmudian yanjiu," 50.

11. According to Feng Junjie 馮俊傑, glazed tiles on the roof ridge of the Water Mirror Terrace are dated to the first year of the Wanli reign period (1573). Personal communication, June 9, 2000.

12. In the *JCZ*, 119, Liu Dapeng states that the name "meeting transcendents" refers to the legend that in past years on the fourteenth day of the fourth month, there were transcendents who met on the bridge. Unfortunately, he does not provide a date for the construction of this bridge. The local name for this bridge is, according to Liu, "Iron Man Bridge" (Tierenqiao 鐵人橋). This name would correspond to the cast-iron warrior statues on the platform to which the bridge leads. It is labeled "Iron Han Chinese[-Man] Bridge" (Tiehanqiao 鐵漢橋) in the painting of the site dating from the Qianlong-reign period (1736–96). However, Liu Dapeng states that the local name for the next axial structure is the Lotus Terrace. I would like to thank Peng Hai for helping me gain access to the Qianlong-period painting.

13. There has been some speculation about the reason for having cast-iron statues here. Liu Dapeng verifies the name for the terrace and suggests that they are water-quelling metal spirits (*zhenshui jinshen* 鎮水金神) established to protect against water disasters; see *JCZ*, 70. After examining their inscriptions, Liu Yongde, *Jinci Fengguang*, 29–30, disagreed. None of the inscriptions mentions anything about quelling water. Additionally, the figures are very similar to those at the Temple to the Central Peak at Songshan, and thus their material is not specific to spring sites. He concludes that they should be considered guardian figures.

14. Liu Yongde, *Jinci Fengguang*, 29; also *JCZ*, 70.

15. Although not always present in the ritual complexes in north China, the bell and drum towers flanking an axial hall before the main compound is a familiar combination during the late Ming and Qing. Three southern Shanxi examples are: the bell and drum towers at Fengshengsi (ca. 1391–1796), Shuanglinsi (Ming-Qing), and Zhenguosi (ca. 1816). However, unlike Jinci, there is little documentation for the bell and drum towers of these complexes.

16. For more information on the statuary of the Sage Mother Hall, see McNair, "On the Date of the Shengmudian Sculptures"; and Zhao Zhiguang et al., *Jinci Songsu*. These figures are considered landmarks of Song-dynasty sculpture, and their configuration within the Sage Mother Hall is thought to be that of an empress's palace hall (Zhao Zhiguang et al., *Jinci Songsu*, 75). This interpretation is problematic for two reasons. First, it depends on the presumption that the Sage Mother was considered to be Yi Jiang when the statues were created, an interpretation that did not exist in the eleventh century. Second, the position of the Sage Mother is not consistent with conventions of ancestral portraiture. I discuss both of these factors in more detail in Chapter 6.

17. A pool north of the Eternal Youth Spring was mentioned in the 1063 documentation of canal expansion at Jinci, see Gongcheng Liangbi,

"Chongguang shuili ji" (1063), reprinted in *SXTZ*, 4705–6, and *TYXZ*, 12/13b.

18. *JCZ*, 66.

19. Liu Dapeng states that the name of the cavern relates to its placement on the east side of Xuanweng Mountain, as the east sides of mountains are called *chaoyang* or "facing the (rising) sun," whereas the west sides of mountains are called *chaoxi* or "facing the evening"; see *JCZ*, 108–9.

20. Peng Hai describes the site as following traditional *fengshui* principles, with the Sage Mother Hall located in the most auspicious position; see *Jinci wenwu*, 99, body text and note 2.

21. Song Naizhong et al., *Jinci lüyou*, 82, and *JCZ*, 77–78.

22. From the eleventh century, the village adjacent to the temple complex was referred to as Jinci Villages (Jincicun 晉祠村); see Gongcheng Liangbi, "Chongguang shuili ji" (1063), reprinted in *TYXZ*, 12/13b; and by the Jin dynasty (1123–1234 CE), Jinci Town (Jincizhen 晉祠鎮) was one of two *zhen* within Pacifying Jin county; see Tuotuo, *Jinshi*, 26/630. By the Song dynasty the word *zhen*, which was used to refer to military garrisons in the early Five Dynasties period, had come to be used for towns that were often centers of local commerce; see Ruth Mostern, "Dividing the Realm" (forthcoming). Thus, from as early as the eleventh century, the primary deity of Jinci would also have been the nominal tutelary deity for the entire community.

23. Naquin, *Peking: Temples and City Life*, 20.

24. For general observations in Shanxi, see Lin Huiyin and Liang Sicheng, "Jin-Fen gujianzhu," 53; and Jing Anning, *The Water God's Temple*, 1. Pomeranz, "Water to Iron, Widows to Warlords," gives three examples of spring-spirit temples located at springs in Hebei province.

25. For a discussion of the text, see Fracasso, "*Shan hai ching*." For a complete English translation of the text, see Birrell, trans., *The Classic of Mountains and Seas*.

26. *Shanhaijing*, 3/9a–b.

27. Ban Gu, *Hanshu*, 28 *shang*/1551.

28. Fan Ye, *Hou Hanshu zhi*, 23/3523. Anomalously, the *Jinshu* places a Jin River in Linjin, Yongzhou, which should be in modern Shaanxi. It is probable, therefore, that there was another Jin River in this period. The temple here to water spirits (*he, shuici*) was named such because it was near the Jin River; see Fang Xuanling, *Jinshu*, 40/430.

29. Fan Ye, *Hou Hanshu*, 5/224–25. Li Xian (Tang dynasty) states that this water-management project was a repair to the system originally built by the Earl of Zhi during the Warring States Period and described by Li Daoyuan in his *Shuijingzhu*; see also Chapter 3; and Yoshinami, "Kinsei Sansei no mizu arasoi o megutte," 365.

30. Wei Shou, *Weishu*, 106/2466. There is a second Jin River mentioned in the *Weishu* that is located in Jinzhou, 106/2477. This river was probably near modern Linfen. If the archaeologists discussed in the previous chapter are correct, this may have been the Jin River for which the Western Zhou state was named. However, it is not discussed in earlier dynastic histories. The explanation that Xuanweng Mountain is also called Dragon Mountain solves part of the inconsistency between the *Shanhaijing* and the *Hanshu* accounts, but the location of Dragon Mountain northwest of Jinyang is still a problem. Later texts regard this as a simple mistake; see the *SJZ* account in Chapter 4.

31. See Goldin, "On the Meaning."

32. Kai-wing Chow, *The Rise of Confucian Ritualism*, translates *ci* as "hall" in the context of *citang* or *dazongci* as "ancestral/lineage hall" and *miao* in the context of *jiamiao* as "ancestral shrine or temple." Wu Hung, *The Wu Liang Shrine*, translates *ci* as "shrine." Susan Naquin, *Peking: Temples and City Life*, acknowledges the plethora of names for ritual buildings as well as their frequent reuse for different types of divinities and dispenses with the issue by rendering them all as "temple." Working on twentieth-century Chinese religion, Jing Jun, *The Temple of Memories*, 23–24, believes that *ci* are buildings erected in honor of great men, *citang* are buildings erected for ancestors, and *miao* are temples dedicated to popular medicine gods, fertility goddesses, flood-control deities, and other divinities, including Confucius. He, too, renders the names of other ritual complexes such as *si* and *guan* as "temple"; see 185*n*8. My thanks to John Janusek for directing me to this source.

33. *Zhongwen dacidian*, 25216.

34. Ibid., 25182.

35. Ibid., entry on Vernal Sacrifice (*chunji*), 14146.427. This entry also describes the Zhou-

dynasty change of naming practice for seasonal sacrifices, whereby *ci* was used to describe the Vernal Sacrifice.

36. *Shangshu*, 8/113; Legge notes that although *ci* here means "to sacrifice," the regular Vernal Sacrifice to which *ci* usually refers is not apparent in the present version of the text; see Legge, *The Chinese Classics*, vol. 3, 191–92.

37. *Zhongwen dacidian*, 25211.

38. Ibid., 25216.17 and 25216.26.

39. Ibid., 9691; and *Erya*, 5/75.

40. *Zhongwen dacidian*, 9691 (for *miao*) and 59565.430 (for *taimiao*). The Taimiao was said to be the name of the ancestral temple for the Duke of Zhou; see *Chunqiu Gongyang zhuan*, Wengong 14/177.

41. Ebrey, *Chu Hsi's Family Rituals*, 6n9. Ebrey notes that though Cheng Yi opposed using images in ancestral rites, he still used this term. This was probably simply the word for the home offering hall, regardless of what type of object was used to stand in for the deceased.

42. *Zhongwen dacidian*, 14210. The character *jin* came to refer to all of Shanxi province and is still used to refer to Shanxi on auto license plates (as well as in other contexts) today.

43. Goldin, "On the Meaning," 84*n*13.

44. Ibid., 84–85.

45. Schafer, *The Divine Woman*, 46. I would like to thank Chang Che-chia for pointing out some problems with the evidence given in this work. The Chang Jiang deity was a *gong* (duke) and not a *wang* at the time Zhang Yue was writing, and it is clear that the *wang* in this text refers to the ruler of the land. However, this does not fundamentally change the nature of Schafer's argument. The title *gong* also implies male gender. For the text in question, see Dong, *Quan Tang wen*, 233/10b. For the title of the Chang Jiang deity during the Tang dynasty, see Wang Pu, *Tang huiyao*, 47/834.

46. Schafer, *The Divine Woman*, 53–55. For the title of the Luo River Goddess during the Tang dynasty, see Liu Xu, *Jiu Tangshu*, 24/925.

47. The connection between water, fertility/fecundity, and female divinities has been well studied; see Stein, *The World in Miniature*. Here I have translated *thanh-mâu* (Chinese *shengmu*) as "sage mother" rather than Stein's "holy mother" for consistency. For a further discussion of femininity, fertility, and its relationship to Jinci, see Peng, *Jinci wenwu*, 46–48.

48. Lin Huiyin and Liang Sicheng note in their documentation of the Water Spirit Temple at Guangsheng Monastery that where there is water, there is a Dragon King and consequently a Dragon King Temple; see "Jin-Fen gujianzhu," 53. For the Guangrenwang Temple at Ruicheng, see Jiu Guanwu, "Wulongmiao," 43–44.

Chapter 3

1. As stated in the previous chapter, this is the primary reason that Jinci and the town to the north of it, Jinyang, have been considered the first Jin fief. If one disregards Jinyang as a possible first fief, there is no source for the name of the Jin state. Many theories have been proposed, none of which can be substantiated. For a bibliography and discussion of the possible meanings of Jin, see Ma Jiandong, "Jin wenhua kao lüe," 56–62.

2. The translation of these titles follows Nienhauser et al., trans., *The Grand Scribe's Record*, vol. 1, 65.

3. The earliest source for this history is the *Zuozhuan*, where the tale is recounted in the commentary on the first year of the Duke of Zhao (Zhao gong). This should be the 4th year of Jingwang, i.e., 541 BCE.

4. Gao Xin was named Ku 嚳 and was the great-grandson of the Yellow Emperor; see Sima Tan and Sima Qian, *Shiji*, 1/12.

5. Legge notes that this is the star Da Huo 大火; see the *Zuozhuan* commentary for Duke Xiang, 9th year, Legge, *The Chinese Classics*, vol. 5, 437.

6. In the *Shiji* it is King Wu who has the dream, and Heaven (*tian* 天), rather than the Thearch, names the child; see Sima Tan and Sima Qian, *Shiji*, 39/1635.

7. Translation follows Legge, *The Chinese Classics*, vol. 5, 580, with minor modifications. See also the *Chunqiu Zuozhuan*, 41/705; and Ban Gu, *Hanshu*, 28 (*xia*)/1648–49.

8. Translation follows Legge, *The Chinese Classics*, vol. 5, 580 (paragraph after note above), with minor modifications. See also the *Chunqiu Zuozhuan*, 41/706.

9. In the next paragraph of this passage, Gongsun Qiao of Zheng rejects the conclusions of the Jin state

diviners on the basis that nature spirits do not attack the health of rulers. Rather, the "spirits of the hills and streams are sacrificed to in times of flood, drought, and pestilence. The spirits of sun, moon, and stars are sacrificed to on the unseasonable occurrence of snow, hoarfrost, wind, or rain." Legge, *The Chinese Classics*, vol. 5, 580.

10. *Sterculia platanifolia*.

11. In the Du Yu (222–84) commentary of the *Zuozhuan*, Duke Xiang, 4th year, the *gong* 工 are referred to as being the musicians; see *Chunqiu Zuozhuan*, 32/563.

12. Lü Buwei, *Lüshi chunqiu*, 1158. The story is also included in the *Shiji*, where Shichi 史佚 rather than the Duke of Zhou reprimands King Cheng. This implies a separate source for the story from the *Lüshi chunqiu*; see Sima Tan and Sima Qian, *Shiji*, 39/1635.

13. He was also known simply as Tang Shu (*Shangshu* 13/196; Legge, vol. 3, 146; and Sima Tan and Sima Qian, *Shiji*, 33/1518) or Jin Tang Shu 晋唐叔 (Sima Tan and Sima Qian, *Shiji*, 4/132).

14. Liu Zongyuan, "Tongye fengdi bian," reprinted in *SXTZ*, 206/1a.

15. Although perhaps the least believable, this story frequently appears in discussions of Shu Yu of Tang. The story appears with reference to Jinci beginning from Li Daoyuan's mention of the shrine in the sixth-century *Shuijingzhu*. However, Liu Dapeng excludes the story in his brief history of Shu Yu of Tang in the *JCZ*, 19–20. Popular tradition at the site continues to include this anecdote, and there are presently four plaques (three from the nineteenth century and one undated) at Jinci that incorporate this legend into four-character phrases; see Guo Yuanzhou and Guo Sujie, *Jinci mingbian*, 14–22.

16. According to the commentary by Du Yu of the *Chunqiu Zuozhuan*, 54/949, Mi Xu is the name of a state.

17. The Legge translation for this sentence reads: "The old capital of Xia was assigned as the center of his state."

18. I have omitted the first two: the son of the Duke of Zhou (named Bo Qin in the Du Yu commentary, 54/13a [947]), who was enfeoffed in Lu and took the place of his father as the first Zhou ruler of the area, and the ninth son of King Wen, the younger brother of King Wu and the Duke of Zhou, Kang Shu. He was made ruler of Wei, which was located by Sima Qian between the Yellow and Qi Rivers (south of modern Anyang); see Sima Qian, *Shiji*, 37/1589.

19. Legge, *The Chinese Classics*, vol. 5, 750 and 754.

20. They are now believed to have been written during the fourth century CE; see Shaughnessy, "Shang shu," 376–89.

21. The Legge translation reads: "The chief of Yue Chang appeared to do homage."

22. Legge, *The Chinese Classics*, vol. 3, 146. Zhou Gong Dan is also known as Zhou Wen Gong; see Zuo Qiuming, *Guoyu*, 2n6.

23. *Shangshu*, 13 (Weizi zhiming)/196. My interpretation follows the Han-dynasty Kong Anguo commentary appended to this edition of the text.

24. *Shangshu*, 13 (Weizi zhiming)/196.

25. Karlgren, "Grammata Serica Recensa," 23.

26. A discussion of the symbolism of this type of grain appears in Fang Xuanling, *Jinshu*, 29/209.

27. For example, this story is alluded to in Zhao Changyan's "Xinxiu Jinci beiming bingxu" of 984; see Gao Ruxing, *Taiyuan xianzhi*, 5/11b; and *JCZ*, 260.

28. For information on the location of the Rong (and Di) peoples living in Shanxi during the Shang and Zhou periods, see Průšek, *Chinese Statelets*; and Pulleyblank, "The Chinese and Their Neighbors," 411–66.

29. Jay Xu notes that the Western Zhou-period Jin cemetery discussed below is surprisingly mainstream Zhou in its artistic style and use of ceremonial bronzes, in contrast to the high Jin style of the sixth and fifth centuries BCE that incorporated influences from the northern steppe. It is possible, then, that the *Zuozhuan* was providing an anachronistic view of early Jin culture as being strongly influenced by the non-Zhou; see Jay Xu, "The Cemetery," 222.

30. Archaeologists concerned about this question have investigated eight areas thought to be capitals (not necessarily the first) of the Jin: (1) Jinyang, (2) Gu Jiangdu 古绛都, (3) Beijiang gucheng 北绛古城, (4) Gu Yicheng 古翼城, (5) Gu Tangcheng 古唐城, (6) Gu Jiangcheng 古绛城, (7) Yongning dongbao 永凝東堡, and (8) Gu Anyicheng 古安邑城. Of these, only Gu Yicheng and Yongning dongbao revealed any early Jin ruins; see Zou et al., "Jin, Yu, E," 11. See below for further discussion of the archaeology of the Hedong region.

31. The best example of the kinds of multiple interpretations possible is the *Guadizhi* by Xiao Deyan, Gu Yin, et al. Although the text was lost, it was heavily quoted in Zhang Shoujie's *Shiji zhengyi*. In the commentary of chapter 39 of the *Shiji*, "Jinshijia" 晉世家, 9, the *Guadizhi* is cited as stating that the ancient walled city of Tang is located twenty *li* west of Yicheng, and in the next section it is cited as stating that the ancient walled city of Tang is located two *li* north of Jinyang; see Sima Tan and Sima Qian, *Shiji*, 39/1636.

32. Zhang Youchun, "Tang Shuyu shifeng," 78–79.

33. Zhang Shoujie's commentaries and notes from the *Guadizhi* are found in Sima Tan and Sima Qian, *Shiji*, 39/1636. Archaeologists working on this question (e.g., Zou) cite *juan* 31, "Hedong Shanxi," of Gu Yanwu's *Rizhilu*. Although I have not found the "Analysis of Tang and Jin," the arguments in question can be found in several essays in *Rizhilu*, including "Dayuan" 大原, 15–16; "Hedong Shanxi" 河東山西, 31–32; "Jinguo" 晉國, 57–58; "Ji" 箕, 59; "Tang" 唐, 59–60; "Jindu" 晉都, 60–61; and "Taiyuan" 太原, 64–65.

34. The name Jinyang indicates that the original city was located north of the Jin River because the north side of a river is the solar (*yang*) side. The earliest reference to the Jin River, the *Shanhaijing*, describes it as originating from Xuanweng Mountain and flowing eastward into the Fen. As it is unlikely that the Fen could have changed its course to the other side of Xuanweng Mountain, it seems reasonable to believe that Jinyang should have originally been located to the west of the Fen River. For more detail on the location of the Jin River, see below. Additional support for this argument can be derived from the *Zuozhuan* passage quoted above, which states that Tai Tai drained the marshes of the Fen and the Tao Rivers. The Tao River has been located southwest of modern Quwo, as can be seen in Fig. 3.4.

35. Ban Gu, *Hanshu*, 28 *xia*/1648–1649.

36. Zheng Xuan, *Maoshipu*, *Tangguo*, 809/33a.

37. *Zuozhuan*, 41/705.

38. *SJZ*, 6/28b.

39. Although I have been unable to find an exact match for this title, in *Shi jizhuan*, 6/1a, Zhu Xi states that the original fief of Tang should be near Taiyuan in his day, which would have been modern Taiyuan.

40. This is probably a reference to Yan Ruoqu's *Sishu shidi xu*. Yan gives his opinion about the location of Tang near Jinyang (or at least that Jinyang was the origin of the Jin state) in his essay on Yi Jiang contained within this work, 1/51b–52a.

41. Ban Gu, *Hanshu*, 28 *xia*/1649; and Zheng Xuan, *Maoshipu*, *Tangguo*, 809/33a.

42. The tradition of Xie Fu moving to the Jin riverside is repeated in Zhang Shoujie's *Zhengyi*; see Sima Qian, *Shiji*, 39/1636 (he cites Xu Cai's *Zongguo duchengji*). Yu's three capitals of Pingyang, Anyi, and Jinyang are given in the "Diwangshiji" 帝王世紀 by Huangfu Mi 皇甫謐 (Jin dynasty 265–420), which is also recorded in the notes of the *Shiji*. Li Mengcun and Chang Jincang (1983), 97, point out that the tradition of Xie Fu moving the capital to Jinyang, and of Jinyang becoming the namesake for the state of Jin, has no pre-Han precedent.

43. The *Book of Documents* and the *Book of Odes* are both considered Western Zhou sources, at least in part. However, the context of their creation and the accuracy of their transmission are debatable; see Shaughnessy, "*Shang shu*," 377–79, and Loewe, "*Shi ching*," 415–16.

44. Artifacts in this region are thought to be in a very provincial style; see Keightley, "The Late Shang State," 535, quoting Bagley, "P'an-lung-ch'eng," 211–12.

45. Shim, "The Early Development," 40–47, uses this to support his argument that multiple non-Shang groups lived in the Jinnan basin during the Shang, but by the eve of the Zhou conquest Shang had recovered hegemony over the area. For a slightly different view on whether the Shang occupied this location until the Zhou conquest, see Keightley, "The Late Shang State," 540. For information on the occupation of this area by the Di, see Průšek, *Chinese Statelets*, 211.

46. Information on the breakdown of archaeological regions comes from Shim, "The Early Development," 19–23.

47. Both Jaroslav Průšek and Jae-hoon Shim agree that the term "Rong" was used in the Western Zhou to mean the "other belligerent group"; see Průšek, *Chinese Statelets*, 210–11; and Shim, "The Early Development," 47–50. The origin of the textual association of the Rong with the place-name Taiyuan and the possible locations of that place are discussed in Průšek,

Chinese Statelets, 73–75. Průšek, *Chinese Statelets*, 210–211, distinguishes the Di as a separate non-Rong or non-"barbarian" peoples interacting with other "statelets" in the area. However, Pulleyblank, "The Chinese and Their Neighbors," 419, argues that the Rong is a broad name of which the Di are a part.

48. The eight sites investigated are given in note 30 above. For an argument showing how the Jin River was named after the state, see Zou, "Jin shifengdi kao," 216.

49. Shaughnessy, "Historical Geography," 18. Shaughnessy was most likely following Qi Sihe's principles laid out in 1946; see Průšek, *Chinese Statelets*, 25.

50. Xie et al., "Jinyang gucheng," 55–58. Because of the location of the city on the banks of the Fen River, Xie et al. also speculated that the eastern portion of the city would have been destroyed over the centuries by the movements of the river (58). From 1979 to 1981, the Shang-Zhou archaeology group from Peking University explored several sites thought to be Shang and Zhou centers in Shanxi, Henan, and Hubei, but their attention was focused on the central Fen River valley from Hongtong to Houma. No excavation of areas north of Hongtong was undertaken at that time (Zou et al., "Jin, Yu, E," 1 and 11). A brief discussion of the failed attempts to find early Shang or Zhou material at Jinyang can be found in Zou, "Jin shifengdi kao," 216–17.

51. See *YHJXTZ*, 13/366; and Gao Ruxing, *Taiyuan xianzhi*, "Jincizhitu," 322.

52. Zou et al., "Jin, Yu, E," 11; and Zhang Han, "Yicheng Quwo," 216. A Li Jinwangmu is discussed in Yi Gou's stele inscription of the 1267 Jinci site; see *JCZ*, 248–51. This may have been a tomb of one of the tenth-century Shatuo Türk rulers (such as Li Keyong, 856–908), who were surnamed Li and based in Taiyuan; see below.

53. Zou et al., "Jin, Yu, E," 1; and Zhang Han et al., "Yicheng Quwo," 124–27.

54. Zhang Han et al., "Yicheng Quwo," 127 and 221. Jay Xu, "The Cemetery," 193*n*2, states that the only site larger than this one is Zhouyuan 周原.

55. Zhang Han et al., "Yicheng Quwo," 221. The chronology of the Tianma-Qucun site is still under debate; see Jay Xu, "The Cemetery," 195–99.

56. Sun Hua et al., "Tianma-Qucun yizhi," 4; Zou, "Lun zaoqi Jindu," 29; and Jay Xu, "The Cemetery," 194.

57. Additionally, several smaller Han tombs were found in the area; see Jay Xu, "The Cemetery," 194 and note 9, on the same page. The 1994 report of the second excavation indicates that more than six hundred Western Zhou tombs had been excavated in the Tianma/Qucun area over the previous decade; see Sun Hua et al., "Tianma-Qucun yizhi," 4.

58. Liu Xu et al., "Tianma-Qucun yizhi J6, J7 qu," 29–36.

59. Ibid., 36. Jay Xu also notes that the early Jin culture represented by the objects found in this excavation is much more closely related to mainstream Zhou material than the more unorthodox material of the Jin during the height of their power in the sixth-fifth centuries BCE; see Jay Xu, "The Cemetery," 222.

60. The *Zuozhuan* and *Shiji* use the character 知 rather than 智; see *Zuozhuan*, Duke Ai, 27th year; and Sima Qian, *Shiji*, 43/1794–95 and 44/1855. According to the *Shiji suoyin*, he was originally surnamed Xun 荀 and was thus also called Xun Yao; see Sima Tan and Sima Qian, *Shiji*, 44/1838.

61. J. I. Crump summarizes the debate over the historicity of the *Zhanguoce* and discusses the extent to which the text is fiction in the introduction of the second edition of his translation, *Chan-kuo tse*, 23–53. However, much of the story related above also appears in the *Shiji*, and Crump himself acknowledges the importance of this work in the cultural history of China. This story as told in the *Zhanguoce* was considered to be historical from before the Han period and has been integrated into the textual history of the Jin Shrines with its mention in Li Daoyuan, *SJZ*, 3/12b. Moreover, the story occurs in eleven passages, and Jinyang is mentioned as the besieged city in eight of those (the only passages that name the city); the Jin River is the river used to flood the city in the two accounts that name the river.

62. The date follows Sima Qian's version of the story in *Shiji*, 43/1794–95.

63. According the *Zhanguoce*, the request for territory was for Cai's Gaolang 蔡皋狼; see Crump, *Chan-kuo tse*, 273.

64. In Sima Qian, *Shiji*, 43/1794–95, the Fen River is used to flood Jinyang. When the story is

retold in 44/1855 (Prince Anli of Wei, 11 or 266 BCE) of this text, the Jin River is the source of the floodwater.

65. It was the Zhao capital until Marquis Cheng of Zhao 趙成侯 moved to Handan 邯鄲, *YHJXTZ*, 13/360. In the *Zhanguoce*, Jinyang was considered the residence of Zhao Xiangzi's father, Jianzi 簡子 and continued to be a Zhao capital after the Earl of Zhi was defeated; see Crump, *Chan-kuo tse*, 274 and 278.

66. *YHJXTZ*, 13/360.

67. According to the *YHJXTZ*, 13/359, the legendary ruler Shun distinguished the plain north of Jizhou 冀州 as Bingzhou, which was then subsumed under Jizhou when Yu the Great established his Nine Prefectures (*Jiuzhou* 九州). Bingzhou was then reestablished as one of the Nine Prefectures of the Zhou.

68. Ban Gu, *Hanshu*, 28/1551; and Fan Ye, *Hou Hanshu*, 23/3523.

69. Graff, *Medieval Chinese Warfare*, 101–2.

70. Wang Zhenfang, "Lun Taiyuan," 53–55. Many thanks to David Graff for directing me to this source.

71. Ibid., 56–57.

72. *YHJXTZ*, 13/363; and Gao Ruxing, *Taiyuan xianzhi*, 1/1a–b.

73. Graff, *Medieval Chinese Warfare*, 165.

747. Wechsler, "The Founding of the T'ang," 156 and 160.

75. *YHJXTZ*, 13/363–65.

76. *TPHYJ*, 40/4b, and *YHJXTZ*, 13/361, both say 690 for this change—but there is some dispute in the sources, where 692 is also given; see *YHJXTZ*, 13/385 ff. 10.

77. *TPHYJ*, 40/9a, the source describes a single walled city, but the location of the city vis-à-vis the Fen River is not stated explicitly here.

78. Mote, *Imperial China*, 12–13.

79. Ibid., 13.

80. Ibid.

81. Xue, *Jiu Wudaishi*, 79/1044–45.

82. Ke Fou and Qing Jing, *Jinyang Haojie*, 109.

83. Mote, *Imperial China*, 13 and 66–67; Ke Fou and Qing Jing, *Jinyang Haojie*, 110; Ouyang, *Xin Wudaishi*, 10/101–2; Ouyang, *Historical Records*, 94; and Xue, *Jiu Wudaishi*, 100/1332.

84. Ke Fou and Qing Jing, *Jinyang Haojie*, 112, and Mote, *Imperial China*, 16. Liu Chong later took the name Liu Min 劉旻; see Ouyang, *Xin Wudaishi*, 70/863; and Ouyang, *Historical Records*, 593.

85. Lorge, "War in the Creation of the Northern Song," 171–74; and Gao Ruxing, *Taiyuan xianzhi*, 1/1b.

86. Lorge, "War in the Creation of the Northern Song," 209–11; and *XCB*, 12/453.

87. Gao Ruxing, *Taiyuan xianzhi*, 1/2a; *TPHYJ*, 40/9a–11b. In the *TPHYJ*, the new city was established north rather than northeast of the old city walls. Within this city were the Pingjin county government and the Destroyed Taiyuan county (Fei Taiyuanxian 廢太原縣) government. The Bingzhou prefectural government was established at Sanjiaozhai/sai 三交寨/塞 on the border of Yangqu county (40/4b). Gao Ruxing cites a Lü Huiqing 呂惠卿 (1032–1111) stele inscription stating that the Bingzhou government was established at Yuci after the destruction of the city of Taiyuan. This is consistent with the account in Tuotuo, *Songshi* 86/2131. The prefectural capital was first moved to Yuci in 979, and then transferred to Sanjiaozhai (*zhai* 寨 in the *XCB*, *sai* 塞 in the *TPHYJ*) in Yangqu county in the second month of 982; see *XCB*, 20/453 and 23/514. For the distance of Pingjinxian to the new county seat, see Gu Yanwu, *Rizhilu*, 614–15.

88. Taiyuan fell to the Jin in the ninth month of the first year of the Jingkang reign period (1126–27); see *XCB shibu* 46/25a–27a, and Lin Ruihan, *Songdai zhengzhi shi*, 306.

89. Gao Ruxing, *Taiyuan xianzhi*, 1/2a.

90. Dreyer, *Early Ming China*, 71; and Gao Ruxing, *Taiyuan xianzhi*, 1/2a–b.

Chapter 4

1. In 569, under the Northern Qi, Jinci was renamed Da Chonghuangsi 大崇皇寺, suggesting that it was a Buddhist institution at this time; I discuss this below.

2. For evidence that Chengzhou was the dynastic capital of the Zhou, see Wu, *Monumentality*, 298, n. 19.

3. *Chunqiu Zuozhuan* Duke He, 24th year. Legge, *The Chinese Classics*, vol. 5, 189 and 192. Terms for the descendents of each ruler are different. For King Wen, they are *zhao* 昭, King Wu *mu* 穆, and the Duke of Zhou *yin* 胤, though they are named individually in the text.

4. See *Kaogongji*, *Zhouli*, 41/642. For more on the decline of the lineage temple system during the Eastern Zhou and its possible impact on the arts, see Wu, "From Temple to Tomb"; and idem, *Monumentality*, 77–142.

5. Wu, *Monumentality*, 88–90.

6. K. C. Chang uses Zhou dynasty ritual texts as a means of understanding Shang dynasty-building practice as well. To what extent the Shang was the model for the Zhou is still unknown, but some degree of continuity between the building techniques of the two dynasties/cultures does exist, particularly in the realm of materials used (e.g., tamped or pounded earth for walls) and the cardinal orientation of walled building compounds and cities, specifically at Erlitou and Panlongcheng; see K. C. Chang, *Shang Civilization*, 158–63. However, since the importance of the Zhou dynasty as a source for legitimacy is of primary significance to Jinci, I am focusing on the established Zhou-dynasty practice.

7. *Maoshi*, 16–2/548. Translation follows Legge, *The Chinese Classics*, vol. 4, 439–40.

8. Wu Hung suggests that the gates described in this passage led to the ancestral temple, whereas Legge states that this section of the hymn described the building of the palace, with the implication that it was a separate complex; see Legge, *The Chinese Classics*, vol. 4, 440; and Wu, *Monumentality*, 87–88.

9. For more on the Fengchu palace-temple, including a discussion of the debate about its function, see Thorp, "Origins of Chinese Architectural Style," 26–31. Builders probably determined north by bisecting an angle made by marking the shadow of the rising and setting sun on the arc of a circle, in a manner similar to that described in the *Kaogongji* (see 41/642). Because modern archaeologists use the magnetic compass to determine orientation, the ten-degree variation is likely due to magnetic declination.

10. By the Northern-Southern Dynasties period, a larger ritual hall in front with a smaller private hall or vestry in the rear (*qianmiao houqin*) was considered to be ancient practice for ancestral temples (*zongmiao*). They were constructed in this fashion to copy the residences of the living where the audience hall would be in front with a sleeping/dressing chamber in the rear (*qianchao houqin*); see Shen Yue, *Songshu*, 16/445. This was the model followed by Ma Duanlin in his diagram of the temple system published in *Wenxian tongkao*, 91/827.

11. Discussion in the dynastic histories tends to focus on the number of individual buildings within the temple compound (five, seven, or nine temples) rather than on the specifics of the temples themselves. The southern orientation and enclosing wall were included in each of these temples. I will describe this below.

12. Ma Duanlin, *Wenxian tongkao*, 91/ 826–27.

13. Duan, *Zhongguo simiao*, 155–59; Bai Zuomin and Shao Junyi, eds., *Tanmiao jianzhu*, 13–14.

14. For example, a temple to the Song-dynasty hero Yue Fei was established in the Southern Song capital of Lin'an (modern Hangzhou, Zhejiang, province) to honor his defense of the Song dynasty when it was under attack by the Jin, even though his ancestral home was in Henan province.

15. See the stele inscription by Yi Gou, reprinted in the *JCZ*, 248–51, where he describes the ruined building complex and his regret in not being able to return it to its previously magnificent scale.

16. Not all official ritual structures were located within the capital city. Important rites and their ritual structures—such as altars to the sacred peaks or marchmounts, the altar and temple to the Earth Queen at Fenyin, or the Mingtang (variously translated as the Bright Hall or Hall of Holiness)—were located outside city walls from at least the Qin dynasty and most likely earlier. Han Wudi and his ritual experts built a Mingtang (the association of this structure with Zhou ancestral worship is documented in the *Kaogongji*) at the foot of Mt. Tai. Additionally, a ritual structure called a Biyong existed in the suburbs of Western Han Chang'an; see Loewe, *Chinese Ideas of Life and Death*, 131–136, and "The Religious and Intellectual Background," 663–65. During Wang Mang's rule (9–23 CE), he had a Mingtang built in the southern suburbs of Chang'an; see Wu, *Monumentality*, 176–87.

17. Zi Xia was a disciple of Confucius also known as Bu Shang (507–420 BCE).

18. Translation of this section is from Legge, *The Chinese Classics*, vol. 4, 55.

19. *SJZ*, 6/28a–29a.

20. The *Zuozhuan* original uses *zhu* 諸 rather than *zhi* 之 in this position; see Legge, vol. 5, 573.

Han; see Huang (1995), 148; and Ono and Hibino, *Godaisan*, 70–71.

39. See drawings of *diantang* structure in *YZFS*, *juan* 31, drawings 11–14. Qi Yingtao, "Jinci Shengmudian yanjiu," 57, describes this building in *YZFS*-like terms, but there is no entry specifically on *diantang* in the building manual. Research on this, and on the *tingtang* 廳堂 system found more commonly in smaller structures with relatively smaller timbers and bracket sets, relies heavily on drawings found in *juan* 31, which are labeled using those terms, in conjunction with size distinctions made for the two types found in the descriptions of individual timber members, e.g., *YZFS*, 5/4a. As both Chen Mingda, *Yingzao fashi damuzuo yanjiu*, 118–25, and Jiang Jianyun, "Qian tan diantang yu tingtang," 38, have observed of the drawings, the interior and peripheral columns are "without exception" the same height (quoting Chen, 119). This is perhaps the most easily discernible feature of the *diantang* structure found in the drawings and differs from the *tingtang*, where interior columns are taller than eaves columns. The structure of the *diantang* hall can thus be divided into three layers: the columns, bracketing system, and roof, thereby facilitating the installation of ceiling panels evenly across the whole interior ceiling.

40. In the transmission of the *YZFS*, the drawings were altered substantially (particularly in the detailed areas of bracketing) because they were copied by people unfamiliar with the details of the buildings; see Glahn, "Unfolding the Chinese Building Standards," 51. They are still useful, however, as the basic massing and columnation of extant Song-period buildings are very similar to what we find in the drawings.

41. One other example is the Moni Hall of Longxingsi in Zhengding, Hebei, mentioned above.

42. Column elimination is considered to be a characteristic of large-scale timber frame buildings from the mid-eleventh through the thirteenth centuries; see Qi Yingtao, "Zenyang jianding gujianzhu," 28–29.

43. According to Chai Zejun, inscriptions with a Song Xuanhe 2nd year (1120) date and a Yuan Zhiyuan 4th year (1267) date were found on a back door frame that was later filled in; see Chai et al., *Taiyuan Jinci Shengmudian*, 11. The present window is visible only from the outside.

44. Peng Hai, "Jinci Shengmudian kance shouhuo," 71.

45. This is the term used in the *YZFS* section on the use of columns; see *YZFS*, 5/4b. The characters 升起 are also used for this meaning. Compare the entries in Wang Xiaoqing, *Gujianzhu shuyu cidian*, 113; and Lü Songyun and Liu Shizhong, *Gudai jianzhu cidian*, 101.

46. This measurement comes from Qi, "Jinci Shengmudian yanjiu."

47. Peng Hai's measurements, "Jinci Shengmudian kance shouhuo," 72, are ambiguous here. I can find no façade on this building that has four "eaves" columns.

48. In *juan* 5 of the *YZFS*, two methods of making a *suozhu* are described. The first one is *gongjuansha* 栱卷殺, the second is called *fupenyang* 覆盆樣; see *YZFS*, 5/4b–5a. According to Qi, "Jinci Shengmudian yanjiu," 58, the style of *juansha* used on the Sage Mother Hall's columns is the *fupenyang*.

49. According to *YZFS*, the degree to which the columns lean should vary according to the façade on which they appear; see *YZFS*, 5/5a.

50. The *pupaifang* is mentioned in the *YZFS*, 4/11a, in the section on balconies (*pingzuo* 平坐). The characters used are the ones I have used above. However, in modern Chinese architectural dictionaries, the characters *pubofang* 普柏枋 are used. This is probably a correction of textual transmission errors.

51. *YZFS*, 4/4b–5a.

52. Ibid.

53. Liang et al., *Yingzao fashi zhushi*, 107–9.

54. Buildings with lute-faced/split-bamboo descending cantilever tips appear in the tenth century, however, at least from extant examples, this only became popular at the end of the eleventh century. Examples include: the Youxiansi Front Hall 游仙寺前殿 (990–95), Gaoping; the Daxiongbao (Mahāvīra) Hall of Kaihuasi 開化寺大雄寶殿 (1073/1092–96), Gaoping; the Shijia (Śākyamuni) Hall of Qingliansi 青蓮寺釋迦殿 (1076–1102), Jincheng; the Three Sages Hall of Hongfusi 洪福寺三聖殿 (ca. 1096), Dingxiang; and the Daxiongbao Hall of Longmensi 龍門寺大雄寶殿 (1098), Pingshun; see Miller, "Constructing Religion," 67–160.

55. For the date of this building, I am following the *Zhongguo mingsheng cidian*, 169, where it is placed between the 1st year of the Song Daguan reign

period and the 7th year of the Zhenghe reign period. In this entry, the complex is called Erxianguan (二仙觀) rather than Erxianmiao. However, stele inscriptions at the site refer to it as a *miao* rather than a *guan*. I have yet to find a historical source where temples to the Two Transcendents in this area are called *guan*, and I have therefore kept with *miao* in this work.

56. For a detailed analysis of the structure of the Sage Mother Hall with respect to other buildings in southern Shanxi province from the tenth through the twelfth centuries, see Miller, "Constructing Religion," 34–167. Although a complete survey of Southern Shanxi Jin-Yuan-dynasty buildings is outside the scope of this book, two examples of this are the curved cantilever tips of the Heavenly Kings Hall (Tianwangdian 天王殿) of Pingshun's Longmensi 龍門寺 (Jin) (as opposed to the lute-faced/split-bamboo versions on the Daoxiongbao Hall of this complex) and, of course, the classic lute-faced descending cantilever tips of the 1325 Hall of the Three Pure Ones (Sanqingdian 三清殿) at Yonglegong, modern Ruicheng.

57. Liang, *Wenji*, vol. 1, 337.

58. Miller, "Water Sprites and Ancestor Spirits."

59. This complex is also called Yuanmiaoguan 元妙觀; see Lin Zhao, "Putian Yuanmiaoguan," 52–53. I follow his dating of the interior Song-period structure to a rebuilding that took place in the 8th year of the Dazhong xiangfu reign period (1015) and is documented with an inscription on the ridge pole in the central bay of the hall.

60. Two twelfth-century buildings in Southern Shanxi (i.e., south of Mt. Wutai) with column-top and intercolumnar bracket sets of the same style are the main halls of Bu'ersi 不二寺 in Yangqu (1195) and Taifuguan 太符觀 in Fenyang 汾陽 (1200).

61. These two features are also present on the Revolving Sūtra Repository (Zhuanluncang dian 轉輪藏殿; sometimes called a *ge* 閣 storied-pavilion because it is two stories in height) of Zhengding's Longxingsi, frequently dated with the Foxiang Storied-pavilion (Foxiangge 佛香閣; also called the Dabeige 大悲閣) to 971. However, the date of this building has not been firmly ascertained. Qi Yingtao suggested that the Sūtra Repository should be placed between the Shanmen (982–88) and the Moni Hall (1052); see Qi, "Jinci Shengmudian yanjiu," 155–56. Puay-peng Ho, "Monumental Innovation," 86, notes that an imperial donation of 1,000 cash for the ritual of the turning of the sūtra may have resulted in the hall's rebuilding during the eleventh or twelfth century. I would go further to suggest that the filled-heart *huagong* and lack of *mangong* 慢栱 date construction of this building as later than that of the Moni Hall.

62. The imperial metaphor used for the Chinese spirit world has been well documented by historians, religious historians, anthropologists, and art historians; examples include Hymes, *Way and Byway;* Katz, *Images of the Immortal;* Kleeman, *A God's Own Tale;* James Watson, "Standardizing the Gods"; and Julia Murray, "The Evolution of Pictorial Hagiography," to name only a few. Exceptions to non-imperial costume for representations of divinities often occurred, particularly in (non-native) Buddhism. However, even in this case, religious iconography was shared. For example, the Ten Kings of Hell, intrinsically tied to Buddhism, were rendered in Chinese official garb, reiterating the power of this belief in the Chinese realm; see Teiser, *The Scripture on the Ten Kings*; and Ledderose, *Ten-Thousand Things*, 163–85. Buddhist influence in representations of native Chinese divinities was also common; see Murray, "The Evolution of Pictorial Hagiography"; and Wu, "Buddhist Elements."

63. Gao Shoutian, "Jinci Shengmudian Song, Yuan tiji," 59. The inscription was discovered in March 1952.

64. McNair specifies that the double dragon was a symbol of the Song imperial house; see McNair, "On the Date of the Shengmudian Sculptures," 242. According to Eberhard, the dragon was considered a symbol of the emperor since the Han dynasty; see Eberhard, *A Dictionary of Chinese Symbols*, 83.

65. Loewe, "The Cult of the Dragon," 195.

66. Anning Jing, *The Water God's Temple*, 70–73. Amy McNair did not overlook the rain symbolism of the dragons but considered it to be secondary; see McNair, "On the Date of the Shengmudian Sculptures," 242.

67. Gao Shoutian, "Jinci Shengmudian Song, Yuan tiji," 59.

68. Peng et al., *Jinci wenwu*, 103.

69. Chai Zejun et al., *Taiyuan Jinci Shengmudian*, 13.

70. Chen Pao-chen, "*The Goddess of the Lo River*," 286.

71. According to Chen Pao-chen (ibid., 18), this is also similar to the iconography of late sixth- and early seventh-century representations of Xiwangmu. However, in Suzanne Cahill's study of this goddess, by the Tang dynasty, she was represented as a "Chinese aristocrat," in a manner consistent with high-status divinities in the Daoist pantheon. In Du Guangting's 杜光庭 (850–933) fullest description of the goddess (quoted in Cahill), her chariot is pulled by the mythical *qilin* 麒麟. His description became the standard for textual and pictorial representations of the goddess during the Tang dynasty; see Cahill, *Transcendence and Divine Passion*, 81–82.

72. Liu Yongde, *Jinci Fengguang*, 41, provides this estimate of the height of the sculpture. For a general description of the guardian sculpture and paintings on the front veranda of the Mingyingwang Hall, see Anning Jing, *The Water God's Temple*, 39.

73. Liu Yongde, *Jinci Fengguang*, 41, describes this as a battle-ax. It does not look like an ax at this point, however, and may have suffered damage in recent years. In images prior to the building's restoration, the weapon looks something like a Lucerne hammer or spear rather than an ax; see Chai et al., *Taiyuan Jinci Shengmudian*, 52, fig. 28.

74. Liu Yongde, *Jinci Fengguang*, 41, and Chai et al., *Taiyuan Jinci Shengmudian*, 53.

75. Liu Yongde, *Jinci Fengguang*, 41.

76. According to Bo Songnian, Door Gods (*menshen* 門神) are frequently depicted as generals in full armor and are then identified by cartouches located on the prints themselves rather than any other specific attribute. Consequently, they are impossible to identify positively from the image alone. The figures of *menshen* from the Song period and earlier were most commonly Shen Tu 神荼 and Yu Lei 鬱壘, spirit guardians of a ghost (or demon) gate mentioned in the *Shanhaijing*. But because of the influence of popular drama (particularly the *Journey to the West*) and the general lack of knowledge of those spirits, by the Yuan dynasty, the *menshen* were more often understood as the seventh-century generals Yuchi Jingde 尉遲敬德 (585–638) and Qin Qiong 秦瓊 (or Qin Shubao 叔寶 [d. 638]); see Bo, *Zhongguo menshen hua*, 10–11, 18–19, and 54–55; and Fong, "Wu Daozi's Legacy," 7–17.

77. Peng Hai, personal communication, August 1998.

78. Peng et al., *Jinci wenwu*, 103.

79. Two smaller statues placed on either side of the Sage Mother were added during the Ming dynasty; see Peng et al., *Jinci wenwu*, 82; Zhao Zhiguang et al., *Jinci Songsu*, 4, 40, 75–77; and Chai et al., *Taiyuan Jinci Shengmudian*, 53.

80. See Shen Congwen, *Zhongguo gudai fushi*, 318–19. McNair, "On the Date of the Shengmudian Sculptures," 251, also remarks on the verisimilitude of these figures, which are much livelier than those of the early twelfth century in the Jincheng Erxianmiao, discussed above. Yuan-dynasty sculpture of the Jincheng Yuhuangmiao takes this type of imagery to a new level with much more realistic postures and facial expressions; see Yang Boda, chief ed., *Yuan, Ming, Qing diaosu*, 9–10.

81. Chai, *Shanxi siguan bihua*, 131. Song paint was found around the doorframe of the original central-bay back door and around the edges of the walls. Additionally, Song-style floral motifs were found under a layer of whitewash on the wall space between the bracket sets on the south wall. These have been restored with the most recent restoration.

82. Chai et al., *Taiyuan Jinci Shengmudian*, 51–52.

83. Chai, *Shanxi siguan bihua*, 132.

84. For the interpretation as either twelve brook transcendents or twelve female officials, see Chai, *Shanxi siguan bihua*, 132 and 324. For the interpretation as a court tour of inspection, see Chai et al., *Taiyuan Jinci Shengmudian*, 55.

85. Chai et al., *Taiyuan Jinci Shengmudian*, 54–55.

86. Chai, *Shanxi siguan bihua*, 132. In the 1950s and 1960s, Yonglegong was moved from its original location in Yongji, near the Yellow River, to Ruicheng so that it would not be destroyed during a dam-building project; see Katz, *Images of the Immortal*, 1.

87. Guo Yuanzhou and Guo Sujian, *Jinci mingbian*, 13. They date the plaque based on the 1111 date of the promotion to Sage Mother of Manifest Aid, as well as on the plaque's style and the cloud patterns painted around the border.

88. Ledderose, *Ten-Thousand Things*, 180–81.

89. Ibid., 164–65.

90. This type of armor can also be seen on sculptures of bodhisattvas found in the Fogongsi

Śākyamuni Pagoda 佛宮寺釋迦塔 in Yingxian built under Liao rule in the second half of the eleventh century; see Chen Mingda, *Yingxian muta*, pl. 136. For images of similar forms in the military context, see Liu Yonghua, *Gudai junrong fushi*, 99–101.

91. This element appears to be an entirely cloth portion more typical of earlier *peijian* in the costume of Daoist goddesses such as Bixia yuanjun and the Earth Queen in later (sixteenth-century) representations; see Little et al., *Taoism and the Arts*, 276–80.

92. For more on these images, see Shi, chief ed., *Wudai, Song diaosu*, 30–31.

93. This site is said to be the only extant Daoist grotto-temple in China, founded by the Perfect Realization (Quanzhen 全眞) master Song Defang 宋德芳 in 1295; see Sun Dazhang and Yu Weiguo et al., eds., *Zongjiao jianzhu*, note to pl. 92.

94. Little et al., *Taoism and the Arts*, 183.

95. See Wu, "Buddhist Elements," 283; and idem, *Monumentality*, 137–42.

96. See Yang Boda, chief ed., *Yuan, Ming, Qing diaosu*, 11.

97. Feuchtwang, *Popular Religion in China*.

98. *JCZ*, 70–71; Song Naizhong et al., *Jinci lüyou*, 15–16.

99. Shi, chief ed., *Wudai, Song diaosu*, 35–36.

100. *JCZ*, 212.

101. Shi, chief ed., *Wudai, Song diaosu*, 36.

102. Knechtges, *Wen Xuan*, vol. 1, xx.

103. Ibid., vol. 1, 292, n. L 564, and vol. 2, 26–29.

104. Liang, *Wenji*, vol. 1, 338.

105. The idea of this being a cantilever bridge follows the understanding of the *feiliangdao* 飛梁道 built by Zhuge Liang 諸葛亮 into Shu, where beams were cantilevered out from the faces of cliffs to make an elevated road; see *Zhongwen dacidian*, 44974.134.

106. *JCZ*, 282. The tank traversed by the bridge may have served a more important function. In some of the rain rituals discussed by Loewe, frogs were released into pools at shrines dedicated to the spirit of the soil in the hope that their voices would help bring about rain; see Loewe, "The Cult of the Dragon," 208–9.

107. *JCZ*, 115.

108. Cahill, "Sex and the Supernatural," 200–201. In painting, the bridge motif can also have the meaning of salvation or releasing from sins; see Susan Shih-Shan Huang, "Summoning the Gods: Paintings of Three Officials of Heaven, Earth, and Water and Their Association with Daoist Ritual Performance in the Southern Song Period (1127–1279)," 41. Thanks to Francois Louis and Shen Hsueh-man for alerting me to this source.

109. *JCZ*, 70–71.

110. See Wang Shiren, "Ji Houtu," 276–77.

111. See *Taiping yulan*, 35/7a–b; Cohen, "Coercing the Rain Deities," 244; and Loewe, "The Cult of the Dragon," 199.

Chapter 7

1. The addition of the gatehouse to the east of the Sage Mother Hall would also have facilitated the *budao* 步禱 ritual of invoking rain, similar to that depicted in the wall paintings of the Water God's Temple of Guangsheng Monastery, in Hongtong, 175 kilometers (108 miles) south of Jinci. In this ritual, the official would walk from town to the temple as an act of humility; see Jing Anning, *The Water God's Temple*, 99–100. By allowing the official to enter through a gatehouse located across from the Sage Mother Hall, the importance of the water spirit may have been emphasized in a time of desperation for the entire population. As mentioned in Chapter 4, Zhang Yipeng speculates that the Jingqing Gatehouse known in the early twentieth century was this eastern gatehouse mentioned in Yi Gou's inscription. Liu Dapeng would have moved the "Jingqing" name plaque originally used on the Song-Jin period south gatehouse to the east gatehouse during the renovation of the complex in 1916; see Zhang, "Jinci wenwu bianzheng," 1099–100.

2. On the 1551 map of the site, there is a King of Jin tomb south of Fengsheng Monastery. This may have been the tomb repaired at this time; however, this structure would not have been located within the compound proper. It is therefore uncertain whether the additional temples mentioned in this section of the 1267 stele, such as the one to Tai Tai, would have been located within Jinci.

3. In his treatment of the Handan Rain Shrine, Kenneth Pomeranz discusses how the speed with which rain fell was considered a reflection of the virtue of the official making the prayer for rain. Although this may be the case here, it is not overtly expressed in the text of the inscription; see Pomeranz, "Water to Iron, Widows to Warlords," 65, 73–

74. I would like to thank Charlotte Furth for directing me to this source.

4. Wang Sicheng (Yuan), "Chongxiu Jinci miaoji" (1342), reprinted in *JCZ*, 262.

5. Ibid., 261–63.

6. Gaochang Xieyu (Yuan), "Chunri you Jinci shixu shike" (1345), reprinted in *JCZ*, 256.

7. *JCZ*, 265.

8. *Ming shilu*, 53/1b, translated by Taylor in "Official Religion in the Ming," 846–47.

9. Gao Ruxing, *Taiyuan xianzhi*, 1/10b–11a. The spirits of Jinci were not the only deities to be affected by this proclamation. The titles of the Spirit of Huo Mountain 霍山, south of Taiyuan, and the Spirit of the Salt Lake, near Yuncheng 運城 in southern Shanxi province, also had their titles stripped at this time; see Jing Anning, *The Water God's Temple*, 111; and *Zhongguo mingsheng cidian*, 187. Although we cannot always be certain that imperial edicts were enacted in the provinces, this one clearly was in Shanxi.

10. The reference to the Earl of Ge is from the *Shangshu*, 8/8a–b (111). Legge translates *xiang* 餉 as "provision carriers"; see Legge, *The Chinese Classics*, vol. 3, 180.

11. Mao Biao (Ming), "Chongxiu Jincimiao beiji," reprinted in *JCZ*, 273.

12. Chow, *The Rise of Confucian Ritualism*, 71.

13. Exams using Zhu Xi's interpretation of Confucianism were established and put into practice from 1313 to 1315; see Hsiao, "Mid-Yuan Politics," 516–17.

14. Brook, "Communications and Commerce," 694.

15. Chow, *The Rise of Confucian Ritualism*, 15–21.

16. Ibid., 1–21.

17. Duara, *Culture, Power, and the State*, 31.

18. Ibid., 32.

19. Ibid.

20. Ibid., 34–35.

21. Harrison, "Village Identity in Rural North China," 99.

22. Ebrey, *Confucianism and Family Rituals*, 6.

23. Ibid., 7.

24. Chow, *The Rise of Confucian Ritualism*, 75.

25. Shang, Rulin waishi *and Cultural Transformation*, 30–31.

26. Chow, *The Rise of Confucian Ritualism*, 100–103.

27. Ibid., 103–5.

28. Su You, "Chongxiu Tang Shu Yu ci ji," reprinted in *JCZ*, 17–18.

29. Chow, *The Rise of Confucian Ritualism*, 104–5.

30. Shang, Rulin waishi *and Cultural Transformation*, 74 and 233–37. Danfu was the grandfather of King Wen of Zhou; see Sima Qian, *Shiji*, 13/492.

31. Chow, *The Rise of Confucian Ritualism*, 207–9.

32. The north-south split extending from the spring is shown in the map of Jinci published in Gao Ruxing's 1551 *Taiyuan xianzhi*, 321, but the subdivision of the shares is not clearly rendered.

33. The measurement was the distance between the Jin Spring and Jinshengcun 金勝村 as the crow flies, according to the map published in Wang Huaibao, *Shanxisheng fenxian dituce*, 17. Dongrucun 董茹村, the northernmost point of the northern canal in the 1543 inscription, is located north of Jinshengcun in the Taiyuan county map published in Gao Ruxing, *Taiyuan xianzhi*, 321.

34. I have been unable to find a firm date for the origin of this system. Su Zhigao's stele inscription simply states that it has been in place for a long time (*zunxing yijiu* 遵行已久); see Su Zhigao, "Shenming shuili jili gongyi beiming" (1543), reprinted in *JCZ*, 795.

35. Ibid., 794–96.

36. Gao Ruxing, *Taiyuan xianzhi*, 1/23b.

37. "Shuili jili yiwenbei" (1589), reprinted in *JCZ*, 797–801.

38. Gao, *Taiyuan xianzhi*, 3/4b. Liu Tongfeng's name is a homophone for "enfeoffed with a paulownia branch" (*tongfeng*), which gives this person a connection with both the popular interpretation of the water goddess and Shu Yu of Tang.

39. Gao, *Taiyuan xianzhi*, 3/4b–5a, states that this legend likely arose from farm workers, old women, and children and was not to be repeated by the educated. Providing a local identity for the Jin Springs water goddess is similar to the identity of Princess Miao-shan, which was given to the bodhisattva Guanyin (Avalokiteśvara) from as early as 1100. More than just another case of euhemerism, as we may understand the interpretation of the water goddess as the historical Yi Jiang, the appearance of the white-clad equestrian in this story suggests that the

identity of Ms. Liu was developed in response to the increasing worship of Guanyin as a popular deity across the Ming dynasty; see Yu, *Kuan-yin*, 293–301.

40. Harrison, "Village Identity in Rural North China," 97.

41. Su You, "Chongxiu Tang Shu Yu ci ji," reprinted in *JCZ*, 17–18.

42. Gao Ruxing, *Taiyuan xianzhi*, 3/4b–5a. My translation of this differs from Harrison, "Village Identity in Rural North China," 97.

43. Gao Ruxing, "Chongxiu Jinci miao beiji" (1567), reprinted in *JCZ*, 282–83.

44. The Dressing Tower almost certainly became the "Water Mother Tower" in the late nineteenth century, after the Spirit of the Jin Springs was officially promoted to Water Mother of Extended Transformation (Fuhua shuimu 専化水母) in 1879; see Liu Yongde, *Jinci fengguang*, 49. There was no additional temple to the Spirit of the Jin Springs at the end of the Ming, though some suggested it to Yan Ruoqu in the latter half of the seventeenth century; see Yan Ruoqu, *Sishu shidi xu*, 52a. The Qianlong-period painting of the site seen in Fig. 7.5 also calls the hall a "dressing tower" (*shuzhuanglou* 梳粧樓).

45. Her seat is widely recognized as being from the traditional story, and the image is interpreted as being in the middle of dressing her hair; see *JCZ*, 17; Liu Yongde, *Jinci fengguang*, 48; and Peng et al., *Jinci wenwu*, 62. Peng also notes here that adding a dressing tower to a goddess temple was an established practice in the Shanxi area. No source I have seen discusses the integration of the lotus blossom into the iconography. This is presumably a carryover from Buddhism, perhaps indicating her divine status. I have also seen no independent dating of the statue; it is presumed to be original to the building.

46. Following the inscription on the *duiyue* plaque, Qi Yingtao, "Jinci Shengmudian yanjiu," 52, states that the Duiyue Memorial Gateway was repaired in the 4th year of the Wanli reign period (1576). Liu Dapeng records that the gateway was built in 1606 without discussing the earlier date of the plaque; see *JCZ*, 73. Because he records the bell and drum towers as being "first built" in 1606, he may mean that the gateway was "rebuilt" in 1606 with the plaque surviving from the initial construction. This plaque was placed on the east side of the gateway during the eighteenth century but was moved to the west side before 1826 when Yang Guotai and Yuan Peilan published their *Taiyuan xianzhi*; see *TYXZ*, drawings/16a. Song Naizhong transcribes the donors listed on the plaque: Taiyuan District Magistrate Gao Bingzhi 高秉直, County Aide Zhang Pengcheng 張鵬程, Instructor Liu Zhihe 劉致和, and Assistant Instructor Huang Qing 黄慶. See Song et al., *Jinci lüyou*, 19. Tradition has it that the characters were done by the local calligrapher Gao Yingyuan 高應元; see Liu Yongde, *Jinci fengguang*, 31; and *JCZ*, 7. A brief biography of Gao Yingyuan can be found in *TYXZ*, 10/36a–b.

47. "Qingmiao," *Maoshi*, 19/583. I would like to thank Song Naizhong for emphasizing this connection in an October 1997 conversation about the site. It is also discussed in Peng et al., *Jinci wenwu*, 105. The translation follows Legge, vol. 4, 568.

48. Pomeranz, "Water to Iron, Widows to Warlords," 73–74, also mentioned in note 3 to this chapter.

49. *JCZ*, 72–75.

50. Chow, *The Rise of Confucian Ritualism*, 44–45.

51. By the nineteenth century, this plaque had been moved to the west side of the gateway and replaced by a plaque reading "Fragrant Flow from Antiquity" (*wangu liufang* 萬古流芳); see *JCZ*, 73; rubbing from an engraved map of the site dated 1877, reproduced in Peng et al., *Jinci wenwu*, 1; and map of Jinci included in *TYXZ*, 39.

52. Three had been established by 1551; see Gao Ruxing, *Taiyuan xianzhi*, 2/27b–28a.

53. In 1551, two women in Taiyuan county had been honored in this way (Gao Ruxing, *Taiyuan xianzhi*, 2/28a); by the end of the dynasty, one more had been added (*TYXZ*, 11/4a–5b).

54. The understanding that the front of a building should be south-facing has been called "conceptual south" by Nancy Berliner. Southern orientation was so customary that craftsmen in the late imperial period would use the names for cardinal directions (north, south, east, west) rather than back, front, left, and right to label building parts prior to assembly. See Berliner, *Yin Yu Tang*, 131. My thanks to Ron Knapp for directing me to this source. This system was also used by Zhu Xi in his discussion of the placement of ritual objects in private ancestral halls; see Bray, *Technology and Gender*, 153; and Ebrey, *Chu Hsi's Family Rituals*, 8.

55. Bai Qianshen, *Fu Shan's World*, 158–59.

56. Zhou Lingshu, "Chongjian Jinci beiting ji" (1672), reprinted in *JCZ*, 68–69.

57. See especially Gu Yanwu, *Jinshi wenziji*, 2/36a, discussed below, and also the *YTZ*, Taiyuanfu, 1/32b–33a.

58. The dates for the Xuanhe reign period are 1119–26. This should be the Jinci Prayer in Thanks for Rain of 1123.

59. Zhou Lingshu, "Chongjian Jinci beiting ji" (1672), reprinted in *JCZ*, 68–69.

60. Murray, "The Evolution of Pictorial Hagiography," 83–92.

61. Mann, "Widows," 45–48, discusses the significance of the chaste widow and how, in many cases, her personal sacrifice to ensure her son's successful passing of the civil service exams served to strengthen the mother-son relationship. Frequently, exam graduates whose mothers were chaste widows were in the best position (as successful, educated men) to petition to have their mothers honored, and in so doing reminded other educated men of the sacrifices their own mothers undertook to ensure their success.

62. See, for example, Johnson, "The City-God Cults," 379–88.

63. Pomeranz, "Water to Iron, Widows to Warlords," 66–90.

64. Zhang Mu, *Yan Ruoqu nianpu*, 1–3; and Bai Qianshen, *Fu Shan's World*, 154–55.

65. Zhang Mu, *Yan Ruoqu nianpu*, 24–25; and Bai Qianshen, *Fu Shan's World*, 155.

66. Bai Qianshen, *Fu Shan's World*, 154–55.

67. The contentious personality of Yan is discussed in Bai Qianshen, *Fu Shan's World*, 166. For Gu's position on Tang, see his *Rizhilu*, 5 *xia*/59. For his opinion of the Sage Mother, see *Jinshi wenzi ji*, 2/36a.

68. In 1672, the year of Zhou Lingshu's essay, Yan argued with Gu at Fu Shan's home about whether the state of Bing (capital at Taiyuan) was included in the original nine states of Yu the Great. Yan supported his thesis that Bing was one of the nine with research into the *Rites of Zhou*; see Bai Qianshen, *Fu Shan's World*, 166.

69. Yan Ruoqu, *Qianqiu zhaji*, 5/34a–36a.

70. Yan Ruoqu, *Sishu shidi xu*, 51b–52a.

71. Song Zhong, ed., *Shiben bazhong*, 216–33.

72. The deities of Jin, including a description of Tai Tai as the spirit of the Fen River and Shi Chen as the spirit of the constellation Shen, are discussed in the *Zuozhuan*; see Legge, vol. 5, 573 and 580; and Chapter 3 of this book.

73. Yan Ruoqu, *Sishu shidi xu*, 51b–52a.

74. None of the inscriptional plaques on the Sage Mother Hall extant at the beginning of this century—some dating from the Qianlong period—mentions her Yi Jiang identity. They only discuss her effectiveness in bringing water. This was a source of confusion for Liu Dapeng, author of the *JCZ*; see *JCZ*, 746–48.

75. As late as 1856, Shen Weijie notes that all who worshiped at Jinci believed the Sage Mother to be a water goddess. He, too, felt it his duty to write about her more noble origins in order to dispel this "myth." See "Jinci Shengmumiao bian," reprinted in *JCZ*, 22–23.

76. Zhu Gui (d. 1806), "Chongxiu Tang Shu Yu ci ji bei," reprinted in *JCZ*, 319.

77. Hu Qijing (Qing), "Chongxiu Yuhuangge Sanqingdong Guandimiao shuming beiji" (1801), reprinted in *JCZ*, 31–32

78. Zhu Gui, "Chongxiu Tang Shu Yu ci ji bei," reprinted in *JCZ*, 319–20.

79. Hu Qijing (Qing), "Chongxiu Yuhuangge Sanqingdong Guandimiao shuming beiji" (dated 1801), reprinted in *JCZ*, 31.

80. Yan Ruoqu, *Qianqiu zhaji*, 5/36a.

81. *TYXZ*, 3/32a.

82. This similarity in temple complexes across sectarian divides has also been discussed by Peng Hai; see Peng et al., *Jinci wenwu*, 100.

83. The representation of the same divinity in different aspects according to the interests of specific groups has been observed in late imperial cults to Mazu, the patron goddess of sailors, by Watson, "Standardizing the Gods."

84. See Pomeranz, "Water to Iron, Widows to Warlords," 64–65, for a criticism of Watson's thesis with respect to miracle-working.

Chapter 8

1. A summary of these inscriptions, including the most recent findings from the 1990s restoration, can be found in Chai et al., *Taiyuan Jinci Shengmudian*, 11–13.

2. See Jing Anning, *The Water God's Temple*, 70–73.

3. Fan Zhongyan, "Ti Jinci," reprinted in *JCZ*, 475.

4. Watson, "Standardizing the Gods," 294–95; and Duara, "Superscribing Symbols," 779–80.

5. Duara, "Superscribing Symbols," 791.

6. David Johnson, "The City-God Cults," 379–88; and Anne Gerritsen, "A Thirteenth-Century Cult," 183–84.

7. Chow, *The Rise of Confucian Ritualism.*

8. Zhou Lingshu, "Chongjian Jinci beiting ji," reprinted in *JCZ*, 68–69.

9. Zhu Xi (1130–1200), *Lunyu jizhu*, 4/16b–17a.

10. Mann, "Widows," 38, 45–48.

11. Pomeranz, "Cult of the Goddess of Taishan"; and idem, "Water to Iron, Widows to Warlords."

12. Pomeranz, "Water to Iron, Widows to Warlords," especially 64.

13. Otto, *Dionysus*, 18–30.

14. Although Mircea Eliade's vision of early religion has undergone much criticism, we should not completely disregard what we have learned from him: that in most places in the world, at most times, people were motivated to create through what they understood to be divine inspiration. As W. F. Otto discussed with respect to the quality of Greek temples and religious sculpture, much of that quality might be due to the significance of the purpose: devotion to the divine.

15. Su You, "Chongxiu Tang Shu Yu ci ji," reprinted in *JCZ*, 17–18.

16. Zhou Lingshu, "Chongjian Jinci beiting ji," reprinted in *JCZ*, 68–69.

17. Yan Ruoqu felt that the difference between the shrines for the two deities was the result of the son allowing himself to be disgraced on behalf of his mother; see *Sishu shidi xu*, 51b.

Appendix A

1. Gao Ruxing, *Taiyuan xianzhi*, 1/11a.

2. *JCZ*, 16.

3. *JCZ*, 319.

4. See *TYXZ*, "Jinci zhi tu," published in 1826, in which the building is labeled 梳庄樓, the character for *zhuang* here being a cursive simplification. The Spirit of the Jin Springs was identified in this text as the Sage Mother, Yi Jiang; see *TYXZ*, 3/32.

5. *SXTZ*, vol. 11, *juan* 73, 5067.

6. *JCZ*, 66.

7. Liu Yongde, *Jinci fengguang*, 83; translation follows Robert G. Henricks, Lao-tzu, *Te Tao ching*, 60.

8. *JCZ*, 249.

9. *JCZ*, 66.

10. Liu Yongde, *Jinci fengguang*, 51; translation follows Richard E. Strassberg, *Inscribed Landscapes*, 515. For an alternative translation, see Legge, *The Chinese Classics*, vol. 4, 617.

11. Lin and Liang, "Jin-Fen gujianzhu," 61.

12. Liu Yongde, *Jinci fengguang*, 34.

13. *JCZ*, 115.

14. In the *JCZ* the date given for the investiture is January 31, 1017. I have not been able to find this in either the *Songshi* or the *XCB* entries for that date. The *Songshi* does have a record of Haotian being added to the title of the Jade Emperor by Huizong in 1116; see *Songshi* 21/396 and 104/2543.

15. *JCZ*, 30–32.

16. Gao Ruxing, *Taiyuan xianzhi*, 1/11a; and *Jinci zhitu*.

17. *JCZ*, 29.

18. Ibid.

19. *JCZ*, 41–43.

20. *JCZ*, 43.

21. *JCZ*, 76–77.

22. Liu Yongde, *Jinci fengguang*, 71.

23. *ZWDCD*, 41132.1 and 41132.2.

24. Song Naizhong, *Jinci lüyou*, 12.

25. *ZWDCD*, 41132.3.

26. *JCZ*, 32–33.

27. *JCZ*, 76.

28. Song Naizhong, *Jinci lüyou*, 10.

29. Feng Junjie 馮俊傑, personal communication, June 9, 2000.

30. *JCZ*, 72.

31. *JCZ*, 77; and Liu Yongde, *Jinci fengguang*, 57–58.

32. Liu Yongde, *Jinci fengguang*, 56.

33. See Legge, *The Four Books*, "King Hui of Liang, Part II," 467–71.

34. *JCZ*, 77–78.

35. Song Naizhong, *Jinci lüyou*, 82.

36. *JCZ*, 70–71.

37. *JCZ*, 73; Peng, *Jinci wenwu*, 105; Liu Yongde, *Jinci fengguang*, 31–32.

38. *JCZ*, 72–73.

39. Liu Yongde, *Jinci fengguang*, 32.
40. JCZ, 74.
41. JCZ, 73.
42. JCZ, 68; Liu Yongde, *Jinci fengguang*, 73.
43. *YHJXTZ*, 13/367.
44. JCZ, 33.
45. JCZ, 249.
46. JCZ, 24–27.
47. Liu Yongde, *Jinci fengguang*, 45.
48. JCZ, 24.
49. JCZ, 28–29.
50. Liu Yongde, *Jinci fengguang*, 85.
51. JCZ, 45; Liu Yongde, *Jinci fengguang*, 86.
52. JCZ, 109–10.
53. JCZ, 40.
54. JCZ, 108–9.
55. "Zhoulian fang Taiyuan Jinci ji shi ke," JCZ, 314.
56. Peng Hai, *Jinci wenwu*, 204.
57. JCZ, 109.
58. JCZ, 41.
59. Liu Yongde, *Jinci fengguan*, 87; Peng Hai, *Jinci wenwu*, 204.
60. JCZ, 72.
61. JCZ, 88.
62. Liu Yongde, *Jinci fengguang*, 89.
63. JCZ, 71.
64. Liu Yongde, *Jinci fengguang*, 88.
65. "Zhoulian fang Taiyuan Jinci ji shi ke," JCZ, 314.
66. JCZ, 78.
67. JCZ, 67.
68. JCZ, 71.
69. Song Naizhong, *Jinci lüyou*, 88–89; Peng Hai, *Jinci wenwu*, 204.
70. Personal communication, August 5, 2006
71. JCZ, 120 and 321–22.
72. JCZ, 120.
73. JCZ, 88.

Select Bibliography

Bagley, Robert W. "P'an-lung-ch'eng: A Shang City in Hupei." *Artibus Asiae* 39.3/4 (1977): 165–219.

Bai Qianshen. *Fu Shan's World: The Transformation of Chinese Calligraphy in the Seventeenth Century*. Cambridge, MA: Harvard University Asia Center Publications, 2003.

Bai Zuomin 白佐民 and Shao Junyi 邵俊儀, eds. *Tanmiao jianzhu* 檀廟建築 (The architecture of altars and temples). *Zhongguo meishu quanji, Jianzhu yishubian*, vol. 6. Beijing: Zhongguo jianzhu gongye chubanshe, 1991.

Ban Gu 班固 (32–92 CE). *Hanshu* 漢書 (History of the Han). Taipei: Dingwen shuju, 1983.

Beijing daxue lishixi kaogu zhuanye Shanxi shixizu 北京大學歷史系考古專業山西實習組 and Shanxi sheng wenwu gongzuo weiyuan hui 山西省文物工作委員會. "Yicheng Quwo kaogu kanchaji" 翼城曲沃考古勘察記 (Yicheng Quwo archaeology investigation report). In Beijing daxue kaoguxi, ed., *Kaoguxue yanjiu*. Beijing: Wenwu chubanshe, 1992, 124–228.

Berliner, Nancy. *Yin Yu Tang: The Architecture and Daily Life of a Chinese House*. Boston: Tuttle Publishing, 2003.

Birrell, Anne, trans. *The Classic of Mountains and Seas*. London: Penguin Press, 2000.

Bo Songnian 薄松年, ed. *Zhongguo menshen hua* 中國門神畫 (Chinese door spirit paintings). Guangzhou: Lingnan meishu chubanshe, 1998.

Bol, Peter K. "The Sung Examination System and the *Shih*." *Asia Major* 3.2 (1990): 149–71.

Boltz, William G. "Chou li 周禮." In Michael Loewe, ed., *Early Chinese Texts: A Bibliographical Guide*. Berkeley, CA: Society for the Study of Early China and Institute of East Asian Studies, 1993, 24–32.

Bosco, Joseph, and Puay-peng Ho. *Temples of the Empress of Heaven*. New York: Oxford University Press, 1999.

Bray, Francesca. *Technology and Gender: Fabrics of Power in Late Imperial China*. Berkeley: University of California Press, 1997.

Brook, Timothy. "At the Margin of Public Authority: The Ming State and Buddhism." In Theodore Huters, R. Bin Wong, and Pauline Yu, eds., *Culture and State in Chinese History: Conventions, Accommodations, and Critiques*. Stanford: Stanford University Press, 1998, 161–81.

———. "Communications and Commerce." In Denis Twitchett and Frederick W. Mote, eds., *The Cambridge History of China*, vol. 8, *The Ming Dynasty, 1368–1644*, pt. II. Cambridge, Eng.: Cambridge University Press, 1998, 579–708.

———. *Praying for Power: Buddhism and the Formation of Gentry Society in Late-Ming China*. Cambridge: Harvard University, Council on East Asian Studies, 1993.

Bujard, Marianne. "Le Joyau de Chen: Culte Historique—Culte Vivant." *Cahiers d'Extrême-Asie* 10 (1998): 131–81.

Cahill, Suzanne E. *Transcendence and Divine Passion: The Queen Mother of the West in Medieval China*. Stanford: Stanford University Press, 1993.

———. "Sex and the Supernatural in Medieval China: Cantos on the Transcendent Who Presides Over the River." *Journal of the American Oriental Society* 105.2 (1985): 197–220.

Chaffee, John W. *The Thorny Gates of Learning in Sung China*. New edition. Albany: State University of New York Press, 1995.

Chai Zejun 柴澤俊. *Jinci* 晉祠. Beijing: Wenwu chubanshe, 1958.

———. "Shanxi gujianzhu gaishu" 山西古建築概述 (An overview of ancient architecture in Shanxi). In *Zhongguo gujianzhu xueshu jiangzuo wenji*. Beijing: Zhanwang chubanshe, 1986.

———. *Shanxi siguan bihua* 山西寺觀壁畫 (Temple murals in Shanxi province). Beijing: Wenwu chubanshe, 1997.

Chai Zejun et al. *Shuozhou Chongfusi Mituodian xiushan gongcheng baogao* 朔州崇福寺彌陀殿修繕工程報告 (Report on the repairs on the Amitābha Hall of Chongfusi in Shuozhou). Beijing: Wenwu chubanshe, 1993.

———. *Taiyuan Jinci Shengmudian xiushan gongcheng baogao* 太原晉祠聖母殿修繕工程報告 (Report on the repairs on the Sage Mother Hall of Jinci in Taiyuan). Beijing: Wenwu chubanshe, 2000.

Chang, Kwang-chih. *Shang Civilization*. New Haven: Yale University Press, 1980.

Chen Mingda 陳明達. "Shanxi—Zhongguo gudai jianzhu de baoku" 山西—中國古代建築的寶庫 (Shanxi: China's treasure-house of ancient architecture). *Wenwu cankao ziliao* 1954.11: 93–96.

———. *Yingxian muta* 應縣木塔 (The timber pagoda in Yingxian). Beijing: Wenwu chubanshe, 1966; 2003 reprint edition.

———. Yingzao fashi *damuzuo yanjiu* 營造法式大木作研究 (Research on the greater carpentry section of the *Yingzao fashi*). Beijing: Wenwu chubanshe, 1981.

Chen Pao-chen. "*The Goddess of the Lo River*: A Study of Early Chinese Narrative Handscrolls." Ph.D. diss., Princeton University, 1987.

Chen Zhongchi 陳仲篪. "*Yingzao fashi* chutan" 營造法式初探 (An initial investigation of the *Yingzao fashi*). *Wenwu* 1962.2: 12–17.

Ching-Chung, Priscilla. *Palace Women in the Northern Sung*. Leiden: E. J. Brill, 1981.

Chow, Kai-wing. *The Rise of Confucian Ritualism in Late Imperial China: Ethics, Classics, and Lineage Discourse*. Stanford: Stanford University Press, 1994.

Chu Dawen 儲大文 (1665–1743) et al., eds. *Shanxi tongzhi* 山西通志 (Shanxi gazetteer). Siku quanshu (Wenyuange) edition. Taipei: Taiwan shangwu yinshuguan, 1983.

Chunqiu Gongyangzhuan zhushu 春秋公羊傳注疏. In Ruan Yuan (1816), ed., *Shisanjing zhushu*. Taipei: Yiwen yinshuguan, 2001.

Chunqiu Zuozhuan zhengyi 春秋左傳正義. In Ruan Yuan (1816), ed., *Shisanjing zhushu*. Taipei: Yiwen yinshuguan, 2001.

Clunas, Craig. *Art in China*. Oxford, Eng.: Oxford University Press, 1997.

Cohen, Alvin P. "Coercing the Rain Deities in Ancient China." *History of Religions* 17.3/4 (1978): 244–65.

Crump, J. I. *Chan-kuo tse*. 2nd edition. Translated and annotated and with an introduction by J. I. Crump. Ann Arbor: University of Michigan Press, 1996.

Demiéville, Paul. "Che-yin Song Li Ming-tchong *Ying tsao fa che*" ('Edition photolithographique de la *Méthode d'architecture* de Li Ming-tchong des Song'), 1920, 8 fascicules." *Bulletin de l'Ecole Française de l'Extrême Orient* 25 (1925): 213–64.

Ding Mingyi 丁明夷 et al. *Jinci* 晉祠. Beijing: Wenwu chubanshe, 1981.

Dong Hao 董浩 (1740–1818), comp. *Quan Tang wen* 全唐文 (Complete prose literature of the Tang). Taipei: Huiwen shuju, 1961.

Dreyer, Edward L. *Early Ming China: A Political History, 1355–1435*. Stanford: Stanford University Press, 1982.

Duan Yuming 段玉明. *Zhongguo simiao wenhua* 中國寺廟文化 (Chinese temple culture). Shanghai: Shanghai renmin chubanshe, 1994.

Duara, Prasenjit. *Culture, Power, and the State: Rural North China, 1900–1942*. Stanford: Stanford University Press, 1988.

———. "Knowledge and Power in the Discourse of Modernity: The Campaigns Against Popular Religion in Early Twentieth-Century China." *Journal of Asian Studies* 50.1 (1991): 67–83.

———. "Superscribing Symbols: The Myth of Guandi, Chinese God of War." *Journal of Asian Studies* 47.4 (1988): 778–95.

Eberhard, Wolfram. *A Dictionary of Chinese Symbols: Hidden Symbols in Chinese Life and Thought*. Translated by G. L. Campbell. London and New York: Routledge, 1986; 1991 reprint edition.

Ebrey, Patricia. *Chu Hsi's Family Rituals: A Twelfth-Century Chinese Manual for the Performance of Cappings, Weddings, Funerals, and Ancestral Rites*. Princeton: Princeton University Press, 1991.

Lin Ruihan 林瑞翰. *Songdai zhengzhi shi* 宋代政治史 (A political history of the Song dynasty). Taipei: Cheng Chung, 1989; 1992 reprint edition.

Lin Zhao 林釗. "Putian Yuanmiaoguan Sanqingdian diaochaji" 莆田元妙觀三清殿調查記 (A record of the survey of the Hall of the Three Pure Ones in Putian's Yuanmiaoguan). *Wenwu* 1957.11: 52–53.

Little, Stephen, et al. *Taoism and the Arts of China.* Chicago: Art Institute of Chicago and Berkeley: University of California Press, 2000.

Liu Dapeng 劉大鵬 (1857–1942). *Jincizhi* 晉祠志 (Jinci gazetteer). Taiyuan: Shanxi renmin chubanshe, 1986.

Liu Dunzhen 劉敦楨 (1896–1968), chief ed. *Zhongguo gudai jianzhu shi* 中國古代建築史 (A history of ancient Chinese architecture). Beijing: Zhongguo jianzhu gongye chubanshe, 1980.

Liu Xu 劉煦 (887–946). *Jiu Tangshu* 舊唐書 (Old history of the Tang). Taipei: Dingwen shuju, 1981.

Liu Xu 劉緒. "Jin yu Jin wenhua de niandai wenti" 晉與晉文化的年代問題 (Problems of dating the Jin and Jin culture). *Wenwu jikan* 1993.4: 83–87.

Liu Xu 劉緒 et al. "Tianma—Qucun yizhi J6, J7 qu Zhoudai juzhi fajue baogao" 天馬曲村遺址 J6，J7 區周代居址發掘簡報 (Report of the Zhou-dynasty vernacular ruins at the Tianma-Qucun J6, J7 area). *Wenwu* 1998.11: 29–36.

Liu Yongde 劉永德. *Jinci fengguang* 晉祠風光 (Scenes of Jinci). Taiyuan: Shanxi renmin chubanshe, 1958.

Liu Yonghua 劉永華. *Zhongguo gudai junrong fushi* 中國古代軍戎服飾 (Ancient Chinese armor). Shanghai: Guji chubanshe, 1995.

Loewe, Michael. *Chinese Ideas of Life and Death: Faith, Myth, and Reason in the Han Period (202 BC–AD 220).* London: George Allen and Unwin, 1982.

———. "The Cult of the Dragon and the Invocation for Rain." In Charles Le Blanc and Susan Blader, eds., *Chinese Ideas About Nature and Society: Studies in Honour of Derk Bodde.* Hong Kong: Hong Kong University Press, 1987, 195–213.

———. *Divination, Mythology, and Monarchy in Han China.* Cambridge, Eng.: Cambridge University Press, 1994.

———. "The Religious and Intellectual Background." In Denis Twitchett and Michael Loewe, eds., *The Cambridge History of China,* vol. 1, *The Ch'in and Han Empires, 221 BC–AD 220.* Cambridge, Eng.: Cambridge University Press, 1986, 649–725.

———. "*Shi ching.*" In Michael Loewe, ed., *Early Chinese Texts: A Bibliographical Guide.* Berkeley, CA: Society for the Study of Early China and Institute of East Asian Studies, 1993, 415–23.

Loewe, Michael, ed. *Early Chinese Texts: A Bibliographical Guide.* Berkeley, CA: Society for the Study of Early China and Institute of East Asian Studies, 1993.

Lorge, Peter. "War in the Creation of the Northern Song State." Ph.D. dissertation, University of Pennsylvania, 1996.

Lü Buwei 呂不韋 (?–235 BCE). *Lüshi chunqiu* (The Lü spring and autumn annals) 呂氏春秋. Annotated by Chen Qiyou 陳奇猷. Shanghai: Xuelin, first published 1984; 1995 reprint edition.

Lü Hongjian 呂鴻鑑 and Zuo Guobao 左國保. "Dougong shenmei tezheng" 枓栱審美特征 (The aesthetic characteristics of bracket sets). *Wenwu jikan* 1996.1: 49–53.

Lü Songyun 呂松雲 and Liu Shizhong 劉詩中. *Zhongguo gudai jianzhu cidian* 中國古代建築辭典 (A dictionary for ancient Chinese architecture). Beijing: Zhongguo shudian, 1992.

Ma Douquan 馬斗全. "Tang Shuyu fengdi zai jin Yongji kao" 唐叔虞封地在今永濟考 (Research into Tang Shuyu's fief being located at modern Yongji). *Jinyang xuekan* 1982.4: 41–42.

Ma Duanlin 馬端臨 (1254–1323). *Wenxian tongkao* 文獻通考 (General history of institutions and critical examination of documents and studies). Shanghai: Zhonghua shuju, 1986; 1991 reprint edition.

Ma Jiandong 馬劍東. "Jin wenhua kao lüe" 晉文化考略 (An outline investigation of Jin culture). *Wenwu jikan* 1990.1: 56–62.

Ma Jikuan 馬吉寬. "Pingshun Longmensi Daxiongbaodian kancha baogao" 平順龍門寺大雄寶殿勘察報告 (A survey report of the Daxiongbao Hall of Longmensi in Pingshun). *Wenwu jikan* 1992.4: 22–28.

Mann, Susan. "Widows in the Kinship, Class, and Community Structures of Qing Dyansty China." *Journal of Asian Studies* 46.1 (1987): 37–56.

Maoshi zhengyi 毛詩正義. In Ruan Yuan (1816), ed., *Shisanjing zhushu*. Taipei: Yiwen yinshuguan, 2001 reprint edition.

McNair, Amy. "On the Date of the Shengmudian Sculptures at Jinci." *Artibus Asiae* 49.3–4 (1988–89): 238–53.

Mengzi zhushu 孟子注疏. In Ruan Yuan (1816), ed., *Shisanjing zhushu*. Taipei: Yiwen yinshuguan, 2001.

Miller, Tracy G. "Constructing Religion: Song Dynasty Architecture and the Jinci Temple Complex." Ph.D. diss., University of Pennsylvania, 2000.

———. "The Influence of Chinese Empire on East Asian Shrine Architecture: An Experiment in Cross-Cultural Comparison." *Asia Major*, forthcoming 2007.

———. "Looking Beyond Empire: Local Expression in the Timber Frame Buildings of 10th-Century China." Paper presented at the Society of Architectural Historians Conference, Providence, RI, 2004.

———. "Northern Song Architecture in Southern Shanxi Province." *Journal of Sung-Yuan Studies* 29 (1999): 135–55.

———. "Synthetic Nature: Sacred Sites, Landscape Gardens, and the Jinci Temple Complex." Paper presented at the American Association for Chinese Studies Annual Conference, Los Angeles, 2002.

———. "Water Sprites and Ancestor Spirits: Reading the Architecture of Jinci." *Art Bulletin* 54.1 (2004): 6–30.

Ming shilu 明實錄. Taipei: Zhongyang yanjiuyuan, Lishi yuyan yanjiusuo edition, 1984.

Mizuno Seiichi 水野清一 (1905–71) and Hibino Takeo 日比野丈夫 (1914–). *Sansei kosekishi* 山西古蹟志 (Historical monuments in Shanxi). Kyoto, 1956.

Mo Zongjiang 莫宗江. "Yingxian Shuoxian ji Taiyuan zhi Jinci zhi gudai jianzhu" 應縣朔縣及太原之晉祠之古代建築 (The ancient architecture of Yingxian, Shuoxian, and Taiyuan's Jinci). *Yanbei wenwu kanchatuan baogao*, 1959. Reprinted in Sun Jinyi 孫進己 et al., eds., *Zhongguo kaogu jicheng Huabei juan* 中國考古集成華北卷, vol. 16 (Song-Liao, vol. 2). Harbin: Harbin chubanshe, 1998, 1175–76.

Mostern, Ruth. "Dividing the Realm in Order to Govern: Spatial Organization and State Power in the Tang-Song Transition." In Peter Lorge, ed., *The Five Dynasties and Ten Kingdoms*, forthcoming.

Mote, Frederick W. *Imperial China, 900–1800*. Cambridge, MA: Harvard University Press, 1999.

Murray, Julia. "The Evolution of Pictorial Hagiography in Chinese Art: Common Themes and Forms." *Arts Asiatiques* 55 (2000): 97.

———. "Illustrations of the Life of Confucius: Their Evolution, Functions, and Significance in Late Ming China." *Artibus Asiae* 57.1–2 (1997): 73–134.

Muzhang'a 穆彰阿 (Qing) et al., comps. *Jiaqing chongxiu Da Qing yitongzhi* (Comprehensive gazetteer of the Qing, Jiaqing-period recompilation) 嘉慶重修大清一統志. Sibu congkan xubian edition. Shanghai: Shanghai shudian, 1984.

Naquin, Susan. *Peking: Temples and City Life, 1400–1900*. Berkeley: University of California Press, 2000.

———. "Sites, Saints, and Sights at the Tanzhe Monastery." *Cahiers d'Extrême-Asie* 10 (1998): 183–211.

Needham, Joseph et al. *Science and Civilisation in China*, vol. 4, pt. 3. Cambridge, Eng.: Cambridge University Press, 1971; 1987 reprint edition.

Nienhauser, William H., Jr., et al., trans. Ssu-ma Ch'ien, *The Grand Scribe's Record*, vols. 1 and 7. Bloomington: Indiana University Press, 1994.

Ono Katsutoshi 小野勝年 and Hibino Takeo 日比野丈夫. *Godaisan* 五臺山. Tokyo: Zauhō kankōkai, 1942.

Otto, Walter Friedrich. *Dionysus: Myth and Cult*. Translated by Robert B. Palmer. Bloomington: Indiana University, 1965.

Ouyang Xiu 區陽修 (1007–72). *Xin Wudaishi* (New history of the Five Dynasties) 新五代史. Taipei: Dingwen, 1998.

Ouyang Xiu 區陽修 (1007–72) and Song Qi 宋祁 (998–1061). *Historical Records of the Five Dynasties*. Translated by Richard L. Davis. New York: Columbia University Press, 2004.

———. *Xin Tangshu* (New history of the Tang) 新唐書. Taipei: Dingwen shuju, 1981.

Pan Guxi 潘谷西. "*Yingzao fashi* chutan" 營造法式初探 (An initial investigation of the *Yingzao fashi*). 2 pts. *Nanjing gongxueyuan xuebao* 1980.4: 35–51; 1981.2: 43–75.

Peng Hai 彭海. "Jinci Shengmudian kance shouhuo—Shengmudian chuangjian niandai" 晉祠聖母殿勘測收獲—聖母殿創建年代 (The reward of the Jinci Sage Mother Hall survey—the date of the first construction of the Sage Mother Hall). *Wenwu* 1996.1: 66–80.

Peng Hai 彭海 et al. *Jinci wenwu toushi* (A cultural perspective of Jinci) 晉祠文物透視. Taiyuan: Shanxi renmin chubanshe, 1997.

Pomeranz, Kenneth. "Power, Gender, and Pluralism in the Cult of the Goddess of Taishan." In Theodore Huters, R. Bin Wong, and Pauline Yu, eds., *Culture and State in Chinese History: Conventions, Accommodations, and Critiques*. Stanford: Stanford University Press, 1997, 182–204.

———. "Water to Iron, Widows to Warlords: The Handan Rain Shrine in Modern Chinese History." *Late Imperial China* 12.1 (1991): 62–99.

Průšek, Jaroslav. *Chinese Statelets and the Northern Barbarians in the Period 1400–300 BC*. Dordrecht-Holland: D. Reidel Publishers, 1971.

Pulleyblank, E. G. "The Chinese and Their Neighbors in Prehistoric and Early Historic Times." In David N. Keightley, ed., *The Origins of Chinese Civilization*. Berkeley: University of California Press, 1983.

Qi Yingtao 祁英濤. "Jinci Shengmudian yanjiu" 晉祠聖母殿研究 (Research on the Shengmudian at Jinci). *Wenwu jikan* 1992.1: 50–68.

———. "Zenyang jianding gujianzhu" 怎樣鑑定古建築 (How to appraise ancient architecture). Reprinted in *Zhongguo jianzhushi lunwen xuanji*, vol. 1. Taipei: Mingwen shuju, 1984 reprint edition, 23–56.

Qi Yingtao 祁英濤 et al. "Liangnianlai Shanxisheng xin faxian de gujianzhu" 兩年來山西省新發現的古建築 (Newly discovered ancient architecture over the past ten years in Shanxi). *Wenwu cankao ziliao* 1954.11: 37–84.

———. "Shanxisheng xin faxian gujianzhu de niandai jianding" 山西省新發現古建築的年代鑑定 (Date appraisal of newly discovered ancient architecture in Shanxi province). *Wenwu cankaoziliao* 1954.11: 87–92.

Qiu Guangming 丘光明. *Zhongguo lidai duliangheng kao* 中國歷代度量衡考 (A study of Chinese historical weights and measures). Beijing: Kexue chubanshe, 1992.

Quanguo zhongdian wenwu baohu danwei Zhenguosi shuomingshu 全國重點文物保護單位鎮國寺説明書 (An introduction to Zhenguosi, a designated monument under national protection). Tourist pamphlet, 1995.

Rawski, Evelyn S. "A Historian's Approach to Chinese Death Ritual." In James L. Watson and Evelyn S. Rawski, eds., *Death Ritual in Late Imperial and Modern China*. Berkeley: University of California Press, 1988.

Ren Yimin 任毅敏. "Jinci Shengmudian xianzhuang ji qi bianxing yuanyin" 晉祠聖母殿現狀及其變形原因 (The present appearance of the Sage Mother Hall at Jinci and the reason for its change). *Wenwu jikan* 1994.1: 68–71.

Ruan Yuan 阮元 (1764–1849) et al., eds. *Shisanjing zhushu* 十三經注疏 (The Thirteen Classics with commentaries and subcommentaries). Taipei: Yiwen yinshuguan reprint edition, 2001.

Ruitenbeek, Klaas. *Carpentry and Building in Late Imperial China: A Study of the Fifteenth-Century Carpenter's Manual* Lu Ban jing. 2nd revised edition. Leiden: E. J. Brill, 1996.

Schafer, Edward. *The Divine Woman: Dragon Ladies and Rain Maidens in T'ang Literature*. Berkeley: University of California Press, 1973.

Shahar, Meir, and Robert P. Weller, eds. *Divinity and Society in China*. Honolulu: University of Hawai'i Press, 1996.

Shang, Wei. Rulin waishi *and Cultural Transformation in Late Imperial China*. Cambridge, MA: Harvard University Asia Center, 2003.

Shangshu 尚書. In Ruan Yuan (1816), ed., *Shisanjing zhushu*. Taipei: Yiwen shuju, 2001 reprint edition.

Shanhaijing 山海經. Sibu beiyao edition. Taipei: Taiwan Zhonghua shuju, 1971.

Shanxi Jinci wenwu baoguansuo 山西晉祠文物保管所. "Jinci." *Wenwu* 1977.6: 64–66.

"Shanxisheng renmin zhengfu guanyu gongbu shengji disanpi zhongdian wenwu baohu danwei de tongzhi" 山西省人民政府關于公布省級第三批重點文物保护單位的通知 (A notification by the People's Government of Shanxi Province regarding the public announcement of objects included as members of the third group of provincial-level important cultural artifacts for preservation). *Wenwu jikan* 1997.3: 91–96.

Shaughnessy, Edward L. "Historical Geography and the Extent of the Earliest Chinese Kingdoms." *Asia Major* 2.2 (1989): 1–22.

———. "Western Zhou History." In Michael Loewe and Edward L. Shaughnessy, eds., *The Cambridge History of Ancient China*. Cambridge: Cambridge University Press, 1999, 292–351.

———. "*Shang shu* 尚書 (*Shu ching* 書經)." In Michael Loewe, ed., *Early Chinese Texts: A Bibliographical Guide*. Berkeley, CA: Society for the Study of Early China and Institute of East Asian Studies, 1993, 376–89.

Shen Congwen 沈從文. *Zhongguo gudai fushi yanjiu* (Research on ancient Chinese costume) 中國古代服飾研究. Taipei: Nantian shuju, 1981.

Shen Kuo 沈括 (1031–95). *Mengxi bitan* (Jottings from the Mengxi) 夢溪筆談. Sibucongkan xubian edition, vol. 53. Shanghai: Shanghai shudian, 1984.

Shen Yue 沈約 (441–513). *Songshu* 宋書. Taipei: Dingwen shuju, 1998.

Shi Yan 石岩, chief editor. *Wudai, Song diaosu* 五代宋雕塑 (Sculpture of the Five Dynasties and Song). *Zhongguo meishu quanji, diaosubian*, vol. 5. Taipei: Jinxiu chuban, 1994 reprint edition.

Shim, Jae-hoon. "The Early Development of the State of Jin: From Its Enfeoffment to the Hegemony of Wen Gong (r. 636–628 B.C.)." Ph.D. dissertation, University of Chicago, 1998..

———. "The 'Jinhou Su *Bianzhong*' Inscription and Its Significance." *Early China* 22 (1997): 43–75.

Sima Guang 司馬光 (1019–86). *Wengong shuyi* 溫公書儀. Xuejin taoyuan edition. Taipei: Yiwen yinshuguan, 1965.

Sima Tan 司馬談 (?180–110 BCE) and Sima Qian 司馬遷 (?145–86 BCE). *Shiji* 史記 (Records of the Grand Historian). Beijing: Zhonghua shuju, 1959; 1994 reprint edition.

Song Naizhong 宋乃忠 et al. *Jinci lüyou: baiwen baida* 晉祠旅游:百問百答 (Touring Jinci: one hundred questions, one hundred answers). Taiyuan: Shanxi guji chubanshe, 1999.

Song Zhong 宋衷, ed. *Shiben bazhong* 世本八種. Han dynasty; reconstructed in the Qing dynasty by Qin Jiamo 秦嘉謨 et al., eds. Shanghai: Shangwu yinshuguan, 1957.

Soper, Alexander C. "Hsiang-kuo-ssu: An Imperial Temple of Northern Sung." *Journal of the American Oriental Society* 68.1 (1948): 19–45.

Stein, Rolf. *The World in Miniature: Container Gardens and Dwellings in Far Eastern Religious Thought*. Translated by Phyllis Brooks. Stanford: Stanford University Press, 1990.

Steinhardt, Nancy S. "Chinese Architecture, 963–966." *Orientations* 26.2 (1995): 46–52.

———. *Liao Architecture*. Honolulu: University of Hawai'i Press, 1997.

Steinhardt, Nancy S., ed. *Chinese Traditional Architecture*. New York: China Institute in America, 1984.

Strassberg, Richard E. *Inscribed Landscapes: Travel Writing from Imperial China*. Berkeley: University of California Press, 1994.

Sui, An-der. "The Construction Bureau and Its Officials in the Song Dynasty." MA thesis, University of Pennsylvania, 1992.

Sun Dazhang 孫大章 and Yu Weiguo 喻維國 et al., eds. *Zhongguo meishu quanji: jianzhu yishu bian, zongjiao jianzhu* 中國美術全集: 建築藝術編, 宗教建築 (The complete collection of Chinese art: the art of architecture series, religious architecture). Beijing: Zhongguo jianzhu gongye chubanshe, 1988.

Sun Hua 孫華 et al. "Tianma-Qucun yizhi Beizhao Jinhou mudi di er ci fajue" 天馬–曲村遺址北趙晉侯墓第二次發掘 (The second excavation of the Beizhao Marquis of Jin tombs at the Tianma-Qucun ruins). *Wenwu* 1994.1: 4–28.

Szonyi, Michael. "The Illusion of Standardizing the Gods: The Cult of the Five Emperors in Late Imperial China." *Journal of Asian Studies* 56.1 (1997): 113–35.

Taiyuan "Jinci" 太原 "晋祠". Zhongguo caisu jinghua zhenshang congshu. Taiyuan: Shanxi renmin chubanshe, 2004.

Taiyuan shi Nanjiao qu difangzhi bianzuan weiyuanhui 太原市南郊區地方志編纂委員會. *Taiyuan shi Nanjiao qu zhi* 太原市南郊區志 (Gazetteer of the southern suburb district of Taiyuan municipality). Beijing: Shenghuo, dushu, xinzhi, sanlian shudian, 1994.

Tan Qixiang 譚其驤, chief ed. *Zhongguo lishi dituji* 中國歷史地圖集 (Collection of historical maps of China). Hong Kong: Sanlian shudian, 1991.

Tanaka Tan 田中淡. "Historical Background of the Formation of the Cai-Fen System." Paper presented at the First International Conference on Chinese Architectural History, Fragrant Hill, Beijing, 1988.

Taylor, Romeyn. "Official Altars, Temples, and Shrines Mandated for All Counties in Ming and Qing." *T'oung Pao* 83 (1997): 93–125.

———. "Official Religion in the Ming." In Denis Twitchett and Frederick W. Mote, eds., *The Cambridge History of China*, vol. 8, *The Ming Dynasty, 1368–1644*, pt. II. Cambridge, Eng.: Cambridge University Press, 1998, 840–92.

Teiser, Steven. *The Scripture on the Ten Kings and the Making of Purgatory in Medieval Chinese Buddhism*. Honolulu: University of Hawai'i Press, 1994.

Thorp, Robert. L. "Origins of Chinese Architectural Style: The Earliest Plans and Building Types." *Archives of Asian Art* 36 (1983): 22–39.

Tian Sulan 田素蘭. "Shanxi Faxingsi xinkao" 山西法興寺新考 (A new examination of Shanxi's Faxingsi). *Beifang wenwu* 1995.3: 94–96, 86.

Tuotuo 脱脱 (Toghto, 1313–1355). *Jinshi* 金史 (History of the Jin). Taipei: Dingwen shuju, 1995.

———. *Songshi* 宋史 (History of the Song). Taipei: Dingwen shuju, 1978.

Twitchett, Denis, and Frederick W. Mote, eds. *The Cambridge History of China*, vol. 3, *Sui and Tang China*, pt. I. Cambridge, Eng.: Cambridge University Press, 1989 reprint edition.

———. *The Cambridge History of China*, vol. 8, *The Ming Dynasty, 1368–1644*, pt. II. Cambridge, Eng.: Cambridge University Press, 1998.

von Falkenhausen, Lothar. "Archaeology and the Study of Chinese Local Religion: A Discussant's Remarks." *Cahiers d'Extrême-Asie* 10 (1998): 411–25.

Wang Huaibao 王懷寶 et al., eds. *Shanxisheng fenxian dituce* 山西分縣地圖册 (Volume of maps of Shanxi province divided by county). Ji'nan: Shandongsheng ditu chubanshe, 1994; 1997 reprint edition.

Wang Hui 王暉. "Zhouchu Tang Shu shoufeng shiji san kao" 周初唐叔受封事蹟三考 (An investigation of three aspects of the enfeoffment and heroic deeds of Tang Shu at the beginning of the Zhou). In Liu Mengze 劉孟澤, chief editor, *Di erci Xizhoushi xueshu taolunhui lunwenji* 第二次西周史學術討論會論文集, vol. 2. Xi'an: Shaanxi renmin jiaoyu chubanshe, 1993, 933–43.

Wang Kelin 王克林. "Jin wenhua yu beifang qingtongqi wenhua guanxi tansuo" 晋文化與北方青銅器文化關系探索 (Probing the relationship between the Jin culture and the bronze culture of north China). *Wenwu jikan* 1995.4: 49–56.

Wang Pu 王溥 (922–82). *Tang huiyao* 唐會要 (Important documents of the Tang). In Congshu jicheng xinbian, vol. 28. Taipei: Xinwenfeng chuban gongsi, 1985.

Wang Shiren 王世仁. "Ji Houtu cimiao maobei" 記后土祠廟貌碑 (A record of the stele image of the Houtu memorial temple). *Kaogu* 1963.5: 273–77.

Wang Xiaoqing 王效青, chief ed. *Zhongguo gujianzhu shuyu cidian* 中國古建築術語辭典 (A dictionary of technical terminology for ancient Chinese architecture). Taiyuan: Shanxi renmin chubanshe, 1996.

Wang Xuan 王軒 (Qing) et al. *Shanxi tongzhi* 山西通志 (Shanxi gazetteer). Guangxu reign period, published 1892. Beijing: Zhonghua shuju, 1990.

Wang Zhenfang 王振芳. "Lun Taiyuan zai Dong Wei Bei Qi shiqi de zhanlüe diwei" 論太原在東魏北齊時期的戰略地位 (Regarding the strategic position of Taiyuan during the Eastern Wei and Northern Qi periods). *Shanxi daxue xuebao* 1991.14: 53–58.

Watson, James L. "Standardizing the Gods: The Promotion of T'ien Hou ('Empress of Heaven') Along the South China Coast, 960–1960." In David Johnson, Andrew J. Nathan, and Evelyn S. Rawski, eds., *Popular Culture in Late Imperial China*. Berkeley: University of California Press, 1985.

———. "The Structure of Chinese Funerary Rites: Elementary Forms, Ritual Sequence, and the Primacy of Performance." In James L. Watson and Evelyn S. Rawski, eds., *Death Ritual in Late Imperial and Modern China*. Berkeley: University of California Press, 1988.

Watson, James L., and Evelyn S. Rawski, eds. *Death Ritual in Late Imperial and Modern China*. Berkeley: University of California Press, 1988.

Wechsler, Howard, J. "The Founding of the T'ang dynasty: Kao-tsu (reign 618–626)." In Denis Twitchett and Frederick W. Mote, eds., *The Cambridge History of China*, vol. 3, *Sui and Tang China*, pt. I. Cambridge, Eng.: Cambridge University Press, 1979 (1989 reprint edition), 150–87.

Wei Shou 魏收 (Northern Qi). *Weishu* 魏書 (History of the Wei). Beijing: Zhonghua shuju 1974; 1997 reprint edition.

Wen Renjun 聞人軍. Kaogongji *daodu tuyi* 考工記導讀圖譯 (A guided reading and pictorial translation of the *Kaogongji*). Taipei: Mingwen shuju reprint, 1990.

Wheatley, Paul. "The Ancient Chinese City as a Cosmological Symbol." *Ekistics* 232 (March 1975): 147–58.

Wilkinson, Endymion. *Chinese History: A Manual*. Cambridge, MA: Harvard University Asia Center, 1998.

Wilson, Thomas A., ed. *On Sacred Grounds: Culture, Society, Politics, and the Formation of the Cult of Confucius*. Cambridge, MA: Harvard University Asia Center, 2002.

Wu Hung. "Buddhist Elements in Early Chinese Art." *Artibus Asiae* 47 (1986): 263–323.

———. "From Temple to Tomb: Ancient Chinese Art and Religion in Transition." *Early China* 13 (1988): 78–115.

———. *Monumentality in Early Chinese Art and Architecture*. Stanford: Stanford University Press, 1995.

———. *The Wu Liang Shrine: The Ideology of Early Chinese Pictorial Art*. Stanford: Stanford University Press, 1989.

Xiao Deyan 蕭德言, Gu Yin 顧胤, et al. (Tang). *Guadizhi* 括地志 (Geographic gazetteer). Recompiled by Sun Xingyan 孫星衍 (1753–1818).

Xiao Tong 蕭統 (501–31). *Wen xuan* (Anthology of literature) 文選. Shanghai: Shanghai guji chubanshe, 1986; 1996 reprint edition.

Xie Yuanlu 謝元璐 et al. "Jinyang gucheng kancha ji" 晉陽古城勘察記 (A record of the investigation of Jinyang's ancient city walls). *Wenwu* 1962.4–5: 55–58.

Xu, Jay. "The Cemetery of the Western Zhou Lords of Jin." *Artibus Asiae* 3/4 (1996): 193–231.

Xu Jiyu 徐繼畬 (1795–1883). *Song Kan quanji* 松龕全集 (The complete works of Pine Niche). Congshu jicheng xubian, vol. 174. Shanghai: Shanghai shudian, 1994.

Xu Pingfang 徐苹芳. "Beisong Kaifeng Da Xiangguosi pingmian fuyuan tushuo" 北宋開封大相國寺平面復原圖説 (A pictorial explanation of the reconstruction of the plan of the Great Xiangguosi in Northern Song Kaifeng). In Editorial Department of Wenwu chubanshe, comp., *Wenwu kaogu lunji*. Beijing: Wenwu chubanshe, 1986, 357–69.

Xu Song 徐宋 (1781–1848), comp. *Song huiyao jigao* 宋會要輯稿 (Draft recovered edition of the *Song huiyao*). Taipei: Xinwenfeng chuban gongsi, 1976.

Xue Juzheng 薛居正 (912–81). *Jiu Wudaishi* 舊五代史 (Old history of the Five Dynasties). Taipei: Dingwen shuju, 1983.

Yan Gengwang 嚴耕望. *Tangdai jiaotong tukao* 唐代交通圖考 (Pictorial examination of communications during the Tang dynasty), vol. 5. Taipei: Zhongyang yanjiuyuan, Lishi yuyan yanjiusuo, 1985; 1998 reprint edition.

Yan Ruoqu 閻若璩 (1636–1704). *Qianqiu zhaji* 潛邱劄記 (Detailed records of Hidden Hill). Siku quanshu (Wenyuange) edition, vol. 510. Taipei: Shangwu yinshuguan, 1986.

———. *Sishu shidi, xu, youxu, sanxu* 四書釋地, 續, 又續, 三續 (An explanation of geography in the *Four Books*, continuation, second continuation, and third continuation). Siku quanshu (Wenyuange) edition, vol. 210. Taipei: Shangwu yinshuguan, 1986.

Yang Boda 楊伯達, chief editor. *Yuan, Ming, Qing diaosu* 元明清雕塑 (Sculpture of the Yuan, Ming, and Qing dynasties). *Zhongguo meishu quanji, diaosubian*, vol. 6. Taipei: Jinxiu chuban shiye, 1994 reprint edition.

Yang Hongxun 陽鴻勛. *Jianzhu kaoguxue lunwenji* 建築考古學論文集 (Essays on the archaeology of architecture). Beijing: Wenwu chubanshe, 1987.

Yang Lie 楊烈. "Shanxi Pingshunxian gujianzhu kanchaji" 山西省平順縣古建築勘察記 (A survey record of the ancient architecture in Pingshunxian, Shanxi). *Wenwu* 1962.2: 40–51.

Yang Zirong 楊子榮. "Lun Shanxi Yuandai yiqian mugou jianzhu de baohu" 論山西元代以前木構建築的保護 (A discussion of the preservation of pre-Yuan wooden architecture in Shanxi). *Wenwu jikan* 1994.1: 62–67.

Yetts, W. Perceval. "A Chinese Treatise on Architecture." *Bulletin of the School of Oriental Studies, London Institution* 4 (1926–28): 473–92.

———. "A Note on the *Ying tsao fa shih*." *Bulletin of the School of Oriental Studies, London Institution* 5.4 (1930): 855–60.

Yoshinami Takashi 好並隆司. "Kinsei Sansei no mizu arasoi o megutte—Shinsui, Kendō ryō kyo no baai" 近世の山西 水爭をめぐって—晋水, 縣東兩渠の場合 (Modern Shanxi water disputes—examples relating to the Jin River and Xiandong canals). In Chūgoku suiri shi kenkyū kai 中国水利史研究会, ed. *Satō Hakushi taikan kinen Chūgoku suiri shi ronsō* 佐藤博士退官記念中国水利史論叢. Tokyo: Kokusho kankōkai, 1984, 365–90.

Yü Chün-fang. *Kuan-yin: The Chinese Transformation of Avalokitesvara*. New York: Columbia University Press, 2001.

Yu Haomin 俞灝敏 and Zhu Guozhao 朱國照. *Fengshui daquan* 風水大全. Zhengzhou: Zhongguo guji chubanshe.

Yuan Peilan 員佩蘭 (Qing) and Yang Guotai 陽國泰 (Qing) et al., eds. *Taiyuan xianzhi* 太原縣志 (Taiyuan county gazetteer). Originally published 1826. Taipei: Chengwen chubanshe, 1976.

Yue Shi 樂史 (930–1007). *Taiping huanyu ji* 太平寰宇記 (Gazetteer of the world during the Taipingxingguo reign period). Taipei: Wenhai chubanshe, 1993 edition.

Yun Shan 雲山. "Jinci" 晉祠. *Shanxi wenwu* 1982.2. Reprinted in Sun Jinyi 孫進已 et al., eds., *Zhongguo kaogu jicheng Huabei juan* 中國考古集成華北卷, vol. 16 (Song-Liao, vol. 2). Harbin: Harbin chubanshe, 1998, 1125–28.

Zeigler, Delphine. "The Cult of the Wuyi Mountains and Its Cultivation of the Past: A Topocultural Perspective." *Cahiers d'Extrême-Asie* 10 (1998): 255–86.

Zhang Gong 張弓. *Han-Tang fosi wenhua shi* 漢唐佛寺文化史 (The history of Buddhist monastic culture during the Han through Tang dynasties). 2 vols. Beijing: Zhongguo shehui kexue, 1997.

Zhang Han et al. "Yicheng Quwo kaogu kancha ji" 翼城曲沃考古勘察記 (Report of the survey of Yicheng Quwo). *Kaoguxue yanjiu* 1992.1: 124–228.

Zhang Mu 張穆 (Qing). *Yan Ruoqu nianpu* 閻若璩年譜 (A chronicle of the life of Yan Ruoqu). Beijing: Zhonghua shuju, 1994.

Zhang Yipeng 張亦彭. "Jinci wenwu bianzheng" 晉祠文物辯證 (Identifying and rectifying the cultural artifacts at Jinci). *Shanxi difangshi yanjiu* 1962.2. Reprinted in Sun Jinyi 孫進已 et al., eds., *Zhongguo kaogu jicheng Huabei juan* 中國考古集成華北卷, vol. 16 (Song-Liao, vol. 2). Harbin: Harbin chubanshe, 1998, 1097–101.

Zhang Youchun 張友椿. "Tang Shuyu shifeng de suozai" 唐叔虞始封所在 (The location of Shu Yu of Tang's initial enfeoffment). *Jinyang xuekan* 1983.2: 78–79.

Zhang Yuhuan 張馭寰. "Taihang gujianzhu" 太行古建築 (Ancient architecture of the Taihang Mountains). In idem, *Gujianzhu kancha yu tanjiu* 古建築勘察與探究. Jiangsu: Guji chubanshe, 1988, 128–48.

Zhang Zhengyi 張正一. "Gaoping gujianzhu gailan" 高平古建築概覽 (A survey of ancient architecture in Gaoping). *Gaoping gujianzhu* 1995.1: 2–18.

Zhangzixian wenwu guanli suo 長子縣文物管理所. *Faxingsi* 法興寺. Tourist pamphlet, n.d.

Zhao Huai'e 趙懷鄂. "Jinci xiandian" 晉祠獻殿 (The offering hall at Jinci). *Wenwu jikan* 1996.1: 18, 44–48.

Zhao Puchu 趙僕初 et al., eds. *Shanxi Fojiao caisu* 山西佛教彩塑 (Buddhist sculpture of Shanxi province). Hong Kong: Zhongguo Fojiao wenhua, 1991.

Zhao Zenggui 趙增貴. "Linli Guandimiao" (The Guandi Temple in Linli) 林里關帝廟. *Wenwu tiandi* 1991.1. Reprinted in Sun Jinyi 孫進已 et al., eds., *Zhongguo kaogu jicheng Huabei juan* 中國考古集成華北卷, vol. 16 (Song-Liao, vol. 2). Harbin: Harbin chubanshe, 1998, 1175–76.

Zhao Zhiguang 趙志光 et al. *Zhongguo Jinci Songsu* (The Song statuary of Jinci, China) 中國晉祠宋塑. Taiyuan: Shanxi renmin chubanshe, 1993.

Zheng Suchun 鄭素春. *Quanzhenjiao yu Da Mengguguo dishi* 全眞教與大蒙古國帝室 (Quanzhen Daoism and the Mongolian kingdom's royal family). Taipei: Taiwan xuesheng shuju, 1987.

Zheng Xuan 鄭玄 (127–200). *Maoshipu* 毛詩譜 (Treatise on the Mao version of the *Book of Odes*). In Yu Minzhong (Qing) et al., eds. *Jingyin chizaotang Sikuquanshu huiyao*, vol. 23. Taipei: Shijie shuju, 1986.

———. *Zhouli Zheng zhu* 周裡鄭注 (The rites of Zhou with Zheng Xuan's commentary). Taibei: Xinxing shuju, 1993.

Zhongguo mingsheng cidian 中國名勝詞典 (A dictionary of famous sites in China). Shanghai: Shanghai cishu chubanshe, 1989.

Zhongwen dacidian 中文大辭典 (The encyclopedic dictionary of the Chinese language). Taipei: Zhongguo wenhua daxue chubanbu, 1993 ed.

Zhouli zhengyi 周禮注疏. In Ruan Yuan (1816), ed., *Shisanjing zhushu*. Taipei: Yiwen yinshuguan, 2001.

Zhu Xi 朱熹 (1130–1200). *Lunyu jizhu* (Collected commentaries on *The Analects*) 論語集注. Congshu jicheng sanbian edition, vol. 13. Taibei: Xinwen chubanshe, 1997.

———. *Shi jizhuan* 詩集傳 (A collection of notes on the *Book of Odes*). *Sibu congkan sanbian edition*, vol. 3. Shanghai: Shanghai shudian, 1985.

Zou Heng 鄒衡. "Jin shifengdi kao" 晉始封地考 (An investigation into the initial Jin fief). In Wu Rongzeng et al., eds., *Jinxinji: Zhang Zhenglang xiansheng bashi qingshou lunwenji* 盡心集：張政烺先生八十慶壽論文集. Beijing: Zhongguo shehui kexue chubanshe, 1996.

———. "Lun zaoqi Jindu" 論早期晉都 (A discussion of the early Jin capital). *Wenwu* 1994.1: 29–32, 34.

Zou Heng 鄒衡 et al. "Jin, Yu, E san sheng kaogu diaocha jianbao" 晉豫鄂三省考古調查簡報 (A findings report on the archaeology of the three regions of Jin, Yu, and E). *Wenwu* 1982.7: 1–16.

Zuo Qiuming (or Zuoqiu ming) 左丘明 (5th c. BCE). *Guoyu* 國語 (Discourses of the states). Shanghai: Guji chubanshe, 1978.

Index

Note: boldface numbers refer to the illustrations; lightface numbers to discussions in the text.

Harvard-Yenching Institute Monograph Series

Titles now in print

11. *Han Shi Wai Chuan: Han Ying's Illustrations of the Didactic Application of the Classic of Songs*, translated and annotated by James Robert Hightower
21. *The Chinese Short Story: Studies in Dating, Authorship, and Composition*, by Patrick Hanan
22. *Songs of Flying Dragons: A Critical Reading*, by Peter H. Lee
24. *Population, Disease, and Land in Early Japan, 645-900*, by William Wayne Farris
25. *Shikitei Sanba and the Comic Tradition in Edo Fiction*, by Robert W. Leutner
26. *Washing Silk: The Life and Selected Poetry of Wei Chuang (834?-910)*, by Robin D. S. Yates
27. *National Polity and Local Power: The Transformation of Late Imperial China*, by Min Tu-ki
28. *Tang Transformation Texts: A Study of the Buddhist Contribution to the Rise of Vernacular Fiction and Drama in China*, by Victor H. Mair
29. *Mongolian Rule in China: Local Administration in the Yuan Dynasty*, by Elizabeth Endicott-West
30. *Readings in Chinese Literary Thought*, by Stephen Owen
31. *Rememhering Paradise: Nativism and Nostalgia in Eighteenth-Century Japan*, by Peter Nosco
32. *Taxing Heaven's Storehouse: Horses, Bureaucrats, and the Destruction of the Sichuan Tea Industry, 1074-1224*, by Paul J. Smith
33. *Escape from the Wasteland: Romanticism and Realism in the Fiction of Mishima Yukio and Oe Kenzaburo*, by Susan Jolliffe Napier
34. *Inside a Service Trade: Studies in Contemporary Chinese Prose*, by Rudolf G. Wagner
35. *The Willow in Autumn: Ryutei Tanehiko, 1783-1842*, by Andrew Lawrence Markus
36. *The Confucian Transformation of Korea: A Study of Society and Ideology*, by Martina Deuchler
37. *The Korean Singer of Tales*, by Marshall R. Pihl

38. *Praying for Power: Buddhism and the Formation of Gentry Society in Late-Ming China*, by Timothy Brook
39. *Word, Image, and Deed in the Life of Su Shi*, by Ronald C. Egan
40. *The Chinese Virago: A Literary Theme*, by Yenna Wu
41. *Studies in the Comic Spirit in Modern Japanese Fiction*, by Joel R. Cohn
42. *Wind against the Mountain: The Crisis of Politics and Culture in Thirteenth-Century China*, by Richard L. Davis
43. *Powerful Relations: Kinship, Status, and the State in Sung China (960-1279)*, by Beverly Bossler
44. *Limited Views: Essays on Ideas and Letters*, by Qian Zhongshu; selected and translated by Ronald Egan
45. *Sugar and Society in China: Peasants, Technology, and the World Market*, by Sucheta Mazumdar
46. *Chinese History: A Manual*, by Endymion Wilkinson
47. *Studies in Chinese Poetry*, by James R. Hightower and Florence Chia-Ying Yeh
48. *Crazy Ji: Chinese Religion and Popular Literature*, by Meir Shahar
49. *Precious Volumes: An Introduction to Chinese Sectarian Scriptures from the Sixteenth and Seventeenth Centuries*, by Daniel L. Overmyer
50. *Poetry and Painting in Song China: The Subtle Art of Dissent*, by Alfreda Murck
51. *Evil and/or/as the Good: Omnicentrism, Intersubjectivity, and Value Paradox in Tiantai Buddhist Thought*, by Brook Ziporyn
52. *Chinese History: A Manual, Revised and Enlarged Edition*, by Endymion Wilkinson
53. *Articulated Ladies: Gender and the Male Community in Early Chinese Texts*, by Paul Rouzer
54. *Politics and Prayer: Shrines to Local Former Worthies in Sung China*, by Ellen Neskar
55. *Allegories of Desire: Esoteric Literary Commentaries of Medieval Japan*, by Susan Blakeley Klein
56. *Printing for Profit: The Commercial Publishers of Jianyang, Fujian (11th-17th Centuries)*, by Lucille Chia
57. *To Become a God: Cosmology, Sacrifice, and Self-Divinization in Early China*, by Michael J. Puett
58. *Writing and Materiality in China: Essays in Honor of Patrick Hanan*, edited by Judith T. Zeitlin and Lydia H. Liu
59. *Rulin waishi and Cultural Transformation in Late Imperial China*, by Shang Wei
60. *Words Well Put: Visions of Poetic Competence in the Chinese Tradition*, by Graham Sanders
61. *Householders: The Reizei Family in Japanese History*, by Steven D. Carter
62. *The Divine Nature of Power: Chinese Ritual Architecture at the Sacred Site of Jinci*, by Tracy Miller